Lecture Notes in Compute

Commenced Publication in 1973
Founding and Former Series Editors:
Gerhard Goos, Juris Hartmanis, and Jan van

Bertrand Meyer   Martin Nordio (Eds.)

Empirical Software Engineering and Verification

International Summer Schools, LASER 2008-2010
Elba Island, Italy
Revised Tutorial Lectures

 Springer

Volume Editors

Bertrand Meyer
Martin Nordio
ETH Zurich
Clausiusstr. 59, 8092 Zurich, Switzerland
E-mail: {bertrand.meyer, martin.nordio}@inf.ethz.ch

ISSN 0302-9743   e-ISSN 1611-3349
ISBN 978-3-642-25230-3   e-ISBN 978-3-642-25231-0
DOI 10.1007/978-3-642-25231-0
Springer Heidelberg Dordrecht London New York

Library of Congress Control Number: Applied for

CR Subject Classification (1998): D.2, D.1, F.3, D.3, K.6.3

LNCS Sublibrary: SL 2 – Programming and Software Engineering

Typesetting: Camera-ready by author, data conversion by Scientific Publishing Services, Chennai, India

Printed on acid-free paper

Springer is part of Springer Science+Business Media (www.springer.com)

Preface

The LASER summer school, organized by the ETH Chair of Software Engineering, brings together the concepts and practice of software engineering. It is intended for professionals from industry (engineers and managers) as well as university researchers, including PhD students. Each year, the LASER school focuses on an important software engineering topic. Since its inception in 2004, the LASER school has featured the following topics and lecturers:

- *2010—Empirical Software Engineering*:
  Victor Basili, Barry Boehm, Natalia Juristo, Tim Menzies, Bertrand Meyer, and Walter F. Tichy

- *2009—Software Testing: The Practice and the Science*:
  Alberto Avritzer, Michel Cukier, Yuri Gurevich, Mark Harman, Bertrand Meyer, Tom Ostrand, Mauro Pezzè, and Elaine Weyuker

- *2008—Concurrency and Correctness*:
  Tryggve Fossum, Maurice Herlihy, Bertrand Meyer, Robin Milner, Peter O'Hearn, and Daniel A. Reed

- *2007—Applied Software Verification*:
  Thomas Ball, Gérard Berry, C.A.R Hoare, Bertrand Meyer, Peter Müller, and Natarajan Shankar

- *2006—Practical Programming Processes*:
  Ralph-Johan Back, Miguel de Icaza, Erik Meijer, Bertrand Meyer, Mary Poppendieck, and Andreas Zeller

- *2005—Software Engineering for Concurrent and Real-Time Systems*:
  Laura K. Dillon, Bertrand Meyer, Jayadev Misra, Amir Pnueli, Wolfgang Pree, and Joseph Sifakis

- *2004—Practical Techniques of Software Quality*:
  Jean-Raymond Abrial, Ernie Cohen, Erich Gamma, Bertrand Meyer, Carroll Morgan, and Pamela Zave

This book contains selected lecture notes from the LASER summer schools 2008–2010, which focused on Concurrency and Correctness in 2008, Software Testing: The Practice and the Science in 2009, and Empirical Software Engineering, in 2010. This volume contains contributions by Mark Harman, Phil Mcminn, Shin Yoo, and Jerffeson Souza on search-based software engineering; by Mauro Pezzè, Pietro Braione and Giovanni Denaro on the integration of software testing and formal analysis; by Yi Wei, Manuel Oriol, and Bertrand Meyer on an empirical study of random testing; by Natalia Juristo and Omar S. Gómez on replication of software engineering experiments; and by Benjamin Morandi, Sebastian Nanz and Bertrand Meyer on a formal reference for SCOOP.

We would like to thank the lecture's and their co-authors for contributing to this volume. We thank Christian Estler, Julian Tschannen, Marco Piccioni, and Nazareno Aguirre for their feedback on drafts of the papers. We are grateful to Claudia Günthart, Julian Tschannen, and the members of the ETH Chair of Software Engineering for assisting with the organization of the LASER summer school.

July 2011

Bertrand Meyer
Martin Nordio

Table of Contents

Search Based Software Engineering: Techniques, Taxonomy, Tutorial

Mark Harman[1], Phil McMinn[2], Jerffeson Teixeira de Souza[3], and Shin Yoo[1]

[1] University College London, UK
[2] University of Sheffield, UK
[3] State University of Ceará, Brazil

Abstract. The aim of Search Based Software Engineering (SBSE) research is to move software engineering problems from human-based search to machine-based search, using a variety of techniques from the metaheuristic search, operations research and evolutionary computation paradigms. The idea is to exploit humans' creativity and machines' tenacity and reliability, rather than requiring humans to perform the more tedious, error prone and thereby costly aspects of the engineering process. SBSE can also provide insights and decision support. This tutorial will present the reader with a step-by-step guide to the application of SBSE techniques to Software Engineering. It assumes neither previous knowledge nor experience with Search Based Optimisation. The intention is that the tutorial will cover sufficient material to allow the reader to become productive in successfully applying search based optimisation to a chosen Software Engineering problem of interest.

1 Introduction

Search Based Software Engineering (SBSE) is the name given to a body of work in which Search Based Optimisation is applied to Software Engineering. This approach to Software Engineering has proved to be very successful and generic. It has been a subfield of software engineering for ten years [45], the past five of which have been characterised by an explosion of interest and activity [48]. New application areas within Software Engineering continue to emerge and a body of empirical evidence has now accrued that demonstrates that the search based approach is definitely here to stay.

SBSE seeks to reformulate Software Engineering problems as 'search problems' [45, 48]. This is not to be confused with textual or hypertextual searching. Rather, for Search Based Software Engineering, a search problem is one in which optimal or near optimal solutions are sought in a search space of candidate solutions, guided by a fitness function that distinguishes between better and worse solutions. The term SBSE was coined by Harman and Jones [45] in 2001, which was the first paper to advocate Search Based Optimisation as a general approach to Software Engineering, though there were other authors who had previously applied search based optimisation to aspects of Software Engineering.

B. Meyer and M. Nordio (Eds.): LASER Summer School 2008-2010, LNCS 7007, pp. 1–59, 2012.

SBSE has been applied to many fields within the general area of Software Engineering, some of which are already sufficiently mature to warrant their own surveys. For example, there are surveys and overviews, covering SBSE for requirements [111], design [78] and testing [3, 4, 65], as well as general surveys of the whole field of SBSE [21, 36, 48].

This paper does not seek to duplicate these surveys, though some material is repeated from them (with permission), where it is relevant and appropriate. Rather, this paper aims to provide those unfamiliar with SBSE with a tutorial and practical guide. The aim is that, having read this paper, the reader will be able to begin to develop SBSE solutions to a chosen software engineering problem and will be able to collect and analyse the results of the application of SBSE algorithms.

By the end of the paper, the reader (who is not assumed to have any prior knowledge of SBSE) should be in a position to prepare their own paper on SBSE. The tutorial concludes with a simple step-by-step guide to developing the necessary formulation, implementation, experimentation and results required for the first SBSE paper. The paper is primarily aimed at those who have yet to tackle this first step in publishing results on SBSE. For those who have already published on SBSE, many sections can easily be skipped, though it is hoped that the sections on advanced topics, case studies and the SBSE taxonomy (Sections 7, 8 and 9) will prove useful, even for seasoned Search Based Software Engineers.

The paper contains extensive pointers to the literature and aims to be sufficiently comprehensive, complete and self-contained that the reader should be able to move from a position of no prior knowledge of SBSE to one in which he or she is able to start to get practical results with SBSE and to consider preparing a paper for publication on these results.

The field of SBSE continues to grow rapidly. Many exciting new results and challenges regularly appear. It is hoped that this tutorial will allow many more Software Engineering researchers to explore and experiment with SBSE. We hope to see this work submitted to (and to appear in) the growing number of conferences, workshops and special issue on SBSE as well as the general software engineering literature.

The rest of the paper is organised as follows. Section 2 briefly motivates the paper by setting out some of the characteristics of SBSE that have made it well-suited to a great many Software Engineering problems, making it very widely studied. Sections 3 and 4 describe the most commonly used algorithms in SBSE and the two key ingredients of representation and fitness function. Section 5 presents a simple worked example of the application of SBSE principles in Software Engineering, using Regression Testing as an exemplar. Section 6 presents an overview of techniques commonly used to understand, analyse and interpret results from SBSE. Section 7 describes some of the more advanced techniques that can be used in SBSE to go beyond the simple world of single objectives for which we seek only to find an optimal result. Section 8 presents four case studies of previous work in SBSE, giving examples of the kinds of results obtained. These cover a variety of topics and involve very different software engineering activities, illustrating how generic and widely applicable SBSE is to a wide range of software engineering problem domains. Section 9 presents a taxonomy of problems so far investigated in SBSE research, mapping these onto the optimisation problems that have been formulated to address these problems. Section 10 describes the next steps a researcher should consider in order to conduct (and submit for publication) their first work on SBSE. Finally, Section 11 presents potential limitations of SBSE techniques and ways to overcome them.

2   Why SBSE?

As pointed out by Harman, Mansouri and Zhang [48] Software Engineering questions are often phrased in a language that simply cries out for an optimisation-based solution. For example, a Software Engineer may well find themselves asking questions like these [48]:

1. What is the smallest set of test cases that cover all branches in this program?
2. What is the best way to structure the architecture of this system?
3. What is the set of requirements that balances software development cost and customer satisfaction?
4. What is the best allocation of resources to this software development project?
5. What is the best sequence of refactoring steps to apply to this system?

All of these questions and many more like them, can (and have been) addressed by work on SBSE [48]. In this section we briefly review some of the motivations for SBSE to give a feeling for why it is that this approach to Software Engineering has generated so much interest and activity.

1. **Generality**
   As the many SBSE surveys reveal, SBSE is very widely applicable. As explained in Section 3, we can make progress with an instance of SBSE with only two definitions: a *representation* of the problem and a *fitness function* that captures the objective or objectives to be optimised. Of course, there are few Software Engineering problems for which there will be no representation, and the readily available representations are often ready to use 'out of the box' for SBSE. Think of a Software Engineering problem. If you have no way to represent it then you cannot get started with any approach, so problem representation is a common starting point for any solution approach, not merely for SBSE. It is also likely that there is a suitable fitness function with which one could start experimentation since many software engineering metrics are readily exploitable as fitness functions [42].
2. **Robustness**
   SBSE's optimisation algorithms are robust. Often the solutions required need only to lie within some specified tolerance. Those starting out with SBSE can easily become immersed in 'parameter tuning' to get the most performance from their SBSE approach. However, one observation that almost all those who experiment will find, is that the results obtained are often robust to

the choice of these parameters. That is, while it is true that a great deal of progress and improvement can be made through tuning, one may well find that all reasonable parameter choices comfortably outperform a purely random search. Therefore, if one is the first to use a search based approach, almost any reasonable (non extreme) choice of parameters may well support progress from the current 'state of the art'.

3. **Scalability Through Parallelism**
   Search based optimisation techniques are often referred to as being 'embarrassingly parallel' because of their potential for scalability through parallel execution of fitness computations. Several SBSE authors have demonstrated that this parallelism can be exploited in SBSE work to obtain scalability through distributed computation [12, 62, 69]. Recent work has also shown how General Purpose Graphical Processing devices (GPGPUs) can be used to achieve scale up factors of up to 20 compared to single CPU-based computation [110].

4. **Re-unification**
   SBSE can also create linkages and relationships between areas in Software Engineering that would otherwise appear to be completely unrelated. For instance, the problems of Requirements Engineering and Regression Testing would appear to be entirely unrelated topics; they have their own conferences and journals and researchers in one field seldom exchange ideas with those from the other.

   However, using SBSE, a clear relationship can be seen between these two problem domains [48]. That is, as *optimisation problems* they are remarkably similar as Figure 1 illustrates: Both involve selection and prioritisation problems that share a similar structure as search problems.

5. **Direct Fitness Computation**
   In engineering disciplines such as mechanical, chemical, electrical and electronic engineering, search based optimisation has been applied for many years. However, it has been argued that it is with Software Engineering, *more than any other engineering discipline*, that search based optimisation has the highest application potential [39]. This argument is based on the nature of software as a unique and very special engineering 'material', for which even the word 'engineering material' is a slight misnomer. After all, software is the only engineering material that can only be sensed by the mind and not through any of the five senses of sight, sounds, smell, taste and touch.

   In traditional engineering optimisation, the artefact to be optimised is often simulated precisely because it is of physical material, so building mock ups for fitness computation would be prohibitively slow and expensive. By contrast, software has no physical existence; it is purely a 'virtual engineering material'. As a result, the application of search based optimisation can often be completely direct; the search is performed directly on the engineering material itself, not a simulation of a model of the real material (as with traditional engineering optimisations).

Selection Problems

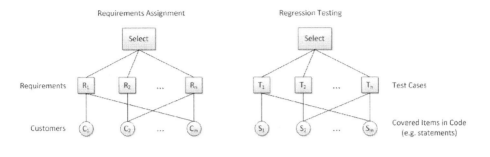

Prioritization Problems

Fig. 1. Requirements Selection and Regression Testing: two different areas of Software Engineering that are Re-unified by SBSE (This example is taken from the recent survey [48]). The task of selecting requirements is closely related to the problem of selecting test cases for regression testing. We want test cases to cover code in order to achieve high fitness, whereas we want requirements to cover customer expectations. Furthermore, both regression test cases and requirements need to be prioritised. We seek to order requirements ensure that, should development be interrupted, then maximum benefit will have been achieved for the customer at the least cost. We seek to order test cases to ensure that, should testing be stopped, then maximum achievement of test objectives is achieved with minimum test effort.

3 Defining a Representation and Fitness Function

SBSE starts with only two key ingredients [36, 45]:

1. The choice of the representation of the problem.
2. The definition of the fitness function.

This simplicity makes SBSE attractive. With just these two simple ingredients the budding Search Based Software Engineer can implement search based opti- misation algorithms and get results.

Typically, a software engineer will have a suitable representation for their problem. Many problems in software engineering also have software metrics as- sociated with them that naturally form good initial candidates for fitness func- tions [42]. It may well be that a would-be Search Based Software Engineer will have to hand, already, an implementation of some metric of interest. With a very little effort this can be turned into a fitness function and so the 'learning curve' and infrastructural investment required to get started with SBSE is among the lowest of any approach one is likely to encounter.

4   Commonly Used Algorithms

Random search is the simplest form of search algorithm that appears frequently in the software engineering literature. However, it does not utilise a fitness function, and is thus unguided, often failing to find globally optimal solutions (Figure 2). Higher quality solutions may be found with the aid of a fitness function, which supplies heuristic information regarding the areas of the search space which may yield better solutions and those which seem to be unfruitful to explore further. The simplest form of search algorithm using fitness information in the form of a fitness function is Hill Climbing. Hill Climbing selects a point from the search space at random. It then examines candidate solutions that are in the 'neighbourhood' of the original; i.e. solutions in the search space that are similar but differ in some aspect, or are close or some ordinal scale. If a neighbouring candidate solution is found of improved fitness, the search 'moves' to that new solution. It then explores the neighbourhood of that new candidate solution for better solutions, and so on, until the neighbourhood of the current candidate solution offers no further improvement. Such a solution is said to be *locally optimal*, and may not represent globally optimal solutions (as in Figure 3a), and so the search is often restarted in order to find even better solutions (as in Figure 3b). Hill Climbing may be restarted as many times as computing resources allow.

Pseudo-code for Hill Climbing can be seen in Figure 4. As can be seen, not only must the fitness function and the 'neighbourhood' be defined, but also the type of 'ascent strategy'. Types of ascent strategy include 'steepest ascent', where all neighbours are evaluated, with the ascending move made to the neighbour offering the greatest improvement in fitness. A 'random' or 'first' ascent strategy, on the other hand, involves the evaluation of neighbouring candidate solutions at random, and the first neighbour to offer an improvement selected for the move.

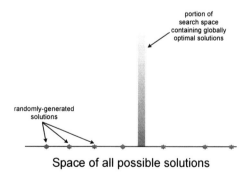

Fig. 2. Random search may fail to find optimal solutions occupying a small proportion of the overall search space (adapted from McMinn [66])

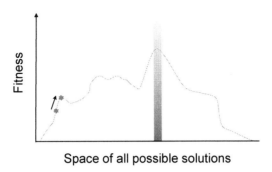

(a) A climb to a local optimum

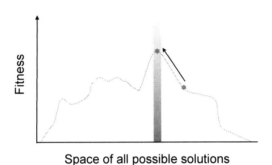

(b) A restart resulting in a climb to the global optimum

Fig. 3. Hill Climbing seeks to improve a single solution, initially selected at random, by iteratively exploring its neighbourhood (adapted from McMinn [66])

Select a starting solution $s \in S$
Repeat
    Select $s' \in N(s)$ such that $fit(s') > fit(s)$ according to ascent strategy
    $s \leftarrow s'$
Until $fit(s) \geq fit(s'), \forall s' \in N(s)$

Fig. 4. High level description of a hill climbing algorithm, for a problem with solution space S; neighbourhood structure N; and fit, the fitness function to be maximised (adapted from McMinn [65])

Simulated Annealing (Figure 5), first proposed by Kirkpatrick et al. [56], is similar to Hill Climbing in that it too attempts to improve one solution. However, Simulated Annealing attempts to escape local optima without the need to continually restart the search. It does this by temporarily accepting candidate solutions of poorer fitness, depending on the value of a variable known as the *temperature*. Initially the temperature is high, and free movement is allowed through the search space, with poorer neighbouring solutions representing

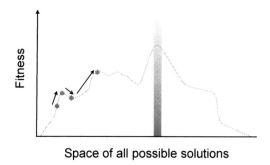

Space of all possible solutions

Fig. 5. Simulated Annealing also seeks to improve a single solution, but moves may be made to points in the search space of poorer fitness (adapted from McMinn [66])

potential moves along with better neighbouring solutions. As the search progresses, however, the temperature reduces, making moves to poorer solutions more and more unlikely. Eventually, *freezing point* is reached, and from this point on the search behaves identically to Hill Climbing. Pseudo-code for the Simulated Annealing algorithm can be seen in Figure 6. The probability of acceptance p of an inferior solution is calculated as $p = e^{-\frac{\delta}{t}}$, where δ is the difference in fitness value between the current solution and the neighbouring inferior solution being considered, and t is the current value of the temperature control parameter.

Select a starting solution $s \in S$
Select an initial temperature $t > 0$
Repeat
    $it \leftarrow 0$
    Repeat
        Select $s' \in N(s)$ at random
        $\Delta e \leftarrow fit(s) - fit(s')$
        If $\Delta e < 0$
            $s \leftarrow s'$
        Else
            Generate random number r, $0 \leq r < 1$
            If $r < e^{-\frac{\delta}{t}}$ Then $s \leftarrow s'$
        End If
        $it \leftarrow it + 1$
    Until $it = num\_solns$
    Decrease t according to cooling schedule
Until Stopping Condition Reached

Fig. 6. High level description of a simulated annealing algorithm, for a problem with solution space S; neighbourhood structure N; num_solns, the number of solutions to consider at each temperature level t; and fit, the fitness function to be maximised (adapted from McMinn [65])

'Simulated Annealing' is named so because it was inspired by the physical process of annealing; the cooling of a material in a heat bath. When a solid material is heated past its melting point and then cooled back into its solid state, the structural properties of the final material will vary depending on the rate of cooling.

Hill Climbing and Simulated Annealing are said to be *local searches*, because they operate with reference to one candidate solution at any one time, choosing 'moves' based on the neighbourhood of that candidate solution. Genetic Algorithms, on the other hand, are said to be *global searches*, sampling many points in the search space at once (Figure 7), offering more robustness to local optima. The set of candidate solutions currently under consideration is referred to as the current *population*, with each successive population considered referred to as a *generation*. Genetic Algorithms are inspired by Darwinian Evolution, in keeping with this analogy, each candidate solution is represented as a vector of components referred to as *individuals* or *chromosomes*. Typically, a Genetic Algorithm uses a binary representation, i.e. candidate solutions are encoded as strings of 1s and 0s; yet more natural representations to the problem may also be used, for example a list of floating point values.

The main loop of a Genetic Algorithm can be seen in Figure 8. The first generation is made up of randomly selected chromosomes, although the population may also be 'seeded' with selected individuals representing some domain information about the problem, which may increase the chances of the search converging on a set of highly-fit candidate solutions. Each individual in the population is then evaluated for fitness.

On the basis of fitness evaluation, certain individuals are selected to go forward to the following stages of crossover, mutation and reinsertion into the next generation. Usually selection is biased towards the fitter individuals, however the possibility of selecting weak solutions is not removed so that the search does not converge early on a set of locally optimal solutions. The very first Genetic Algorithm, proposed by Holland[1], used 'fitness-proportionate' selection, where the expected number of times an individual is selected for reproduction is proportionate to the individual's fitness in comparison with the rest of the population. However, fitness-proportionate selection has been criticised because highly-fit individuals appearing early in the progression of the search tend to dominate the selection process, leading the search to converge prematurely on one sub-area of the search space. Linear ranking [100] and tournament selection [23] have been proposed to circumvent these problems, involving algorithms where individuals are selected using relative rather than absolute fitness comparisons.

In the crossover stage, elements of each individual are recombined to form two offspring individuals. Different choices of crossover operator are available, including 'one-point' crossover, which splices two parents at a randomly-chosen position in the string to form two offspring. For example, two strings '111' and '000' may be spliced at position 2 to form two children '100' and '011'. Other

---

[1] This was introduced by Holland [54], though Turing had also briefly mentioned the idea of evolution as a computational metaphor [94].

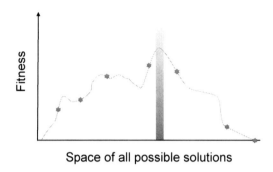

Fig. 7. Genetic Algorithms are global searches, taking account of several points in the search space at once (adapted from McMinn [66])

Randomly generate or seed initial population P
Repeat
 Evaluate fitness of each individual in P
 Select parents from P according to selection mechanism
 Recombine parents to form new offspring
 Construct new population P' from parents and offspring
 Mutate P'
 $P \leftarrow P'$
Until Stopping Condition Reached

Fig. 8. High level description of a Genetic Algorithm, adapted from McMinn [65]

operators may recombine using multiple crossover points, while 'uniform' crossover treats every position as a potential crossover point.

Subsequently, elements of the newly-created chromosomes are mutated at random, with the aim of diversifying the search into new areas of the search space. For GAs operating on binary representation, mutation usually involves randomly flipping bits of the chromosome. Finally, the next generation of the population is chosen in the 'reinsertion' phase, and the new individuals are evaluated for fitness. The GA continues in this loop until it finds a solution known to be globally optimal, or the resources allocated to it (typically a time limit or a certain budget of fitness evaluations) are exhausted. Whitley's tutorial papers [101, 102] offer a further excellent introductory material for getting starting with Genetic Algorithms in Search Based Software Engineering.

5   Getting the First Result: A Simple Example for Regression Testing

This section presents an application of a search-based approach to the Test Case Prioritisation (TCP) in regression testing, illustrating the steps that are necessary to obtain the first set of results. This makes concrete the concepts of representation, fitness function and search based algorithm (and their operators) introduced in the previous sections. First, let us clarify what we mean by TCP.

Regression testing is a testing activity that is performed to gain confidence that the recent modifications to the System Under Test (SUT), e.g. bug patches or new features, did not interfere with existing functionalities [108]. The simplest way to ensure this is to execute all available tests; this is often called *retest-all* method. However, as the software evolves, the test suite grows too, eventually making it prohibitively expensive to adopt the retest-all approach. Many techniques have been developed to deal with the cost of regression testing.

Test Case Prioritisation represents a group of techniques that particularly deal with the permutations of tests in regression test suites [28, 108]. The assumption behind these techniques is that, because of the limited resources, it may not be possible to execute the entire regression test suite. The intuition behind Test Case Prioritisation techniques is that more important tests should be executed earlier. In the context of regression testing, the 'important' tests are the ones that detect regression faults. That is, the aim of Test Case Prioritisation is to maximise *earlier fault detection rate*. More formally, it is defined as follows:

Definition 1. *Test Case Prioritisation Problem*

Given: *A test suite, T, the set of permutations of T, PT, and a function from PT to real numbers, $f : PT \rightarrow \mathbb{R}$.*

Problem: *To find $T' \in PT$ such that $(\forall T'')(T'' \in PT)(T'' \neq T')[f(T') \geq f(T'')]$.*

Ideally, the function f should be a mapping from tests to their fault detection capability. However, whether a test detects some faults or not is only known *after* its execution. In practice, a function f that is a surrogate to the fault detection capability of tests is used. Structural coverage is one of the most popular choices: the permutation of tests that achieves structural coverage as early as possible is thought to maximise the chance of early fault detection.

5.1   Representation

At its core, TCP as a search problem is an optimisation in a permutation space similar to the Travelling Salesman Problem (TSP), for which many advanced representation schemes have been developed. Here we will focus on the most basic form of representation. The set of all possible candidate solutions is the set of all possible permutations of tests in the regression test suite. If the regression test suite contains n tests, the representation takes the form of a vector with n elements. For example, Figure 9 shows one possible candidate solution for TCP with size n, i.e. with a regression test suite that contains 6 tests, $\{t_0, \ldots, t_5\}$.

Depending on the choice of the search algorithm, the next step is either to define the neighbouring solutions of a given solution (local search) or to define the genetic operators (genetic algorithm).

t1	t3	t0	t2	t5	t4

Fig. 9. One possible candidate solution for TCP with a regression test suite with 6 tests, $\{t_0, \ldots, t_5\}$

Neighbouring Solutions. Unless the characteristics of the search landscape is known, it is recommended that the neighbouring solutions of a given solution for a local search algorithm is generated by making the smallest possible changes to the given solution. This allows the human engineer to observe and understand the features of the search landscape.

It is also important to define the neighbouring solutions in a way that produces a manageable number of neighbours. For example, if the set of neighbouring solutions for TCP of size n is defined as the set of all permutations that can be generated by swapping two tests, there would be $n(n-1)$ neighbouring solutions. However, if we only consider swapping adjacent tests, there would be $n-1$. If the fitness evaluation is expensive, i.e. takes non-trivial time, controlling the size of the neighbourhood may affect the efficiency of the search algorithm significantly.

Genetic Operators. The following is a set of simple genetic operators that can be defined over permutation-based representations.

- **Selection:** Selection operators tend to be relatively independent of the choice of representation. It is more closely related to the design of the fitness function. One widely used approach that is also recommended as the first step is n-way tournament selection. First, randomly sample n solutions from the population. Out of this sample, pick the fittest individual solution. Repeat once again to select a pair of solutions for reproduction.
- **Crossover:** Unlike selection operators, crossover operators are directly linked to the structure of the representation of solutions. Here, we use the crossover operator following Antoniol et al. [6] to generate, from parent solutions p_1 and p_2, the offspring solutions o_1 and o_2:
  1. Pick a random number k $(1 \leq k \leq n)$
  2. The first k elements of p_1 become the first k elements of o_1.
  3. The last $n - k$ elements of o_1 are the sequence of $n - k$ elements that remain when the k elements selected from p_1 are taken from p_2, as illustrated in Figure 10.
  4. o_2 is generated similarly, composed of the first $n - k$ elements of p_2 and the remaining k elements of p_1.
- **Mutation:** Similarly to defining the neighbouring solutions for local search algorithms, it is recommended that, initially, mutation operators are defined to introduce relatively small changes to individual solutions. For example, we can swap the position of two randomly selected tests.

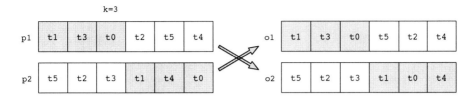

Fig. 10. Illustration of crossover operator for permutation-based representations following Antoniol et al.

5.2   Fitness Function

The recommended first step to design the fitness function is to look for an existing metric that measures the quality we are optimising for. If one exists, it often provides not only a quick and easy way to evaluate the search-based approach to the problem but also a channel to compare the results to other existing techniques.

The metric that is widely used to evaluate the effectiveness of TCP techniques is Average Percentage of Faults Detected (APFD) [28]. Higher APFD values mean that faults are detected earlier in testing. Suppose that, as the testing progresses, we plot the percentage of detected faults against the number of tests executed so far: intuitively, APFD would be the area behind the plot.

However, calculation of APFD requires the knowledge of which tests detected which faults. As explained in Section 5, the use of this knowledge defies the purpose of the prioritisation because fault detection information is not available until all tests are executed. This forces us to turn to the widely used surrogate, structural coverage. For example, Average Percentage of Blocks Covered (APBC) is calculated in a similar way to APFD but, instead of percentage of detected faults, percentage of blocks covered so far is used. In regression testing scenarios, the coverage information of tests are often available from the previous iteration of testing. While the recent modification that we are testing against might have made the existing coverage information imprecise, it is often *good enough* to provide guidance for prioritisation, especially when regression testing is performed reasonably frequently.

5.3   Putting It All Together

The representation of solutions and the fitness function are the only problem-specific components in the overall architecture of SBSE approach in Figure 11. It is recommended that these problem specific components are clearly separated from the search algorithm itself: the separation not only makes it easier to reuse the search algorithms (that are problem independent) but also helps testing and debugging of the overall approach (repeatedly used implementations of search algorithms can provide higher assurance).

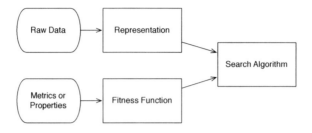

Fig. 11. Overall Architecture of SBSE Approach

6   Understanding Your Results

6.1   Fair Comparison

Due to the stochastic nature of optimisation algorithms, searches must be repeated several times in order to mitigate against the effects of random variation. In the literature, experiments are typically repeated 30-50 times.

When comparing two algorithms, the best fitness values obtained by the searches concerned are an obvious indicator to how well the optimisation process performed. However, in order to ensure a fair comparison, it is important to establish the amount of effort expended by each search algorithm, to find those solutions. This effort is commonly measured by logging the *number of fitness evaluations* that were performed. For example, it could be that an algorithm found a solution with a better fitness value, but did so because it was afforded a higher number of trials in which to obtain it. Or, there could be trade-offs, for example search A may find a solution of good fitness early in the search, but fail to improve it, yet search B can find solutions of slightly better fitness, but requiring many more fitness evaluations in which to discover it. When a certain level of fitness is obtained by more than one search algorithm, the *average number of fitness evaluations* over the different runs of the experiments by each algorithm is used to measure the cost of the algorithm in obtaining that fitness, or to put it another way, its relative *efficiency*.

For some types of problem, e.g. test data generation, there is a specific goal that must be attained by the search; for example the discovery of test data to execute a particular branch. In such cases, merely 'good' solutions of high fitness are not enough - a solution with a certain very high fitness value must be obtained, or the goal of the search will not be attained. In such cases, best fitness is no longer as an important measure as the *success rate*, a percentage reflecting the number of times the goal of the search was achieved over the repetitions of the experiment. The success rate gives an idea of how *effective* the search was at achieving its aim.

6.2   Elementary Statistical Analysis

The last section introduced some *descriptive* statistics for use in Search Based Software Engineering experiments, but also *inferential* statistics may be applied to discern whether one set of experiments are significantly different in some aspect from another.

Suppose there are two approaches to address a problem in SBSE, each of which involves the application of some search based algorithm to a set of problem instances. We collect results for the application of both algorithms, A and B, and we notice that, over a series of runs of our experiment, Algorithm A tends to perform better than Algorithm B. The performance we have in mind, may take many forms. It may be that Algorithm A is faster than B, or that after a certain number of fitness evaluations it has achieved a higher fitness value, or a higher average fitness. Alternatively, there may be some other measurement that we can make about which we notice a difference in performance that we believe is worth reporting.

In such cases, SBSE researchers tend to rely on inferential statistics as a means of addressing the inherently stochastic nature of search based algorithms. That is, we may notice that the mean fitness achieved by Algorithm A is higher than that of Algorithm B after 10 executions of each, but how can we be *sure* that this is not merely an observation arrived at by *chance*? It is to answer precisely these kinds of question that statistical hypothesis testing is used in the experimental sciences, and SBSE is no exception.

A complete explanation of the issues and techniques that can be used in applying inferential statistics in SBSE is beyond the scope of this tutorial. However, there has been a recent paper on the topic of statistical testing of randomised algorithms by Arcuri and Briand [8], which provides more detail. In this section we provide an overview of some of the key points of concern.

The typical scenario with which we are concerned is one in which we want to explore the likelihood that our experiments found that Algorithm A outperforms Algorithm B purely by chance. Usually we wish to be in a position to make a claim that we have evidence that suggests that Algorithm A is better than Algorithm B. For example, as a sanity check, we may wish to show that our SBSE technique comfortably outperforms a random search. But what do we mean by 'comfortably outperforms'?

In order to investigate this kind of question we set a threshold on the degree of chance that we find acceptable. Typically, in the experimental sciences, this level is chosen to be either 1% or 5%. That is, we will have either a less than 1 in 100 or a less than 5 in 100 chance of believing that Algorithm A outperforms Algorithm B based on a set of executions when in fact it does not. This is the chance of making a so-called 'Type I' error. It would lead to us concluding that some Algorithm A was better than Algorithm B when, in fact, it was not.

If we choose a threshold for error of 5% then we have a 95% confidence level in our conclusion based on our sample of the population of all possible executions of the algorithm. That is, we are '95% sure that we can claim that Algorithm A really is better than Algorithm B'. Unpacking this claim a little, what we find is that there is a population involved. This is the population of all possible runs of the algorithm in question. For each run we may get different behaviour due to the stochastic nature of the algorithm and so we are not in a position to say exactly what the value obtained will be. Rather, we can give a range of values.

However, it is almost always impractical to perform all possible runs and so we have to sample. Our '95% confidence claim' is that we are 95% confident that the evidence provided by our sample allows us to infer a conclusion about the algorithm's performance on the whole population. This is why this branch of statistics is referred to as 'inferential statistics'; we *infer* properties of a whole population based on a sample.

Unfortunately a great deal of 'ritualistic' behaviour has grown up around the experimental sciences, in part, resulting for an inadequate understanding of the underlying statistics. One aspect of this ritual is found in the choice of a suitable confidence level. If we are comparing some new SBSE approach to the state of the art, then we are asking a question as to whether the new approach is worthy of consideration. In such a situation we may be happy with a 1 in 10 chance of a Type I error (and could set the confidence level, accordingly, to be 90%). The consequences of considering a move from the status quo may not be so great.

However, if we are considering whether to use a potently fatal drug on a patient who may otherwise survive we might want a much higher confidence that the drug would, indeed, improve the health of the patent over the status quo (no treatment). For this reason it is important to think about what level of confidence is suitable for the problem in hand.

The statistical test we perform will result in a p-value. The p-value is the chance that a Type I error has occurred. That is, we notice that a sample of runs produces a higher mean result for a measurement of interest for Algorithm A than for Algorithm B. We wish to reject the so-called 'null hypothesis'; the hypothesis that the population of all executions of Algorithm A is no different to that of Algorithm B. To do this we perform an inferential statistical test. If all the assumptions of the test are met and the sample of runs we have is unbiased then the p-value we obtain indicates the chance that the populations of runs of Algorithm A and Algorithm B are identical given the evidence we have from the sample. For instance a p-value equal to or lower than 0.05 indicates that we have satisfied the traditional (and somewhat ritualistic) 95% confidence level test. More precisely, the chance of committing a Type I error is p.

This raises the question of how large a sample we should choose. The sample size is related to the statistical power of our experiment. If we have too small a sample then we may obtain high p-values and incorrectly conclude that there is no significant difference between the two algorithms we are considering. This is a so-called Type II error; we incorrectly accept the null hypothesis when it is, in fact, false. In our case it would mean that we would incorrectly believe Algorithm A to be no better than Algorithm B. More precisely, we would conclude, *correctly*, that we have no evidence to claim that Algorithm A is significantly better than Algorithm B at the chosen conference level. However, had we chosen a larger sample, we may have had just such evidence. In general, all else being equal, the larger the sample we choose the less likely we are to commit a Type II error. This is why researchers prefer larger sample sizes where this is feasible.

There is another element of ritual for which some weariness is appropriate: the choice of a suitable statistical test. One of the most commonalty performed tests in work on search based algorithms in general (though not necessarily SBSE in particular) is the well-known t test. Almost all statistical packages support it and it is often available at the touch of a button. Unfortunately, the t test makes assumptions about the distribution of the data. These assumptions may not be borne out in practice thereby increasing the chance of a Type I error. In some senses a type I error is worse than a Type II error, because it may lead to the publication of false claims, whereas a Type I error will most likely lead to researcher disappointment at the lack of evidence to support publishable results.

To address this potential problem with parametric inferential statistics SBSE researchers often use nonparametric statistical tests. Non-parametric tests make fewer assumptions about the distribution of the data. As such, these tests are weaker (they have less power) and may lead to the false acceptance of the null hypothesis for the same sample size (a Type II error), when used in place of a more powerful parametric test that is able to reject the null hypothesis. However, since the parametric tests make assumptions about the distribution, should these assumptions prove to be false, then the rejection of the null hypothesis by a parametric test may be an artefact of the false assumptions; a form of Type I error.

It is important to remember that all inferential statistical techniques are founded on probability theory. To the traditional computer scientist, particularly those raised on an intellectual diet consisting exclusively of formal methods and discrete mathematics, this reliance on probability may be as unsettling as quantum mechanics was to the traditional world of physics. However, as engineers, the reliance on a confidence level is little more than an acceptance of a certain 'tolerance' and is quite natural and acceptable.

This appreciation of the probability-theoretic foundations of inferential statistics rather than a merely ritualistic application of 'prescribed tests' is important if the researcher is to avoid mistakes. For example, armed with a non parametric test and a confidence internal of 95% the researcher may embark on a misguided 'fishing expedition' to find a variant of Algorithm A that outperforms Algorithm B. Suppose 5 independent variants of Algorithm A are experimented with and, on each occasion, a comparison is made with Algorithm B using an inferential statistical test. If variant 3 produces a p-value of 0.05, while the others do not it would be a mistake to conclude that *at the 95% confidence level* Algorithm A (variant 3) is better than Algorithm B.

Rather, we would have to find that Algorithm A variant 3 had a p-value lower than 0.05/5; by repeating the same test 5 times, we raise the confidence required for each test from 0.05 to 0.01 to retain the same overall confidence. This is known as a 'Bonferroni correction'. To see why it is necessary, suppose we have 20 variants of Algorithms A. What would be the expected likelihood that one of these would, *by chance*, have a p-value equal or lower than 0.05 in a world where none of the variants is, in fact, any different from Algorithm B? If we repeat a statistical test sufficiently many times without a correction to the confidence level, then we are increasingly likely to commit a Type I error. This situation is amusingly captured by an xkcd cartoon [73].

Sometimes, we find ourselves comparing, not vales of measurements, but the success rates of searches. Comparison of success rates using inferential statistics requires a categorical approach, since a search goal is either fulfilled or not. For this Fisher's Exact test is a useful statistical measure. This is another non-parametric test. For investigative of correlations, researchers use Spearman and Pearson correlation analysis. These tests can be useful to explore the degree to which increases in one factor are correlated to another, but it is important to understand that correlations does not, of course, entail causality.

7   More Advanced Techniques

Much has been achieved in SBSE using only a single fitness function, a simple representation of the problem and a simple search technique (such as hill climbing). It is recommended that, as a first exploration of SBSE, the first experiments should concern a single fitness function, a simple representation and a simple search technique. However, once results have been obtained and the approach is believed to have potential, for example, it is found to outperform random search, then it is natural to turn one's attention to more advanced techniques and problem characterisations.

This section considers four exciting ways in which the initial set of results can be developed, using more advanced techniques that may better model the real world scenario and may also help to extend the range and type of results obtained and the applicability of the overall SBSE approach for the Software Engineering problem in hand.

7.1   Multiple Objectives

Though excellent results can be obtained with a single objective, many real world Software Engineering problems are multiple objective problems. The objectives that have to be optimised are often in competition with one another and may be contradictory; we may find ourselves trying to balance the different optimisation objectives of several different goals.

One approach to handle such scenarios is the use of Pareto optimal SBSE, in which several optimisation objectives are combined, but without needing to decide which take precedence over the others. This approach is described in more detail elsewhere [48] and was first proposed as the 'best' way to handle multiple objectives for all SBSE problems by Harman in 2007 [36]. Since then, there has been a rapid uptake of Pareto optimal SBSE to requirements [27, 31, 84, 90, 113], planning [5, 98], design [17, 88, 95], coding [9, 99], testing [33, 35, 47, 76, 90, 96, 107], and refactoring [52].

Suppose a problem is to be solved that has n fitness functions, $f_1, \ldots, f_n$ that take some vector of parameters $\bar{x}$. Pareto optimality combines a set of measurements, f_i, into a single ordinal scale metric, F, as follows:

$$F(\overline{x_1}) > F(\overline{x_2})$$
$$\Leftrightarrow$$
$$\forall i. f_i(\overline{x_1}) \geq f_i(\overline{x_2}) \ \land \ \exists i. f_i(\overline{x_1}) > f_i(\overline{x_2})$$

Under Pareto optimality, one solution is better than another if it is better according to at least one of the individual fitness functions and no worse according to all of the others. Under the Pareto interpretation of combined fitness, no overall fitness improvement occurs no matter how much almost all of the fitness functions improve, should they do so at the slightest expense of any one of their number. The use of Pareto optimality is an alternative to simply aggregating fitness using a weighted sum of the n fitness functions.

When searching for solutions to a problem using Pareto optimality, the search yields a set of solutions that are non–dominated. That is, each member of the non-dominated set is no worse than any of the others in the set, but also cannot be said to be better. Any set of non–dominated solutions forms a Pareto front.

Consider Figure 12, which depicts the computation of Pareto optimality for two imaginary fitness functions (Objective 1 and Objective 2). The longer the search algorithm is run the better the approximation becomes to the real Pareto front. In the figure, points $S1$, $S2$ and $S3$ lie on the Pareto front, while $S4$ and $S5$ are dominated.

Pareto optimality has many advantages. Should a single solution be required, then coefficients can be re-introduced in order to distinguish among the non–dominated set at the current Pareto front. However, by refusing to conflate the individual fitness functions into a single aggregate, the search may consider solutions that may be overlooked by search guided by aggregate fitness. The approximation of the Pareto front is also a useful analysis tool in itself. For example, it may contain 'knee points', where a small change in one fitness is accompanied by a large change in another. These knee points denote interesting parts of the solution space that warrant closer investigation.

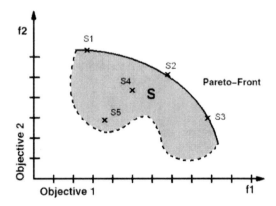

Fig. 12. Pareto Optimality and Pareto Fronts (taken from the survey by Harman et al. [48])

7.2   Co Evolution

In Co–Evolutionary Computation, two or more populations of solutions evolve simultaneously with the fitness of each depending upon the current population of the other. Adamopoulos et al. [2] were the first to suggest the application of co-evolution to an SBSE problem, using it to evolve sets of mutants and sets of test cases, where the test cases act as predators and the mutants as their prey. Arcuri and Yao [10] use co-evolution to evolve programs and their test data from specifications using co-evolution.

Arcuri and Yao [11] also developed a co-evolutionary model of bug fixing, in which one population essentially seeks out patches that are able to pass test cases, while test cases can be produced from an oracle in an attempt to find the shortcomings of a current population of proposed patches. In this way the patch is the prey, while the test cases, once again, act as predators. The approach assumes the existence of a specification to act the oracle.

Many aspects of Software Engineering problems lend themselves to a co-evolutionary model of optimisation because software systems are complex and rich in potential populations that could be productively co-evolved (using both competitive and co-operative co-evolution). For example: components, agents, stakeholder behaviour models, designs, cognitive models, requirements, test cases, use cases and management plans are all important aspects of software systems for which optimisation is an important concern. Though all of these may not occur in the same system, they are all the subject of change. If a suitable fitness function be found, the SBSE can be used to co-evolve solutions.

Where two such populations are already being evolved in isolation using SBSE, but participate in the same overall software system, it would seem a logical 'next step', to seek to evolve these populations together; the fitness of one is likely to have an impact on the fitness of another, so evolution in isolation may not be capable of locating the best solutions.

7.3   SBSE as Decision Support

SBSE has been most widely used to find solutions to complex and demanding software engineering problems, such as sets of test data that meet test adequacy goals or sequences of transformations that refactor a program or modularisation boundaries that best balance the trade off between cohesion and coupling. However, in many other situations it is not the actual solutions found that are the most interesting nor the most important aspects of SBSE.

Rather, the value of the approach lies in the insight that is gained through the analysis inherent in the automated search process and the way in which its results capture properties of the structure of software engineering solutions. SBSE can be applied to situations in which the human will decide on the solution to be adopted, but the search process can provide insight to help guide the decision maker.

This insight agenda, in which SBSE is used to gain insights and to provide decision support to the software engineering decision maker has found natural resonance and applicability when used in the early aspects of the software engineering lifecycle, where the decisions made can have far–reaching implications.

For instance, addressing the need for negotiation and mediation in requirements engineering decision making, Finkelstein et al. [31] explored the use of different notions of fairness to explore the space of requirements assignments that can be said to be fair according to multiple definitions of 'fairness'. Saliu and Ruhe [84] used a Pareto optimal approach to explore the balance of concerns between requirements at different levels of abstraction, while Zhang et al, showed how SBSE could be used to explore the tradeoff among the different stakeholders in requirements assignment problems [112].

Many of the values used to define a problem for optimisation come from estimates. This is particularly the case in the early stages of the software engineering lifecycle, where the values available necessarily come from the estimates made by decision makers. In these situations it is not optimal solutions that the decision maker requires, so much as guidance on which of the estimates are most likely to affect the solutions. Ren et al. [46] used this observation to define an SBSE approach to requirements sensitivity analysis, in which the gaol is to identify the requirements and budgets for which the managers' estimates of requirement cost and value have most impact. For these *sensitive* requirements and budgets, more care is required. In this way SBSE has been used as a way to provide *sensitivity analysis*, rather than necessarily providing a proposed set of requirement assignments.

Similarly, in project planning, the manager bases his or her decisions on estimates of work package duration and these estimates are notoriously unreliable. Antoniol et al. [5] used this observation to explore the trade off between the completion time of a software project plan and the risk over overruns due to misestimation. This was a Pareto efficient, bi–objective approach, in which the two objectives were the completion time and the risk (measured in terms of overrun due to misestimation). Using their approach, Antoniol et al., demonstrated that a decision maker could identify safe budgets for which completion times could be more assured.

Though most of the work on decision support through SBSE has been conducted at the early stages of the lifecycle, there are still opportunities for using SBSE to gain insight at later stages in the lifecycle. For example, White et al. [99] used a bi-objective Pareto optimal approach to explore the trade off between power consumption and functionality, demonstrating that it was possible to find knee points on the Pareto front for which a small loss of functionality could result in a high degree of improved power efficiency.

As can be seen from these examples, SBSE is not merely a research programme in which one seeks to 'solve' software engineering problems; it is a rich source of insight and decision support. This is a research agenda for SBSE that Harman has developed through a series of keynotes and invited papers, suggesting SBSE as a source of additional insight and an approach to decision support for predictive modelling [38], cognitive aspects of program understanding [37], multiple objective regression testing [40] and program transformation and refactoring [41].

7.4   Augmenting with Other Non SBSE Techniques

Often it is beneficial to augment search algorithms with other techniques, such as clustering or static analysis of source code. There is no hard rules for augmentation: different non-SBSE techniques can be considered appropriate depending on the context and challenge that are unique to the given software engineering problem. This section illustrates how some widely used non-SBSE techniques can help the SBSE approach.

Clustering. Clustering is a process that partitions objects into different subsets so that objects in each group share common properties. The clustering criterion determines which properties are used to measure the commonality. It is often an effective way to reduce the size of the problem and, therefore, the size of the search space: objects in the same cluster can be replaced by a single representative object from the cluster, resulting in reduced problem size. It has been successfully applied when the human is in the loop [109].

Static Analysis. For search-based test data generation approaches, it is common that the fitness evaluation involves the program source code. Various static analysis techniques can improve the effectiveness and the efficiency of code-related SBSE techniques. Program slicing has been successfully used to reduce the search space for automated test data generation [43]. Program transformation techniques have been applied so that search-based test data generation techniques can cope with flag variables [15].

Hybridisation. While hybridising different search algorithms are certainly possible, hybridisation with non-SBSE techniques can also be beneficial. Greedy approximation has been used to *inject* solutions into MOEA so that MOEA can reach the region close to the true Pareto front much faster [107]. Some of more sophisticated forms of hybridisation use non-SBSE techniques as part of fitness evaluation [105].

8   Case Studies

This section introduces four case studies to provide the reader with a range of examples of SBSE application in software engineering. The case studies are chosen to represent a wide range of topics, illustrating the way in which SBSE is highly applicable to Software Engineering problem; with just a suitable representation, fitness function and a choice of algorithm it is possible to apply SBSE to the full spectrum of SBSE activities and problems and to obtain interesting and potentially valuable results. The case studies cover early lifecycle activities such as effort estimation and requirements assignment through test case generation to regression testing, exemplifying the breadth of applications to which SBSE has already been put.

8.1   Case Study: Multi-objective Test Suite Minimisation

Let us consider another class of regression testing techniques that is different from Test Case Prioritisation studied in Section 5: test suite minimisation. Prioritisation techniques aim to generate an ideal test execution order; minimisation techniques aim to reduce the size of the regression test suite when the regression test suite of an existing software system grows to such an extent that it may no longer be feasible to execute the entire test suite [80]. In order to reduce the size of the test suite, any *redundant* test cases in the test suite need to be identified and removed.

Regression Testing requires optimisation because of the problem posed by large data sets. That is, organisations with good testing policies quickly accrue large pools of test data. For example, one of the regression test suites studied in this paper is also used for a smoke-test by IBM for one of its middleware products and takes over 4 hours if executed in its entirety. However, a typical smoke-test can be allocated only 1 hour maximum, forcing the engineer either to select a set of test cases from the available pool or to prioritise the order in which the test cases are considered.

The cost of this selection or prioritisation may not be amortised if the engineer wants to apply the process with every iteration in order to reflect the most recent test history or to use the whole test suite more evenly. However, without optimisation, the engineer will simply run out of time to complete the task. As a result, the engineer may have failed to execute the most optimal set of test cases when time runs out, reducing fault detection capabilities and thereby harming the effectiveness of the smoke test.

One widely accepted criterion for redundancy is defined in relation to the coverage achieved by test cases [16, 20, 53, 74, 81]. If the test coverage achieved by test case t_1 is a subset of the test coverage achieved by test case t_2, it can be said that the execution of t_1 is redundant as long as t_2 is also executed. The aim of test suite minimisation is to obtain the smallest subset of test cases that are not redundant with respect to a set of test requirements. More formally, test suite minimisation problem can be defined as follows [108]:

Definition 2. *Test Suite Minimisation Problem*

Given: A test suite of n tests, T, a set of m test goals $\{r_1, \ldots, r_m\}$, that must be satisfied to provide the desired 'adequate' testing of the program, and subsets of T, T_is, one associated with each of the r_is such that any one of the test cases t_j belonging to T_i can be used to achieve requirement r_i.

Problem: Find a representative set, T', of test cases from T that satisfies all r_is.

The testing criterion is satisfied when every test-case requirement in $\{r_1, \ldots, r_m\}$ is satisfied. A test-case requirement, r_i, is satisfied by any test case, t_j, that belongs to T_i, a subset of T. Therefore, the representative set of test cases is the hitting set of T_is. Furthermore, in order to maximise the effect of minimisation, T' should be the minimal hitting set of T_is. The minimal hitting-set problem is an NP-complete problem as is the dual problem of the minimal set cover problem [34].

The NP-hardness of the problem encouraged the use of heuristics and meta-heuristics. The greedy approach [74] as well as other heuristics for minimal hitting set and set cover problem [20, 53] have been applied to test suite minimisation but these approaches were not cost-cognisant and only dealt with a single objective (test coverage). With the single-objective problem formulation, the solution to the test suite minimisation problem is one subset of test cases that maximises the test coverage with minimum redundancy.

Later, the problem was reformulated as a multi-objective optimisation problem [106]. Since the greedy algorithm does not cope with multiple objectives very well, Multi-Objective Evolutionary Algorithms (MOEAs) have been applied to the multi-objective formulation of the test suite minimisation [63, 106]. The case study presents the multi-objective formulation of test suite minimisation introduced by Yoo and Harman [106].

Representation. Test suite minimisation is at its core a set-cover problem; the main decision is whether to include a specific test into the minimised subset or not. Therefore, we use the binary string representation. For a test suite with n tests, $\{t_1, \ldots, t_n\}$, the representation is a binary string of length n: the i-th digit is 1 if t_i is to be included in the subset and 0 otherwise. Binary tournament selection, single-point crossover and single bit-flip mutation genetic operators were used for MOEAs.

Fitness Function. Three different objectives were considered: structural coverage, fault history coverage and execution cost. Structural coverage of a given candidate solution is simply the structural coverage achieved collectively by all the tests that are selected by the candidate solution (i.e. their corresponding bits are set to 1). This information is often available from the previous iteration of regression testing. This objective is to be maximised.

Fault history coverage is included to compliment structural coverage metric because achieving coverage may not always increase fault detection capability. We collect all known previous faults and calculate *fault coverage* for each candidate solution by counting how many of the previous faults could have been detected by the candidate solution. The underlying assumption is that a test that has detected faults in the past may have a higher chance of detecting faults in the new version. This objective is to be maximised.

The final objective is execution cost. Without considering the cost, the simplest way to maximise the other two objectives is to select the entire test suite. By trying to optimise for the cost, it is possible to obtain the trade-off between structural/fault history coverage and the cost of achieving them. The execution cost of each test is measured using a widely-used profiling tool called `valgrind`.

Algorithm. A well known MOEA by Deb et al. [24], NSGA-II, was used for the case study. Pareto optimality is used in the process of selecting individuals. This leads to the problem of selecting one individual out of a non-dominated pair. NSGA-II uses the concept of crowding distance to make this decision; crowding distance measures how far away an individual is from the rest of the population. NSGA-II tries to achieve a wider Pareto frontier by selecting individuals that are far from the others. NSGA-II is based on elitism; it performs the non-dominated sorting in each generation in order to preserve the individuals on the current Pareto frontier into the next generation.

The widely used single-objective approximation for set cover problem is greedy algorithm. The only way to deal with the chosen three objectives is to take the weighted sum of each coverage metric per time, i.e.:

Results. Figure 13 shows the results for the three objective test suite minimisation for a test suite of a program called `space`, which is taken from Software Infrastructure Repository (SIR). The 3D plots display the solutions produced by the weighted-sum additional greedy algorithm (depicted by + symbols connected with a line), and the reference Pareto front (depicted by × symbols). The reference Pareto front contains all non-dominated solutions from the combined results of weighted-sum greedy approach and NSGA-II approach. While the weighted-sum greedy approach produces solutions that are not dominated, it can be seen that NSGA-II produces a much richer set of solutions that explore wider area of the trade-off surface.

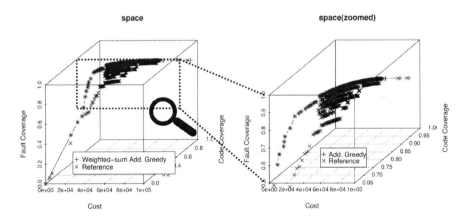

Fig. 13. A plot of 3-dimensional Pareto-front from multi-objective test suite minimisation for program `space` from European Space Agency, taken from Yoo and Harman [106]

8.2   Case Study: Requirements Analysis

Selecting a set of software requirements for the release of the next version of a software system is a demanding decision procedure. The problem of choosing the optimal set of requirements to include in the next release of a software system has become known as the Next Release Problem (NRP) [13, 113] and the activity of planning for requirement inclusion and exclusion has become known as release planning [82, 84].

The NRP deals with the selecting a subset of requirements based on their desirability (e.g. the expected revenue) while subject to constraints such as a limited budget [13]. The original formulation of NRP by Bagnall et al. [13] considered maximising the customer satisfaction (by inclusion of their demanded requirements in the next version) while not exceeding the company's budget.

More formally, let $C = \{c_1, \ldots, c_m\}$ be the set of m customers whose requirements are to be considered for the next release. The set of n possible software requirements is denoted by $R = \{r_1, \ldots, r_n\}$. It is assumed that all requirements are independent, i.e. no requirement depends on others[2]. Finally, let $cost = [cost_1, \ldots, cost_n]$ be the cost vector for the requirements in R: $cost_i$ is the associate cost to fulfil the requirement r_i.

We also assume that each customer has a degree of importance for the company. The set of relative weights associated with each customer $c_j (1 \leq j \leq m)$ is denoted by $W = \{w_1, \ldots, w_m\}$, where $w_j \in [0, 1]$ and $\sum_{j=1}^{m} w_j = 1$. Finally, it is assumed that all requirements are not equally important for a given customer. The level of satisfaction for a given customer depends on the requirements that are satisfied in the next release of the software. Each customer $c_j (1 \leq j \leq m)$ assigns a value to requirement $r_i (1 \leq i \leq n)$ denoted by $value(r_i, c_j)$ where $value(r_i, c_j) > 0$ if customer c_j gets the requirement r_i and 0 otherwise.

Based on above, the overall $score$, or importance of a given requirement $r_i (1 \leq i \leq n)$, can be calculated as $score_i = \sum_{j=1}^{m} w_j \cdot value(r_i, c_j)$. The score of a given requirement is represented as its overall $value$ to the organisation.

The aim of the Multi-Objective NRP (MONRP) is to investigate the trade-off between the score and cost of requirements. Let $score = [score_1, \ldots, score_n]$ be the score vector calculated as above. Let $x = [x_1, \ldots, x_n] \in \{0, 1\}^n$ a solution vector, i.e. a binary string identifying a subset of R. Then MONRP is defined as follows:

Definition 3. Given: *The cost vector,* $cost = [cost_1, \ldots, cost_n]$ *and the score vector (calculated from the customer weights and customer-assigned value of requirements)* $score = [score_1, \ldots, score_n]$.

Problem: *Maximise* $\sum_{i=1}^{n} score_i \cdot x_i$ *while minimising* $\sum_{i=1}^{n} cost_i \cdot x_i$.

Representation. Similar to the test suite minimisation problem in Section 8.1, the candidate solution for NRP should denote whether each requirement will be *selected*, i.e. implemented in the next release. For a set of n requirements, $\{r_1, \ldots, r_n\}$, a candidate solution can be represented with a binary string of length n: the i-th digit is 1 if r_i is to be included in the subset and 0 otherwise.

---

[2] Bagnall et al. [13] describe a method to remove dependences in this context by computing the transitive closure of the dependency graph and regarding each requirement and all its prerequisites as a new single requirement.

Fitness Function. The *cost* and *profit* function can be directly used as fitness functions for each objectives for MOEAs: *cost* should be minimised while *profit* should be maximised.

Algorithm. The case study compares three different evolutionary algorithms to random search: NSGA-II, Pareto-GA and a single-objective GA. Pareto-GA is a variation of a generic single-objective GA that uses Pareto-optimality only for the selection process. The single-objective GA is used to deal with the multi-objective formulation of NRP by adopting different sets of weights with the weighted-sum approach. When using weighted-sum approach for two objective functions, f_1 and f_2, the overall fitness F of a candidate solution x is calculated as follows:

$$F(x) = w \cdot f_1(x) + (1 - w) \cdot f_2(x)$$

Depending on the value of the weight, w, the optimisation will target different regions on the Pareto front. The case study considered 9 different weight values ranging from 0.1 to 0.9 with step size of 0.1 to achieve wider Pareto fronts.

Results. Figure 14 shows results for an artificial instance of NRP with 40 requirements and 15 customers. Random search produces normally distributed solutions, whereas the weighted-sum, single-objective GA tends to produce solutions at the extremes of the Pareto front. Pareto-GA does produce some solutions that dominate most of the randomly generated solutions, but it is clear

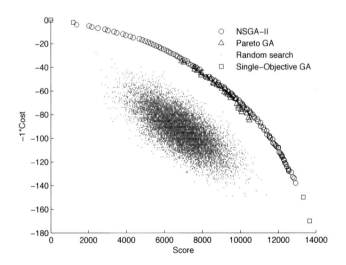

(**a**) 15 customers; 40 requirements

Fig. 14. Plot of results for NRP from different algorithms taken from Zhang and Harman [113]

that the Pareto front is dominantly produced by NSGA-II. Solutions generated by NSGA-II form the widest Pareto front that represents the trade-off between the cost and the expected profit (score).

8.3   Case Study: Structural Test Data Generation

Since the costs of manual software testing are extremely high, the software engineering community has devoted a lot of attention to researching methods of automating the process. The problem of generating structural test data, i.e. test data that attempts to execute all of a program's paths, program statements or true and false decisions, is one area that has attracted a lot of interest, particularly with respect to branch coverage; motivated by the prevalence of its variants in software testing standards.

To motivate the use of Search Based Software Engineering in this context, the program of Figure 15 will be studied, with the aim of generating a test suite that covers each of its individual branches. It is a program for evaluating a Chemical Abstracts Service (CAS) registry number assigned to chemicals. Each number is a string of digits separated by hyphens, with the final digit serving as a check digit. The routine takes a pointer to the first character of the string, processes it, and returns zero if the number is valid. An error code is returned in the case the number is not valid.

Definition. Let $I = (i_1, i_2, ...i_{len})$ be a vector of the input variables of a program under test, p. The domain D_{i_n} of the input variable i_n is the set of all values that i_n can hold, $1 \leq n \leq len; len = |I|$. The *input domain* of p is a cross product of the domains of each of the individual input variables: $D = D_{i_1} \times D_{i_2} ... \times D_{i_{len}}$. An *input* i to the function under test is a specific element of the function's input domain, that is, $i \in D$.

Given a target structure t in p, the problem is to find an input vector $I \in D$ such that t is executed.

Representation. Defining a representation for structural test data generation simply involves a method of encoding the input vector to a program. This is straightforward for program units such as functions involving primitive types such as integers, reals or characters, as the input vector can be manipulated directly by the search algorithm or trivially encoded into a binary format. However, programs involving arrays or dynamic data structures require more careful handling. In order to avoid a multi-length encoding, the size and shape of the data structure may need to be fixed. However research has been undertaken to remove this restriction [60]. For the CAS check routine, the representation is a sequence of integer values in the range 0-255, fixed to a length of 15. In this case, the whole range of the char type is used. For primitive types with large domains, however, the tester may wish to restrict the domains to sensible limits or a legal range of values.

```
(1) int cas_check(char* cas) {
(2)    int count = 0, checksum = 0, checkdigit = 0, pos;
(3)
(4)    for (pos=strlen(cas)-1; pos >= 0; pos--) {
(5)      int digit = cas[pos] - '0';
(6)
(7)      if (digit >= 0 && digit <= 9) {
(8)        if (count == 0)
(9)          checkdigit = digit;
(10)       if (count > 0)
(11)         checksum += count * digit;
(12)
(13)       count ++;
(14)     }
(15)   }
(16)
(17)   if (count >= 4)
(18)     if (count <= 10)
(19)       if (checksum % 10 == checkdigit)
(20)         return 0;
(21)       else return 1;
(22)     else return 2;
(23)   else return 3;
(24) }
```

Fig. 15. C routine for validating CAS registry numbers of chemical substances (e.g. '7732-18-5', the CAS number of water), taken from McMinn [66]

Fitness Function. In this case study, each branch is taken as the focus of a separate test data search, using the fitness function defined by Wegener et al. [97]. Fitness is computed according to the function $fit(t, i) \rightarrow \mathbb{R}$, that takes a structural target t and individual input i, and returns a real number that scores how 'close' the input was to executing the required branch. This assessment is based on a) the path taken by the input, and b) the values of variables in predicates at critical points along the path.

The path taken by the input is assessed and used to derive the value of a metric known as the 'approach level'. The approach level is essentially a count of the target's control dependencies that were not executed by the path. For structured programs, the approach level reflects the number of unpenetrated levels of nesting levels surrounding the target. Suppose, for example, a string is required for the execution of the true branch from line 19, i.e. where the string corresponds to a valid registry number. A diagram charting the computation of fitness can be seen in Figure 16. The approach level will be 2 if no invalid characters are found in the string, but there are too few digits in the string to form a valid CAS number, and the false branch is taken at line 17. If instead the string has too many digits, the true branch is taken at node 17, but the target is then missed because the false branch was taken at node 18, and the approach level is 1. When the checksum calculation is reached at line 19, the approach level is zero.

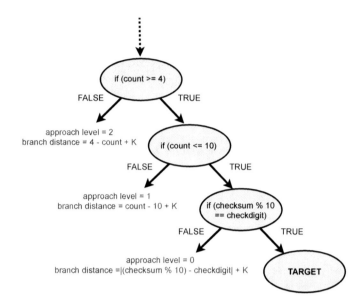

Fig. 16. Fitness function computation for execution of the true branch from line 19 of the CAS registry number check program of Figure 15, taken from McMinn [66]

When execution of a test case diverges from the target branch, the second component, the *branch distance*, expresses how close an input came to satisfying the condition of the predicate at which control flow for the test case went 'wrong'; that is, how close the input was to descending to the next approach level. For example, suppose execution takes the false branch at node 17 in Figure 15, but the true branch needs to be executed. Here, the branch distance is computed using the formula $4 - count + K$, where K is a constant added when the undesired, alternate branch is taken. The closer count is being greater than 4, the 'closer' the desired true branch is to being taken. A different branch distance formula is applied depending on the type of relational predicate. In the case of y >= x, and the >= relational operator, the formula is $x - y + K$. For a full list of branch distance formulae for different relational predicate types, see Tracey et al. [93].

The complete fitness value is computed by normalising the branch distance and adding it to the approach level:

$$fit(t, i) = approach\_level(t, i) + normalise(branch\_distance(t, i))$$

Since the maximum branch distance is generally not known, the standard approach to normalisation cannot be applied [7]; instead the following formula is used:

$$normalise(d) = 1 - 1.001^{-d}$$

Algorithm. A popular Genetic Algorithm for Search Based Structural Test Data Generation is that of Wegener et al. [97], which we will refer to as the 'Wegener GA' hereinafter. The GA uses a population size of 300 individuals, divided across 6 subpopulations, initially made up of 50 individuals each. It uses a linear ranking method [100] as part of the selection phase. Linear ranking sorts the population into fitness order as assigns new ranked fitness values such that the best individual is awarded a ranked fitness of Z, the median individual a value of 1 and the worst individual a value of $Z - 2$. The Wegener GA uses a value of $Z = 1.7$. Stochastic universal sampling [14] is then used as a selection method, whereby individuals are selected with a probability proportionate to its ranked fitness value. The selection method therefore favours fitter individuals, but the use of ranked fitness values rather than direct values helps prevent super-fit individuals from being selected as many times as they would have been normally, which may go on to dominate the next generation and cause the search to converge prematurely.

The Wegener GA uses a special type of mutation that is well-suited for test data generation problems involving real values. The mutation operator is derived from the Breeder GA [71]. Mutation is applied with a probability p_m of $1/len$, where len is the length of the input vector. The mutation operator applies a different mutation step size, 10^{-pop}, depending on the subpopulation pop, $1 \leq pop \leq 6$. A mutation range r is defined for each input parameter by the product of pop and the domain size of the parameter. The 'mutated' value of an input parameter can thus be computed as $v' = v \pm r \cdot \delta$. Addition or subtraction is chosen with an equal probability. The value of δ is defined to be $\sum_{y=0}^{15} \alpha_y \cdot 2^{-y}$, where each α_y is 1 with a probability of $1/16$ else 0. If a mutated value is outside the allowed bounds of a variable, its value is set to either the minimum or maximum value for that variable. Discrete recombination [71] is used as a crossover operator. Discrete recombination is similar to uniform crossover. However with uniform crossover, genes (input values) are guaranteed to appear in one of the offspring. With discrete recombination offspring individuals receive 'genes' (*i.e.* input variable values) from either parent with an equal probability. Thus a particular gene may be copied into both children, one of the children or neither child.

The Wegener GA, uses an elitist reinsertion strategy, with the top 10% of a current generation retained and used in the next, with the remaining 90% discarded and replaced by the best offspring.

Finally the Wegener GA incorporates competition and migration between each of its subpopulations. A progress value, $prog$, is computed for each population at the end of a generation. This value is obtained using the formula $0.9 \cdot prog + 0.1 \cdot rank$. The average fitness $rank$ for a population is obtained by linearly ranking its individuals as well as the populations amongst themselves (again with $Z = 1.7$). After every 4 generations, the populations are ranked according to their progress value and a new slice of the overall population is computed for each, with weaker subpopulations transferring individuals to stronger ones. However, no subpopulation can lose its last 5 individuals, preventing it from dying out. Finally, a general migration of individuals takes place after every 20th generation, where subpopulations randomly exchange 10% of their individuals with one another.

Results. Results with the CAS check example can be found in Table 1. The search for test data was repeated 50 times with both the GA outlined in the last section and random search. Random search simply constructs an input by constructing a string where each of the 15 characters is selected at random. Both algorithms were given a budget of 100,000 inputs to generate and execute the program with, in order to find test data for a particular branch. Each branch is denoted as $LT|F$, where L is the line number of the branch, while T and F denote which of the true or false branches is being referred to.

The performance of the GA is compared with random search. In the table, the average number of test data evaluations (fitness function evaluations for the GA) is reported, unless the branch was not covered over the 50 runs with a 100% success rate, in which case the success rate is reported instead. As can be seen from the table, random search is very effective, covering all the branches of the example except 1 (branch 18F). The GA, on the other hand, achieves 100% coverage. Statistical tests were also performed, as outlined in Section 6.2. For the majority of branches, there was no statistical difference in performance between the two searches. However, for 18F and 19T, the GA was significantly

Table 1. Results with the CAS registry number checking program of Figure 15. The average number of test data evaluations over 50 runs is reported for the branch and algorithm if the success rate of finding test data to execute the branch was 100%, else the success rate is reported instead. A figure appears in bold for the GA if its performance was significantly better than random search.

Branch	Search	
	Random	Genetic Algorithm
4T	1	1
4F	1	1
7T	2	2
7F	1	1
8T	2	2
8F	8	8
10T	8	8
10F	2	2
17T	465	329
17F	1	1
18T	465	329
18F	0%	**3,230**
19T	4,270	**802**
19F	519	363

better. Random search never covered 18F, and requires 5 times as much effort (test data evaluations) in order to cover 19T.

8.4 Case Study: Cost Estimation for Project Planning

Software effort estimation is an important activity performed in the planning phase of a software project. Its importance can be easily realised by the fact that the effort estimation will drive the planning of basically all remaining activities in the software development. Given such significance, many approaches have been proposed in the attempt to find effective techniques for software estimation. Nevertheless, as a result of the high complexity of this activity, the search for efficient and effective estimation models is still underway. An interesting example on the application of a search based approach - genetic programming, in this case - to tackle the software estimation problem can be found in [25].

In this application, the software estimation problem is modeled as a search problem, considering as search space the set of cost predictive functions which will have their predictive capability evaluated based on some particular measure. A search algorithm would then seek functions which maximise this evaluation measure.

Therefore, the Software Cost Estimation problem can be defined, as in [25], as follows:

Definition 4. *Software Cost Estimation Problem*

Given: *Well-formed equations, which can be used to produce cost predictions.*

Problem: *Find the equation with best predictive capability, calculated by measures such as mean squared error or correlation coefficient.*

Representation. For this problem, solutions are represented as trees, expressing well-formed equations. In each tree, terminal nodes represent constants or variables, and each non-terminal node stores a simple function, from a predetermined set of available functions that can be used in the composition of an equation. The available functions proposed in the original paper were: plus, minus, multiplication, division, square, square root, natural logarithm and exponential.

Fitness Function. As pointed out by Dolado [25], classical measures used to evaluate the fitting of equations to some data can be use as fitness functions for this software estimation problem. In the paper, the following measures were considered: *mean squared error*, which quantifies the error of the considered function being used as estimator, and the *correlation coefficient*, which measures the variation between the predicted and the actual values.

Algorithm. Genetic programming (GP), as a variation of the well-known genetic algorithm (GA), can be used to manipulate complex individuals, expressed by data structures representing trees, source codes, design projects, or any other structure. Similarly to GA, GP performs genetic operations such as selection, crossover and mutation to evolve its populations to seek for more adapted solutions. Dolado [25] employs genetic programming to find a function for software cost estimation.

In that application, as previously described, the candidate functions are described by trees, representing well-formed equations. Given that representation, the usual evolutionary process is performed. Initially, an initial population P, with N individuals (equations) is generated. While a terminate condition in not met, new populations are produced iteratively. First, the members of the current population are evaluated using the fitness function. Next, individuals are selected as input to the genetic operators, including crossover and mutation, which create new individuals that will form the new population.

Results. The proposed search based approach was evaluated over twelve datasets and compared to standard regression analysis. To evaluate the candidate functions, the *mean magnitude of relative error* (MMRE) and the *prediction at level l* (PRED(l)) were used. As reported, the proposed Genetic Programming strategy performed better, considering the PRED(0.25) measure, in eleven out of the twelve cases, but with a slight worse value of the MMRE in some cases.

Even though, from the predictive point of view, both methods did not show considerably satisfactory results, authors pointed out that since GP allows the exploration of a large space of candidate cost functions, this method can provide confidence in the limits of prediction. Additionally, results showed that linear models, regardless of the approach employed, obtained the best predictions in general.

Other authors have also reported interesting applications of search based approaches in software estimation [18, 26, 58].

9   A Taxonomy of Optimisation Problems and Their Mapping to Software Engineering

The Search Based Software Engineering (SBSE) research field has grown rapidly. From its formal definition to this date, a huge number of software engineering problems have been mathematically formulated as optimisation problems and tackled with a considerable variety of search techniques. This growth has taken place in several directions, but more concentrated in a few particular areas. As this natural development occurs, and the number of SBSE problems increases, also grows the necessity of strategies that would help structuring the field. This section introduces a taxonomy, of Search Based Software Engineering problems and instantiates it with the four examples described in the case studies of this the paper.

Our goal in introducing the taxonomy is four fold:

i. to allow researchers to understand the relationship among problems and hypothesise about these relationships.

ii. to highlight to future research directions by identifying unexplored opportunities.

iii. to allow the development of automated search tools to enable effective and efficient search of SBSE problems in any particular repository.

iv. to facilitate re-use, especially regarding approximation algorithms and theoretical bounds.

The proposed taxonomy of Search Based Software Engineering problems will involve Perspectives, Dimensions and Characteristics.

The two Perspectives, SOFTWARE ENGINEERING and OPTIMISATION, will reflect the different points of view under which a particular SBSE problem can be analysed. The Dimensions, as in other taxonomies, will represent, for each Perspective, the SBSE problem features. Finally, for each Dimension, the Characteristics will correspond to the possible feature values under which a particular SBSE problem can be identified. For all Dimensions, the Characteristics are collectively exhaustive. However, only the Dimensions "Objective Space Dimensionality", "Instance Space Characterisation", "Constrained" and "Problem Linearity" are mutually exclusive, for all others, more than one Characteristic may be selected for a particular SBSE problem.

In Tables 2 and 3, the proposed taxonomy of Search Based Software Engineering problems is presented.

For the SOFTWARE ENGINEERING Perspective (Table 2), four Dimensions are identified: "Software Development Stage(s)", "Software Development Model(s)", "Main Subject Descriptor(s)" and "Main Implicit Subject Descriptor(s)".

1. The **"Software Development Stage(s)"** positions the problem under one, or more, stages in the software engineering process. The Characteristics available for this Dimension are representative of the standard software development process.

2. Next, the **"Software Development Model(s)"** identifies a particular set of development models in which the problem occurs.

3. The Dimension named **"Main Subject Descriptor(s)"** describes the software engineering subject addressed by the problem. The Characteristics present in this Dimension were obtained from the 1998 version of the ACM Computing Classification System [1]. More specifically, the possible values for this feature are those defined as a "Subject Descriptor" under the level D.2 (SOFTWARE ENGINEERING), in the third level of the classification structure, with values, and corresponding subjects, ranging from D.2.0 (General) to D.2.13 (Reusable Software) and D.2.m (Miscellaneous).

4. Finally, the **"Main Implicit Subject Descriptor(s)"** Dimension details the previous subject descriptor(s), by allowing the selection of the more specific subject descriptors present in the fourth level of the ACM Computing Classification System [1], once again under the level D.2 (SOFTWARE ENGINEERING).

Table 2. Taxonomy of Search Based Software Engineering Problems - SOFTWARE ENGINEERING Perspective

---

A. SOFTWARE ENGINEERING Perspective

---

1. Software Development Stage(s)
   (a) Software Planning
   (b) Requirement Engineering
   (c) Software Design
   (d) Implementation/Coding
   (e) Integration
   (f) Testing/Validation
   (g) Deployment
   (h) Maintenance
2. Software Development Model(s)
   (a) Waterfall Model
   (b) Spiral Model
   (c) Iterative and Incremental Development
   (d) Agile Development
3. Main Subject Descriptor(s)
   (a) Subject Descriptors under SOFTWARE ENGINEERING (D.2), in the 1998 ACM Computing Classification System.
4. Main Implicit Subject Descriptor(s)
   (a) Implicit Subject Descriptors under SOFTWARE ENGINEERING (D.2), in the 1998 ACM Computing Classification System.

For the OPTIMISATION Perspective, other six Dimensions are defined.

1. The **"Objective Space Dimensionality"** is descriptive of the number of objective functions present in the formulation.
2. **"The Instance Space Characterisation"** Dimension evaluates the problem variables as continuous or discrete.
3. Next, **"Constrained"** accounts for the presence of restrictions.
4. **"Problem Linearity"** indicates, for both objective and restriction functions, their linearity.
5. The following Dimension, **"Base NPO Problem Type(s)"**, attempts to extract the problem category, using the classification proposed by Garey and Johnson [34] and employed in the Compendium of NP Optimisation Problems [22]. The general types present in the Compendium are: Graph Theory, Network Design, Sets and Partitions, Storage and Retrieval, Sequencing and Scheduling, Mathematical Programming, Algebra and Number Theory,

Games and Puzzles, Logic, Automata and Language Theory, Program Optimisation and Miscellaneous.

6. Finally, **"Base NPO Problem"** tries to relate the considered SBSE problem with a generally defined NP optimisation problem, in a way one could employ the known results, including approximation algorithms and theoretical bounds, previously available in the literature regarding that general problem. For that purpose, once again, the "Compendium of NP Optimisation Problems" will be used.

At this point, it is worth mentioning that the "Compendium of NP Optimisation Problems" presents a considerable variety of optimisation problems in the most different categories, however, it lacks a formal definition of a basic optimisation problem, under which several known problems could be classified. To tackle this absence, the definition of a **BASIC OPTIMISATION PROBLEM**, which would fall under the **MISCELLANEOUS** type, defined with the same basic ingredients employed in the Compendium, is presented below.

BASIC OPTIMISATION PROBLEM

Instance: Finite or infinite set U, for each $u \in U$ a fitness value $f(u) \in Z^+$.
Solution: An element, $u' \in U$.
Measure: Fitness value of u, i.e., $f(u)$.

9.1   Classification Examples

In order to illustrate the representation of Search Based Software Engineering problems under the proposed taxonomy, it is presented, next, the classification of SBSE problems discussed in section 8: The Regression Test Case Selection problem (Table 4), the Next Release problem (Table 5), the Structural Test Case Generation problem (Table 6) and the Software Cost Estimation problem (Table 7).

The Multi-Objective Regression Test Case Selection problem [106] extends previously published mono-objective formulations. The paper discusses two variations, one which considers two objectives (code coverage and execution time), used here, and the other covering three objectives (code coverage, execution time and fault detection). Consider, for this problem, the special case where a set of test cases which covers 100% of the code is sought. In addition, consider that all test cases have the same execution time. In that case, the Test Case Selection Problem problem can be seen as a application of the **MINIMUM SET COVER** problem.

MINIMUM SET COVER

Instance: Collection C of subsets of a finite set S.
Solution: A set cover for S, i.e., a subset $C' \subseteq C$ such that every element in S belongs to at least one member of C'.
Measure: Cardinality of the set cover, i.e., $|C'|$.

S will represent the set of all statements in the source code. Collection C will contain the test cases that can be selected. Each test case covers a number of

Table 3. Taxonomy of Search Based Software Engineering Problems - OPTIMISATION Perspective

---

A. OPTIMISATION Perspective

---

1. Objective Space Dimensionality
   (a) Mono-objective
   (b) Multi-objective
2. Instance Space Characterisation
   (a) Discrete
   (b) Continuous
3. Constrained
   (a) Yes
   (b) No
4. Problem Linearity
   (a) Linear
   (b) Nonlinear
5. Base NPO Problem Type(s)
   (a) Problem Categories as defined in the Compendium of NP Optimisation Problems
6. Base NPO Problem(s)
   (a) Problems as defined in the Compendium of NP Optimisation Problems

---

statements in the source code, which means that each test case can be representative of a subset of S. Thus, the solutions are set covers for S, that is, a subset of test cases, $C' \subseteq C$, such that all statements in S are covered, meaning that each statement is covered by, at least, one of the members of C'. The solution sought is the one with the lowest cardinality, which will have lowest execution time, since all test cases have the same execution time.

For the other dimensions in the OPTIMISATION perspective (Table 4), the Multi-Objective Test Case Selection Problem can be classified as Multi-objective, having a Discrete instance space, Unconstrained and Linear. Over the SOFT-WARE ENGINEERING perspective, the problem falls under the Testing/Validation development stage and is not particular to any specific development model. Furthermore, it has as main subject descriptor the choice "D.2.5 Testing and Debugging", and "Testing Tools" as implicit subject descriptor.

The Next Release Problem (NRP), in its original formulation as a constrained mono-objective optimisation problem [13], involves determining a set of customers which will have their selected requirements delivered in the next software release. This selection prioritises customers with higher importance to the company (maximise $\sum_{i=1}^{n} w_i$), and must respect a pre-determined budget (subject to $\sum_{i=1}^{n} c_i \leq B$).

Table 4. Typification of the Regression Test Case Selection under the Proposed Taxonomy

---

A. SOFTWARE ENGINEERING Perspective
  1. Software Development Stage(s)
     Testing/Validation

  2. Software Development Model(s)
     Waterfall Model

     Spiral Model

     Iterative and Incremental Development

     Agile Development

  3. Main Subject Descriptor(s)
     D.2.5 Testing and Debugging

  4. Main Implicit Subject Descriptor(s)
     Testing Tools

B. OPTIMISATION Perspective
  1. Objective Space Dimensionality
     Multi-objective

  2. Instance Space Characterisation
     Discrete

  3. Constrained
     No

  4. Problem Linearity
     Linear

  5. Base NPO Problem Type(s)
     SETS AND PARTITIONS

  6. Base NPO Problem(s)
     MINIMUM SET COVER

In typifying this problem under the proposed taxonomy, it is easy to see that, regarding the SOFTWARE ENGINEERING perspective (Table 5), the NRP is positioned under the Requirement Engineering software development stage, occurring specially in the Iterative and Incremental and Agile Development Models. In addition, the Next Release Problem addresses the subject "D.2.1 Requirements/Specifications", present in the ACM Computing Classification System. Under the OPTIMISATION perspective, as stated above, it is a mono-objective problem, since it aims to solely maximise the importance of the customers which will have their requirements delivered. It has a discrete instance space and should be classified as a constrained problem, since considers a pre-defined budged as restriction. Since both objective and restriction functions are linear, the overall

Table 5. Typification of the Next Release Problem under the Proposed Taxonomy

---

A. SOFTWARE ENGINEERING Perspective
  1. Software Development Stage(s)
       Requirement Engineering
  2. Software Development Model(s)
       Iterative and Incremental Development
       Agile Development
  3. Main Subject Descriptor(s)
       D.2.1 Requirements/Specification
  4. Main Implicit Subject Descriptor(s)

B. OPTIMISATION Perspective
  1. Objective Space Dimensionality
       Mono-objective
  2. Instance Space Characterisation
       Discrete
  3. Constrained
       Yes
  4. Problem Linearity
       Linear
  5. Base NPO Problem Type(s)
       MATHEMATICAL PROGRAMMING
  6. Base NPO Problem(s)
       MAXIMUM KNAPSACK

---

problem can be considered linear as well. Finally, it involves the solution of a MATHEMATICAL PROGRAMMING problem, as defined in the "Compendium of NP Optimisation Problems". In fact, the Next Release Problem can be seen as a specialisation of the MAXIMUM KNAPSACK Problem, as discussed next.

Consider the mathematical definition of the **MAXIMUM KNAPSACK** problem, as presented in [22]:

MAXIMUM KNAPSACK

Instance: Finite set U, for each $u \in U$ a size $s(u) \in Z^+$ and a value $v(u) \in Z^+$, a positive integer $B \in Z^+$.
Solution: A subset $U' \subseteq U$ such that $\sum_{u \in U'} s(u) \leq B$.
Measure: Total weight of the chosen elements, i.e., $\sum_{u \in U'} v(u)$.

As defined in **Instance**, the set U can represent the customers which may have their requirements delivered in the next software release. Each customer, $u \in U$, has an importance, represented here by $v(u)$, which expresses the function w_i in the NRP definition. The goal is to maximise the sum of the importance of the selected customers. However, only solutions respecting the problem restriction can be considered. In the definition of the MAXIMUM KNAPSACK problem, each element $u \in U$ has a size, $s(u) \in Z^+$, which will limit the amount of elements that can be selected. In the Next Release problem, the function $s(u)$ will represent the overall cost of implementing all requirements desired by customer u, that is, $s(u) = c_i$.

For the Structural Test Data Generation problem, the classification under the proposed taxonomy, as shown in Table 6, considering the SOFTWARE ENGINEERING perspective, would place this problem under the Testing/Validation

Table 6. Typification of the Structural Test Data Generation Problem under the Proposed Taxonomy

---

A. SOFTWARE ENGINEERING Perspective
1. Software Development Stage(s)
   Testing/Validation

2. Software Development Model(s)
   Waterfall Model

   Spiral Model

   Iterative and Incremental Development

   Agile Development

3. Main Subject Descriptor(s)
   D.2.5 Testing and Debugging

4. Main Implicit Subject Descriptor(s)
   Testing Tools

B. OPTIMISATION Perspective
1. Objective Space Dimensionality
   Mono-objective

2. Instance Space Characterisation
   Continuous

3. Constrained
   No

4. Problem Linearity
   Linear

5. Base NPO Problem Type(s)
   MISCELLANEOUS

6. Base NPO Problem(s)
   BASIC OPTIMISATION PROBLEM

---

development stage. Regarding development models, this test data generation issue arises in all models covered by the taxonomy. "D.2.5 Testing and Debugging" would be the main subject descriptor of such problem and "Testing Tools" would work as implicit descriptor.

Considering now the OPTIMISATION perspective, this problem could be characterised as mono-objective, since it composes two measures (approach level and branch distance) in a single evaluation function. Additionally, it works with a usually continuous instance space formed of input vectors. It is also an unconstrained and linear problem. Finally, the Structural Test Data Generation problem can be seen as a simple instantiation of the BASIC OPTIMISATION PROBLEM described earlier, where, given a target structure t in p, the problem involves simply searching for an input vector $i \in D$, representing elements in the instance space U, with minimum value given by evaluation function $fit(t, i)$, representing $f(u)$ in the description of the BASIC OPTIMISATION PROBLEM.

Finally, the Software Cost Estimation problem is associated with the Software Planning development phase and all development models (Table 7). The most adequate mains and implicit subject descriptors would be "D.2.9 Management" and "Cost Estimation", respectively.

Similarly to the Test Data Generation problem, this problem is an instantiation of the BASIC OPTIMISATION PROBLEM. In this case, the problem seeks solutions represented by well-formed functions, forming the instance set U, looking for a solution with minimum value given by function $f(u)$, associated with measures such as *minimum squared error* or *correlation coefficient*. Additionally, the problem should be classified as mono-objective, continuous, unconstrained and nonlinear.

10 Next Steps: Getting Started

This section is primarily aimed at those who have not used SBSE before, but who have a software engineering application in mind for which they wish to apply SBSE. Throughout this section the emphasis is unashamedly on obtaining the first set of results as quickly as possible; SBSE is attractive partly because it has a shallow learning curve that enables beginner to quickly become productive. There is an excitement that comes with the way in which one can quickly assemble a system that suggests potentially well optimised solutions to a problem that the experimenter had not previously considered.

By minimising the time from initial conception to first results, we seek to maximise this excitement. Of course subsequent additional work and analysis will be required to convert these initial findings into a sufficiently thorough empirical study for publication. The goal of the section is to take the reader from having no previous work on SBSE to the point of being ready to submit their first paper on SBSE in seven simple steps. The first four of these steps are sufficient to gain the first results (and hopefully also the excitement that comes with the surprises and insights that many authors have experienced through using SBSE for the first time).

Table 7. Typification of the Software Cost Estimation Problem under the Proposed Taxonomy

---

A. SOFTWARE ENGINEERING Perspective
    1. Software Development Stage(s)
        Software Planning
    2. Software Development Model(s)
        Waterfall Model

        Spiral Model

        Iterative and Incremental Development

        Agile Development
    3. Main Subject Descriptor(s)
        D.2.9 Management
    4. Main Implicit Subject Descriptor(s)
        Cost Estimation

B. OPTIMISATION Perspective
    1. Objective Space Dimensionality
        Mono-objective
    2. Instance Space Characterisation
        Continuous
    3. Constrained
        No
    4. Problem Linearity
        Nonlinear
    5. Base NPO Problem Type(s)
        MISCELLANEOUS
    6. Base NPO Problem(s)
        BASIC OPTIMISATION PROBLEM

Step 1: The first step is to choose a representation of the problem and a fitness function (see Section 3). The representation is important because it must be one that can be readily understood; after all, you may find that you are examining a great many candidate solutions that your algorithms will produce.

One should, of course, seek a representation that is suitable for optimisation. A great deal has been written on this topic. For the first exploration of a new SBSE application the primary concern is to ensure that a small change to your representation represents a small change to the real world problem that your representation denotes. This means that a small change in the representation (which will be reflected by a move in a hill climb or a mutation in a genetic algorithm) will cause the search to move from one solution to a 'near neighbour' solution in the solution space. There are many other considerations when it comes to representation, but for a first approach, this should be sufficient to contend with.

Perhaps for the first experiments, the most important thing is to get some results. These can always be treated as a baseline, against which you measure the progress of subsequent improvements, so 'getting it a bit wrong' with the initial choices need not be a wasted effort; it may provide a way to assess the improvements brought to the problem by subsequent development.

Step 2: Once there is a way to represent candidate solutions, the next step is to chose a fitness function. There may be many candidate fitness functions. Choose the simplest to understand and the easiest to implement to start off with. Once again, this may provide a baseline against which to judge subsequent choices. Ideally, the fitness function should also be one that your implementation will be able to compute inexpensively, since there will be a need for many fitness evaluations, regardless of the search technique adopted.

Step 3: In order to ensure that all is working, implement a simple random search. That is, use a random number generator to construct an entirely arbitrary set of candidate solutions by sampling over the representation at random. This allows you to check that the fitness function is working correctly and that it can be computed efficiently. One can also examine the spread of results and see whether any of the randomly found solutions is any good at solving the problem. Despite its simplicity, random search is simple and fast and many researchers have found that it is capable of finding useful solutions for some Software Engineering applications (for instance, in testing, where it has been very widely studied [55, 79]).

Step 4: Having conducted steps 1-3 we are in a position to conduct the first application of a search based technique. It is best to start with hill climbing. This algorithm is exceptionally easy to implement (as can be seen from Section 4). It has the advantage that is is fast and conceptually easy to understand. It can also be used to understand the structure of the search space. For instance, one can collect a set of results from multiple restart hill climbing and examine the peaks reached. If all peaks found are identical then hill climbing may have located a large 'basin of attraction' in the search space. If all peaks are of very different heights (that is, they have different fitness values) then the search space is likely to be multimodal. If many hill climbs make no progress then the search space contains many plateaux (which will be a problem for almost any search based optimisation technique).

It is possible that simply using hill climbing, the results will be acceptable. If this is the first time that SBSE has been applied to the Software Engineering problem in hand, then the results may already be at the level at which publication would be possible. If the peaks are all acceptable but different then the approach already solves the problem well and can give many diverse solutions.

This was found to be the case in several software engineering applications. For instance, in software modularisation [68], the hill climbing approach produced exceptionally good results for determining the module boundaries of source code that remained unsurpassed by more sophisticated algorithms from 1998 [64] until 2011 [77]. Furthermore, the multi objective genetic algorithm that found better solutions only managed to do so at a cost of two orders of magnitude more fitness evaluations [77].

Korel [59] was one of the first authors to apply a search based optimisation approach to a software engineering problem. He used a hill climbing approach for software test input generation. Though this problem has been very widely studied, this hill climbing approach still proved to be an attractive approach 17 years later, when it was studied and (favourably) compared empirically and theoretically to a more sophisticated genetic algorithm [49], suggesting that a hybrid that combined both hill climbing (local search) and genetic algorithms (global search) was the best approach for test data generation [50].

Hill climbing can also be used to help to understand the nature of the solutions found. For example, through multiple hill climbs, we can find the set of common building blocks that are found in all good solutions. This can help to understand the problem and also may be a way to make subsequent techniques more effective. This approach to locating building blocks using multiple runs of a hill climber was applied by Mahdavi et al. [62], who used a distributed cluster of machines to perform multiple hill climbs in parallel for the software modularisation problem. The results were the building blocks of 'good modules' (those which were cohesive and exhibited low coupling) for a particular architecture of dependencies. Mahdavi et al. also showed that the initial identification of building blocks could improve the performance of the subsequent search.

For all these reasons, faced with a large number of possible algorithms with which to start, it seems sensible to adopt hill climbing as the first optimisation algorithm. If the results are promising then within a very short space of time, the novice SBSE researcher will have migrated from finishing reading this tutorial to starting to write their own first SBSE paper; perhaps in as little as a matter of days.

Step 5: The natural next step is to try some different search based algorithms. A good place to start is those described in Section 4 since these have been commonly applied and so there will be a wealth of previous results with which to compare. Following this, the SBSE researcher is already going beyond what can be covered in a single tutorial such as this and is thus referred to the literature on search based optimisation. A good overview of search techniques can be found in the text book by Burke and Kendall [19].

Step 6: Having implemented several SBSE algorithms and obtained results, the next step is to analyse these results. In this paper we have set out some of the common statistical techniques used to analyse SBSE work in Section 6. Naturally, this can only provide an overview of some commonly used approaches, but it should be sufficient to address some of the most obvious initial questions; those to which a referee would naturally expect answers. Using these techniques the results can be developed to become the basis for an experimental or empirical study, by selecting some non trivial real world examples to which the new SBSE approach can be applied. The most natural questions to address are those of efficiency and effectiveness. That is, the study should, at least, answer the questions: how good are the solutions you find and how much computational (and/or human) effort is required to obtain them?

Step 7: One of the attractive aspects of SBSE is the way it re-unites different areas of software engineering, as explained in Section 2. A good paper on SBSE will contain a thorough account of the related work and this may help to achieve this re-unification goal, drawing together apparently unrelated areas of software engineering. In so doing, SBSE work can play a vital role in the development of the wider field of Software Engineering itself, providing a more solid search-based understanding of the underlying optimisation problems that are found in each application area.

Using SBSE, we seek to apply search algorithms to software engineering problems so there are two natural sources of related work for any paper on SBSE; the previous work that tries to solve the same (or similar) Software Engineering problem(s) and the previous work that uses a similar search based approach. You may find that two apparently quite different software engineering problems have been attacked using the same (or similar) search based formulation (perhaps representation is shared or a similar fitness can be used).

An SBSE paper can be considerably enhanced by exploring these links, since such connections mean that the paper can have an impact on at least two software engineering domains, rather than merely the one for which the results are presented. Hopefully, in developing a related work section, the taxonomy in Section 9 will be helpful. The many surveys on SBSE are also a source of valuable summary information concerning potentially related techniques and application areas.

Step 8: At this point, the researcher has sufficient information and results to consider writing a paper. Naturally, there will be a choice about where to send the paper that can only be made by the author(s). There is also the question of how to set the problem formulation, research questions and results into as format that will appeal to (firstly) referees and (ultimately) readers.

There are many excellent papers that give guidance on how to write good software engineering papers, such as that by Mary Shaw [86]. Those papers that present results on SBSE generally (though not exclusively) fall in the category of empirical software engineering papers, for which the systematic review of Ali et al. [4] sets out useful guidelines relevant to SBSE.

11   SBSE Limitations and Techniques for Overcoming Them

In this final section we review some of the problems and issues that can arise when using SBSE and some simple techniques for overcoming them. Many of these issues are common to all approaches to optimisation based on algorithms guided by fitness and many of the solution approaches could be described as the application of 'common sense' (though some may be slightly surprising or counter-intuitive). Where possible, we provide pointers to the SBSE literature, indicating where the proposed solution approaches have already been explored in the specific context of Software Engineering problem domains.

11.1 My Ideal Fitness Function Is Too Computationally Expensive

The most natural fitness function for a problem may turn out to be computationally expensive and this may mean that the whole search process takes a long time. In most applications of SBSE, it is the computation of fitness that occupies the largest part of the overall computational cost of the SBSE implementation. As such, it makes sense to consider techniques for controlling and reducing this cost, where it is manageable. This issue, therefore, can be considered to be the problem of 'how can we compute fitness faster?'. We consider three approaches: use a cheaper surrogate, parallelise and imbue the search with domain knowledge.

Find a cheaper surrogate: Often, a computationally demanding fitness function can be reserved for evaluating the final result or for occasional fitness computation, while a surrogate (or surrogates) is/are used for most of the fitness evaluations used to guide the search. Even if the surrogate fitness function is not a perfect guide, it can be computationally cheaper overall, to use a less accurate fitness function (that still provides *some* guidance for the majority of fitness computations). This approach has been used very little in Software Engineering, partly because many of the fitness functions used in SBSE tend to be computationally inexpensive (they often come from works on metrics [42], which are pre-designed to be computationally practical). Even when the metrics used as fitness functions do prove to be computationally expensive, it is typically hard to find surrogates. However, as SBSE increasingly finds applications in new software engineering areas there may also be a wider choice of available metrics and it may turn out that the most suitable metrics are also those that are more computationally expensive. We can therefore expect that there will be a greater reliance on surrogate fitness computations in future work on SBSE. To minimise the negative impact of using a surrogate that only captures part of the true fitness or which includes noise, it may be advantageous to use multiple surrogate fitness computations (as discussed later on in this section).

Parallelise: SBSE algorithms are known as 'embarrassingly parallel' [32] because of their potential for scalability through parallel execution of fitness computations [72]. Recent work has shown how this parallelism can be exploited on General Purpose Graphical Processing devices (GPGPUs) [110] with scale ups in overall computation time up to a factor of 20. Because of the inherent parallelism of SBSE algorithms and the wide availability of cheap multicore devices we can expect a great deal more scalability research in future work on SBSE. In the era of multicore computing, SBSE is well placed to make significant strides forward in simple effective and scalable parallel solutions.

Use domain knowledge: Domain Knowledge can be used to guide the search to fruitful areas of the landscape, without actually determining the precise solution. For example, in selection and prioritisation problems, we may know that the solution we seek must include certain items (for selection these can be hard wired onto the solution) or we may know that a certain relative placement of some individuals in an ordering is highly likely. This can happen often as the result of human considerations concerned with management and business properties. For instance, in selecting and prioritising requirements, it is not always possible to take account of all the socio-political issues that may determine the ideal solution set. The manager may simply say something like 'whatever the solution you adopt, we must include these five requirements, because the CEO deems them essential for our business strategy, going forward'. This can be an advantage for search, because it simultaneously and effortlessly adapts the solution to the business needs while reducing the size of the search space. Wherever possible, domain knowledge should be incorporated into the SBSE approach.

11.2 My Fitness Function Is Too Vague and Poorly Understood to Make It Something I Can *Compute*

It is a popular misconception that SBSE must use a fitness function that is both precise and accurate. It is true that this is advantageous and valuable (if possible), but neither is essential. In software measurement, we seek metrics that meet the 'representation condition' [87], which states that the ordering imposed by the metric on the individuals it measures should respect the 'true ordering' of these individuals in the real world.

It is a natural condition to require of a metric, M; if $M(a) > M(b)$ then we should reasonably expect that the real world entity a is truly 'better' than b in some sense and *vice versa*. However this requirement is not essential for SBSE. If a fitness function merely *tends* to give the right answer, then it may well be a useful, if inefficient, fitness function candidate. That is, if the probability is greater than 0.5 that a pairwise fitness comparison on two individuals a and b with metric M will produce the correct outcome, then may potentially be used in SBSE should it prove to have compensatory properties; our search will be guided to some extent, though it may make many wrong moves.

However, if a metric is simply not defined for some part of the candidate solutions space or can only be defined by subjective assessment for all or part of the solution space, then we need a way to handle this. There are two natural approaches to this problem: use a human or use multiple fitness functions.

Involve Human Judgement: Fitness functions do not need to be calculated entirely automatically. If they can be fully automated, then this is advantageous, because one of the overall advantages of SBSE is the way it provides a generic approach to the problem of Automating Software Engineering [36]. However, it has been argued [37] that some Software Engineering tasks, such as those associated with comprehension activity are inherently subjective and require a human input to the fitness computation. This is easily accommodated in SBSE, since may algorithms allow for 'human-in-the-loop fitness computation. Such subjective, human-guided, fitness has been used in interactive evolutionary algorithms for SBSE applied to design-oriented problems [89] and Requirements Engineering [92].

Use Multiple Fitness Functions: It is not necessary to use only the 'best' fitness function to guide the search. If the best fitness function is still only the best at capturing *part* of the search space there is nothing to prevent the use of other fitness functions that capture different, perhaps smaller, parts of the solution space. Fitness functions can be combined in a number of ways to provide an 'agglomerated' fitness function. Both weighting and Pareto optimal approaches have been widely studied in the SBSE literature [36]. However, using several fitness functions, each of which applies to different parts of the solutions space has not been explored in the literature. Given the complicated and heterogenous nature of many Software Engineering problems, this approach is under-explored and should receive more attention. In future work on SBSE, we may seek to bundle patchworks of different fitness functions to solve a single problem, deploying different fitness functions at different times, for different stake holders, or for different parts of the solutions space.

11.3   My Search Space Is Too Difficult for Search to Work Well

The performance of a search based optimisation algorithms depends crucially on the search landscape that a fitness function creates when used to guide the search for a specific problem. If a particular search algorithm performs poorly on a search space then there are two obvious solutions that immediately present themselves; do something to modify the way fitness is computed or choose a different algorithm (one that is better suited to the landscape). In order to take either course of action, it is important to undertake research into the properties of the search landscape in order to understand which is the best algorithm to apply. There has been much work on analysis and characterisation of SBSE landscapes and fitness functions, but more is required in order to provide a more complete understanding of the properties to which SBSE is applied.

Analyse Different Fitness Functions: Different characterisations of fitness can achieve very different results. This has been demonstrated empirically, in SBSE problems, where the choice of fitness can have different robustness to noise in the data [51]. The initial choice of fitness function may lead to a search landscape contains too many plateaux, or other features that make search hard (needle in a haystack, multimodal features, deceptive basins of attraction etc.). In these situations, it makes sense to analyse the effect of different fitness functions; each will characterise the problems differently and may have very different behaviours, even if all agree on the local or global optima.

Use Multiple Fitness Functions: Even if your search problem is inherently single objective in nature, it may make sense to consider experimenting with multi objective approaches. It has been shown in previous work on SBSE for module clustering [77] that better results can be obtained for using a multi objective optimisation on a single objective problem. This happens because the other objectives may help the search to find routes to the global optima in the single objective space. Therefore, searching for solutions that satisfy multiple objectives may, perhaps counter-intuitively, help to solve a single objective problem. If you find that one of your fitness characterisation has an unattractive search landscape, yet it provides useful guidance in some cases, you might consider incorporating additional fitness functions.

Use Secondary Fitness: For problems in which there are too many plateaux, you may consider the use of a secondary fitness function, to be used to distinguish candidate solutions that lie on a plateaux according to the primary fitness function. This has been used in the SBSE problem of search based transformation. In transformation, the goal is to find a new version of the program that is better (according to some metric) by searching the space of transformations of the original program (or the transformations sequences that can be applied to it). This is a very well studied area of SBSE [21, 29, 30, 52, 75, 85], dating back to the work of Ryan and Williams [83, 104] on auto-parallelisation transformations.

One of the problems for this SBSE problem, is that there are many transformations the application of which fails to affect the primary fitness function. For example, suppose we seek to shrink the size of a program by either removing redundant computation or by slicing [44]. In this situation, there are many transformations that will not reduce the size of the program to which they are applied. All such transformations will lie on a plateau of fitness with regard to their effect on code reduction for some specific program. However, we can distinguish among such transformations. Those that are not applicable are worse than those that are applicable. Those that are applicable, but have no effect at all are worse than those that alter the code without reducing its size. In the early stages of the search those transformations that have a larger effect on the syntax may also be preferred. This suggests a secondary fitness that can be used to guide a search to the edges of a plateaux in the search space induced by the primary fitness function. This has been employed to improve the performance of search based slicing [30].

Landscape Analysis: In the more general optimisation literature, the issue of landscape analysis and algorithmic characterisation is well studied [103]. For example, there has been work on the analysis of plateaux in search landscapes [91]. There has also been much work on SBSE landscape analysis and algorithm characterisation. Early work in this area for the project estimate feature selection [57] and modularisation [67] has been championed in the SBSE literature [36] as exemplary of the kinds of analyse that can be achieved, empirically, using a simple (but effective) multiple restart simple hill climbing approach. There has also been recent theoretical analysis of SBSE algorithm performance [61] and theoretical and empirical analyses of search based testing for structural test data generation [7, 49, 50].

Choose the Right Algorithm for the Search Space: Choosing the right algorithm for the problem is as fundamental to search as choosing the right tool for the job is in any engineering endeavour. The field of optimisation is well known for its many versions of the 'no free lunch theorem' [102]. There is plenty of evidence [3, 48, 78] to indicate that SBSE problems are as wide and varied as those found in the general optimisation literature. It is, therefore, foolhardy to believe that one search based optimisation technique will be superior for all possible problems that one might encounter.

The most popular algorithms (by far) that have been used hitherto in SBSE work are variations on the theme of population-based evolutionary algorithm [48]. This is not the result of evidence that evolutionary algorithms are superior to other algorithms. Quite the contrary in fact: There is evidence to suggest that, for some problems, such as structure test data generation (a very widely studied problem), simpler local search algorithms may be better [49], and that some form of hybridisation that seeks to achieve the best of both local and global search [50] may be the best performing approach so far known.

11.4   The Final Fitness I Obtained Is Simply Too Poor: The Solutions Are Just not Good Enough

Usually, even with a relatively 'out of the box' choice of fitness function and search based optimisation technique, the results obtained will be better than those obtained using a purely random search. However, you may still feel that the results are not as good as you would like, or, if you have as specific threshold fitness value in mind, you may find that your algorithm fails to achieve this threshold, even when you allow it considerable computation resources. In this situation, you should not give up and assume that 'SBSE does not work' (it is just possible that it may not, but it is certainly too soon to be sure!). It may be that your algorithm is performing poorly because of some of the parameter choices or because it is the wrong algorithm for this particular problem. Even should all else fail, you may be able to extract useful information from the suboptimal results you have obtained.

Avoid Premature Convergence: Premature convergence on a local optima often turns out to underlie the observation that an SBSE algorithm fails to produce 'good enough' results. This can happen because, for example, too much elitism has been incorporated into an evolutionary approach, or because some domain knowledge has been injected in a way that strongly biases solutions towards only one part of the search space. In general, it may be helpful to think of your search process as a compromise between exploration and exploitation (a common distinction in the more general optimisation literature). If you fail to explore sufficiently, then premature convergence will result. If you fail to exploit sufficiently, then you may have a broad spread of solutions across the search space, none of which is of particularly high quality. It is a good overarching principle to seek to favour exploration in the earlier stages of the search process and exploitation subsequently. This principle is captured, elegantly, by the cooling parameter of simulated annealing, though there are ways to incorporating similar ideas into almost all search algorithms.

Try Other Search Algorithms: As noted above, the reasons for poor performance could simply be that the wrong search algorithm is used for the search space in hand. If the fitness landscape resembles one enormous hill (or lots of hills of equal fitness) then hill climbing is clearly an attractive candidate. For landscapes with so-called 'royal road' properties [70], an evolutionary algorithm will be favourable. These distinctions are starting to be explored in the SBSE literature [49]. It is always advisable to explore with several search based algorithms in any SBSE work, to include (as a sanity check) random search, together with at least one local and one global search technique, simply to get a sense for the variabilities involved. Of course, comparing these will require some thought and careful planning, as explained in Section 6.

Look for Building Blocks: It is unlikely, but suppose you discover that you cannot get the higher quality results you seek after trying several fitness functions and many different algorithms. What then? Well, in this situation, you will have a large set of results, albeit a set of sub optimal results. There is a great deal of value that can be obtained from such a set of results. You can use them to understand the structure of the search space. This may helpful to explain why your results turn out the way they do. Furthermore, you can search for building blocks in the solutions, that can help you to identify *partial* solutions or fragments of good solutions that can help to identify better solutions. Such building blocks may lead a human to a 'eureka' moment, when they gain insight into the structure of some essential or sufficient ingredient of a good solution. They can also be used to constrain subsequent search based approaches, that may then prove more successful. This two-stage search approach has been shown to be effective in SBSE work; it has been used to identify the building blocks of good software modularisations for a subsequent search over a constrained (and therefore much smaller) landscape in which the building blocks are now fixed [62].

12   Conclusion

We hope that this tutorial paper has been a useful guide to the development of the reader's (perhaps first) SBSE paper. We look forward to reading and learning from your work on SBSE.

References

1. ACM. The 1998 ACM computing classification system (2009),
   http://www.acm.org/about/class/1998
2. Adamopoulos, K., Harman, M., Hierons, R.M.: How to Overcome the Equivalent Mutant Problem and Achieve Tailored Selective Mutation Using Co-evolution. In: Deb, K., et al. (eds.) GECCO 2004. LNCS, vol. 3103, pp. 1338–1349. Springer, Heidelberg (2004)

3. Afzal, W., Torkar, R., Feldt, R.: A systematic review of search-based testing for non-functional system properties. Information and Software Technology 51(6), 957–976 (2009)
4. Ali, S., Briand, L.C., Hemmati, H., Panesar-Walawege, R.K.: A systematic review of the application and empirical investigation of search-based test-case generation. IEEE Transactions on Software Engineering (2010) to appear
5. Antoniol, G., Gueorguiev, S., Harman, M.: Software project planning for robustness and completion time in the presence of uncertainty using multi objective search based software engineering. In: ACM Genetic and Evolutionary Computation COnference (GECCO 2009), Montreal, Canada, July 8-12, pp. 1673–1680 (2009)
6. Antoniol, G., Di Penta, M., Harman, M.: Search-based techniques applied to optimization of project planning for a massive maintenance project. In: 21st IEEE International Conference on Software Maintenance, pp. 240–249. IEEE Computer Society Press, Los Alamitos (2005)
7. Arcuri, A.: It does matter how you normalise the branch distance in search based software testing. In: Proceedings of the International Conference on Software Testing, Verification and Validation, pp. 205–214. IEEE (2010)
8. Arcuri, A., Briand, L.: A practical guide for using statistical tests to assess randomized algorithms in software engineering. In: 33rd International Conference on Software Engineering (ICSE 2011), pp. 1–10. ACM, New York (2011)
9. Arcuri, A., White, D.R., Yao, X.: Multi-objective Improvement of Software Using Co-evolution and Smart Seeding. In: Li, X., Kirley, M., Zhang, M., Green, D., Ciesielski, V., Abbass, H.A., Michalewicz, Z., Hendtlass, T., Deb, K., Tan, K.C., Branke, J., Shi, Y. (eds.) SEAL 2008. LNCS, vol. 5361, pp. 61–70. Springer, Heidelberg (2008)
10. Arcuri, A., Yao, X.: Coevolving Programs and Unit Tests from their Specification. In: Proceedings of the 22nd IEEE/ACM International Conference on Automated Software Engineering (ASE 2007), Atlanta, Georgia, USA, November 5-9, pp. 397–400. ACM (2007)
11. Arcuri, A., Yao, X.: A Novel Co-evolutionary Approach to Automatic Software Bug Fixing. In: Proceedings of the IEEE Congress on Evolutionary Computation (CEC 2008), Hongkong, China, June 1-6, pp. 162–168. IEEE Computer Society (2008)
12. Asadi, F., Antoniol, G., Guéhéneuc, Y.-G.: Concept locations with genetic algorithms: A comparison of four distributed architectures. In: Proceedings of 2nd International Symposium on Search based Software Engineering (SSBSE 2010), Benevento, Italy. IEEE Computer Society Press (2010) to appear
13. Bagnall, A.J., Rayward-Smith, V.J., Whittley, I.M.: The next release problem. Information and Software Technology 43(14), 883–890 (2001)
14. Baker, J.E.: Reducing bias and inefficiency in the selection algorithm. In: Proceedings of the 2nd International Conference on Genetic Algorithms and their Application, Hillsdale, New Jersey, USA, Lawrence Erlbaum Associates (1987)
15. Binkley, D., Harman, M., Lakhotia, K.: FlagRemover: A testability transformation for transforming loop assigned flags. ACM Transactions on Software Engineering and Methodology. (2010) to appear
16. Black, J., Melachrinoudis, E., Kaeli, D.: Bi-criteria models for all-uses test suite reduction. In: Proceedings of the 26th International Conference on Software Engineering (ICSE 2004), pp. 106–115. ACM Press (May 2004)

17. Bowman, M., Briand, L.C., Labiche, Y.: Solving the Class Responsibility Assignment Problem in Object-Oriented Analysis with Multi-Objective Genetic Algorithms. Technical Report SCE-07-02, Carleton University (August. 2008)

18. Burgess, C.J., Lefley, M.: Can genetic programming improve software effort estimation? a comparative evaluation. Information and Software Technology 43, 863–873 (2001)

19. Burke, E., Kendall, G.: Search Methodologies. Introductory tutorials in optimization and decision support techniques. Springer, Heidelberg (2005)

20. Chen, T.Y., Lau, M.F.: Heuristics towards the optimization of the size of a test suite. In: Proceedings of the 3rd International Conference on Software Quality Management, vol. 2, pp. 415–424 (1995)

21. Clark, J., Dolado, J.J., Harman, M., Hierons, R.M., Jones, B., Lumkin, M., Mitchell, B., Mancoridis, S., Rees, K., Roper, M., Shepperd, M.: Reformulating software engineering as a search problem. IEE Proceedings — Software 150(3), 161–175 (2003)

22. Crescenzi, P., Kann, V. (eds.): A compendium of NP-optimization problems, http://www.nada.kth.se/

23. Deb, K., Goldberg, D.: A comparative analysis of selection schemes used in genetic algorithms. In: Foundations of Genetic Algorithms, pp. 69–93. Morgan Kaufmann, San Francisco (1991)

24. Deb, K., Pratap, A., Agarwal, S., Meyarivan, T.: A fast and elitist multiobjective genetic algorithm: NSGA-II. IEEE Transactions on Evolutionary Computation 6, 182–197 (2002)

25. Dolado, J.J.: On the problem of the software cost function. Information and Software Technology 43(1), 61–72 (2001)

26. Dolado, J.J.: A Validation of the Component-based Method for Software Size Estimation. IEEE Transactions on Software Engineering 26(10), 1006–1021 (2000)

27. Durillo, J.J., Zhang, Y., Alba, E., Nebro, A.J.: A Study of the Multi-Objective Next Release Problem. In: Proceedings of the 1st International Symposium on Search Based Software Engineering (SSBSE 2009), Cumberland Lodge, Windsor, UK, May 13-15, pp. 49–58. IEEE Computer Society Press (2009)

28. Elbaum, S.G., Malishevsky, A.G., Rothermel, G.: Prioritizing test cases for regression testing. In: International Symposium on Software Testing and Analysis, pp. 102–112. ACM Press (2000)

29. Fatiregun, D., Harman, M., Hierons, R.: Evolving transformation sequences using genetic algorithms. In: 4th International Workshop on Source Code Analysis and Manipulation (SCAM 2004), pp. 65–74. IEEE Computer Society Press, Los Alamitos (2004)

30. Fatiregun, D., Harman, M., Hierons, R.: Search-based amorphous slicing. In: 12th International Working Conference on Reverse Engineering (WCRE 2005), pp. 3–12. Carnegie Mellon University, Pittsburgh (2005)

31. Finkelstein, A., Harman, M., Afshin Mansouri, S., Ren, J., Zhang, Y.: "Fairness Analysis" in Requirements Assignments. In: Proceedings of the 16th IEEE International Requirements Engineering Conference (RE 2008), Barcelona, Catalunya, Spain, September 8-12, pp. 115–124. IEEE Computer Society (2008)

32. Foster, I.: Designing and building parallel programs:Concepts and tools for parallel software. Addison-Wesley (1995)

33. Sapna, P.G., Mohanty, H.: Automated Test Scenario Selection Based on Levenshtein Distance. In: Janowski, T., Mohanty, H. (eds.) ICDCIT 2010. LNCS, vol. 5966, pp. 255–266. Springer, Heidelberg (2010)

34. Garey, M.R., Johnson, D.S.: Computers and Intractability: A guide to the theory of NP-Completeness. W. H. Freeman and Company (1979)
35. Gu, Q., Tang, B., Chen, D.: Optimal regression testing based on selective coverage of test requirements. In: International Symposium on Parallel and Distributed Processing with Applications (ISPA 2010), pp. 419–426 (September 2010)
36. Harman, M.: The current state and future of search based software engineering. In: Briand, L., Wolf, A. (eds.) Future of Software Engineering 2007, pp. 342–357. IEEE Computer Society Press, Los Alamitos (2007)
37. Harman, M.: Search based software engineering for program comprehension. In: 15th International Conference on Program Comprehension (ICPC 2007), Banff, Canada, pp. 3–13. IEEE Computer Society Press (2007)
38. Harman, M.: The relationship between search based software engineering and predictive modeling. In: 6th International Conference on Predictive Models in Software Engineering, Article Number 1, Timisoara, Romania (2010) (keynote paper)
39. Harman, M.: Why the Virtual Nature of Software Makes It Ideal for Search Based Optimization. In: Rosenblum, D.S., Taentzer, G. (eds.) FASE 2010. LNCS, vol. 6013, pp. 1–12. Springer, Heidelberg (2010)
40. Harman, M.: Making the case for MORTO: Multi objective regression test optimization. In: 1st International Workshop on Regression Testing (Regression 2011), Berlin, Germany (March 2011)
41. Harman, M.: Refactoring as testability transformation. In: Refactoring and Testing Workshop (RefTest 2011), Berlin, Germany (March 2011)
42. Harman, M., Clark, J.: Metrics are fitness functions too. In: 10th International Software Metrics Symposium (METRICS 2004), pp. 58–69. IEEE Computer Society Press, Los Alamitos (2004)
43. Harman, M., Hassoun, Y., Lakhotia, K., McMinn, P., Wegener, J.: The impact of input domain reduction on search-based test data generation. In: ACM Symposium on the Foundations of Software Engineering (FSE 2007), Dubrovnik, Croatia, pp. 155–164. Association for Computer Machinery (September 2007)
44. Harman, M., Hierons, R.M.: An overview of program slicing. Software Focus 2(3), 85–92 (2001)
45. Harman, M., Jones, B.F.: Search based software engineering. Information and Software Technology 43(14), 833–839 (2001)
46. Harman, M., Krinke, J., Ren, J., Yoo, S.: Search based data sensitivity analysis applied to requirement engineering. In: ACM Genetic and Evolutionary Computation Conference (GECCO 2009), Montreal, Canada, July 8-12, pp. 1681–1688 (2009)
47. Harman, M., Lakhotia, K., McMinn, P.: A Multi-Objective Approach to Search-based Test Data Generation. In: Proceedings of the 9th annual Conference on Genetic and Evolutionary Computation (GECCO 2007), London, England, July 7-11, pp. 1098–1105. ACM (2007)
48. Harman, M., Mansouri, A., Zhang, Y.: Search based software engineering: A comprehensive analysis and review of trends techniques and applications. Technical Report TR-09-03, Department of Computer Science, King's College London (April 2009)
49. Harman, M., McMinn, P.: A theoretical and empirical analysis of evolutionary testing and hill climbing for structural test data generation. In: International Symposium on Software Testing and Analysis (ISSTA 2007), London, United Kingdom, pp. 73–83. Association for Computer Machinery (2007)

50. Harman, M., McMinn, P.: A theoretical and empirical study of search based testing: Local, global and hybrid search. IEEE Transactions on Software Engineering 36(2), 226–247 (2010)
51. Harman, M., Swift, S., Mahdavi, K.: An empirical study of the robustness of two module clustering fitness functions. In: Genetic and Evolutionary Computation Conference (GECCO 2005), Washington DC, USA, pp. 1029–1036. Association for Computer Machinery (2005)
52. Harman, M., Tratt, L.: Pareto optimal search-based refactoring at the design level. In: GECCO 2007: Proceedings of the 9th Annual Conference on Genetic and Evolutionary Computation, pp. 1106–1113. ACM Press, London (2007)
53. Jean Harrold, M., Gupta, R., Lou Soffa, M.: A methodology for controlling the size of a test suite. ACM Transactions on Software Engineering and Methodology 2(3), 270–285 (1993)
54. Holland, J.H.: Adaptation in Natural and Artificial Systems. University of Michigan Press, Ann Arbor (1975)
55. Ince, D.C., Hekmatpour, S.: Empirical evaluation of random testing. The Computer Journal 29(4) (August 1986)
56. Kirkpatrick, S., Gellat, C.D., Vecchi, M.P.: Optimization by simulated annealing. Science 220(4598), 671–680 (1983)
57. Kirsopp, C., Shepperd, M., Hart, J.: Search heuristics, case-based reasoning and software project effort prediction. In: GECCO 2002: Proceedings of the Genetic and Evolutionary Computation Conference, July 9-13, pp. 1367–1374. Morgan Kaufmann Publishers, San Francisco (2002)
58. Kirsopp, C., Shepperd, M.J., Hart, J.: Search heuristics, case-based reasoning and software project effort prediction. In: Proceedings of the Genetic and Evolutionary Computation Conference, GECCO 2002, pp. 1367–1374. Morgan Kaufmann Publishers Inc., San Francisco (2002)
59. Korel, B.: Automated software test data generation. IEEE Transactions on Software Engineering 16(8), 870–879 (1990)
60. Lakhotia, K., Harman, M., McMinn, P.: Handling dynamic data structures in search based testing. In: Proceedings of the Genetic and Evolutionary Computation Conference (GECCO 2008), pp. 1759–1766. ACM Press, Atlanta (2008)
61. Lehre, P.K., Yao, X.: Runtime analysis of search heuristics on software engineering problems. Frontiers of Computer Science in China 3(1), 64–72 (2009)
62. Mahdavi, K., Harman, M., Mark Hierons, R.: A multiple hill climbing approach to software module clustering. In: IEEE International Conference on Software Maintenance, pp. 315–324. IEEE Computer Society Press, Los Alamitos (2003)
63. Maia, C.L.B., do Carmo, R.A.F., de Freitas, F.G., Lima de Campos, G.A., de Souza, J.T.: A multi-objective approach for the regression test case selection problem. In: Proceedings of Anais do XLI Simpòsio Brasileiro de Pesquisa Operacional (SBPO 2009), pp. 1824–1835 (2009)
64. Mancoridis, S., Mitchell, B.S., Rorres, C., Chen, Y.-F., Gansner, E.R.: Using automatic clustering to produce high-level system organizations of source code. In: International Workshop on Program Comprehension (IWPC 1998), pp. 45–53. IEEE Computer Society Press, Los Alamitos (1998)
65. McMinn, P.: Search-based software test data generation: A survey. Software Testing, Verification and Reliability 14(2), 105–156 (2004)
66. McMinn, P.: Search-based testing: Past, present and future. In: Proceedings of the 3rd International Workshop on Search-Based Software Testing (SBST 2011). IEEE, Berlin (to appear, 2011)

67. Mitchell, B.S., Mancoridis, S.: Using heuristic search techniques to extract design abstractions from source code. In: GECCO 2002: Proceedings of the Genetic and Evolutionary Computation Conference, July 9-13, pp. 1375–1382. Morgan Kaufmann Publishers, San Francisco (2002)

68. Mitchell, B.S., Mancoridis, S.: On the automatic modularization of software systems using the bunch tool. IEEE Transactions on Software Engineering 32(3), 193–208 (2006)

69. Mitchell, B.S., Traverso, M., Mancoridis, S.: An architecture for distributing the computation of software clustering algorithms. In: IEEE/IFIP Proceedings of the Working Conference on Software Architecture (WICSA 2001), pp. 181–190. IEEE Computer Society, Amsterdam (2001)

70. Mitchell, M., Forrest, S., Holland, J.H.: The royal road for genetic algorithms: Fitness landscapes and GA performance. In: Varela, F.J., Bourgine, P. (eds.) Proc. of the First European Conference on Artificial Life, pp. 245–254. MIT Press, Cambridge (1992)

71. Mühlenbein, H., Schlierkamp-Voosen, D.: Predictive models for the breeder genetic algorithm: I. continuous parameter optimization. Evolutionary Computation 1(1), 25–49 (1993)

72. Munawar, A., Wahib, M., Munetomo, M., Akama, K.: A survey: Genetic algorithms and the fast evolving world of parallel computing. In: 10th IEEE International Conference on High Performance Computing and Communications (HPCC 2008), pp. 897–902. IEEE (2008)

73. Munroe, R.: XKCD: Significant, http://xkcd.com/882/

74. Offutt, J., Pan, J., Voas, J.: Procedures for reducing the size of coverage-based test sets. In: Proceedings of the 12th International Conference on Testing Computer Software, pp. 111–123 (June 1995)

75. O'Keeffe, M., Ó Cinnéide, M.: Search-based refactoring: an empirical study. Journal of Software Maintenance 20(5), 345–364 (2008)

76. Pinto, G.H.L., Vergilio, S.R.: A multi-objective genetic algorithm to test data generation. In: 22nd IEEE International Conference on Tools with Artificial Intelligence (ICTAI 2010), pp. 129–134. IEEE Computer Society (2010)

77. Praditwong, K., Harman, M., Yao, X.: Software module clustering as a multi-objective search problem. IEEE Transactions on Software Engineering (to appear, 2011)

78. Räihä, O.: A survey on search–based software design. Computer Science Review 4(4), 203–249 (2010)

79. Reid, S.C.: An empirical analysis of equivalence partitioning, boundary value analysis and random testing. In: 4th International Software Metrics Symposium. IEEE Computer Society Press, Los Alamitos (1997)

80. Rothermel, G., Harrold, M., Ronne, J., Hong, C.: Empirical studies of test suite reduction. Software Testing, Verification, and Reliability 4(2), 219–249 (2002)

81. Rothermel, G., Harrold, M.J., Ostrin, J., Hong, C.: An empirical study of the effects of minimization on the fault detection capabilities of test suites. In: Proceedings of International Conference on Software Maintenance (ICSM 1998), Bethesda, Maryland, USA, pp. 34–43. IEEE Computer Society Press (November 1998)

82. Ruhe, G., Greer, D.: Quantitative Studies in Software Release Planning under Risk and Resource Constraints. In: Proceedings of the International Symposium on Empirical Software Engineering (ISESE 2003), Rome, Italy, September 29 - October 4, pp. 262–270. IEEE (2003)

83. Ryan, C.: Automatic re-engineering of software using genetic programming. Kluwer Academic Publishers (2000)

84. Saliu, M.O., Ruhe, G.: Bi-objective release planning for evolving software systems. In: Crnkovic, I., Bertolino, A. (eds.) Proceedings of the 6th Joint Meeting of the European Software Engineering Conference and the ACM SIGSOFT International Symposium on Foundations of Software Engineering (ESEC/FSE) 2007, pp. 105–114. ACM (September 2007)

85. Seng, O., Stammel, J., Burkhart, D.: Search-based determination of refactorings for improving the class structure of object-oriented systems. In: Genetic and Evolutionary Computation Conference (GECCO 2006), Seattle, Washington, USA, July 8-12, vol. 2, pp. 1909–1916. ACM Press (2006)

86. Shaw, M.: Writing good software engineering research papers: minitutorial. In: Proceedings of the 25th International Conference on Software Engineering (ICSE 2003), Piscataway, NJ, May 3-10, pp. 726–737. IEEE Computer Society (2003)

87. Shepperd, M.J.: Foundations of software measurement. Prentice Hall (1995)

88. Simons, C.L., Parmee, I.C.: Agent-based Support for Interactive Search in Conceptual Software Engineering Design. In: Keijzer, M. (ed.) Proceedings of the 10th Annual Conference on Genetic and Evolutionary Computation (GECCO 2008), Atlanta, GA, USA, July 12-16, pp. 1785–1786. ACM (2008)

89. Simons, C.L., Parmee, I.C., Gwynllyw, R.: Interactive, evolutionary search in upstream object-oriented class design. IEEE Transactions on Software Engineering 36(6), 798–816 (2010)

90. de Souza, J.T., Maia, C.L., de Freitas, F.G., Coutinho, D.P.: The human competitiveness of search based software engineering. In: Proceedings of 2nd International Symposium on Search based Software Engineering (SSBSE 2010), Benevento, Italy, pp. 143–152. IEEE Computer Society Press (2010)

91. Sutton, A.M., Howe, A.E., Whitley, L.D.: Estimating Bounds on Expected Plateau Size in MAXSAT Problems. In: Stützle, T., Birattari, M., Hoos, H.H. (eds.) SLS 2009. LNCS, vol. 5752, pp. 31–45. Springer, Heidelberg (2009)

92. Tonella, P., Susi, A., Palma, F.: Using interactive ga for requirements prioritization. In: Proceedings of the 2nd International Symposium on Search Based Software Engineering (SSBSE 2010), Benevento, Italy, September 7-9, pp. 57–66. IEEE (2010)

93. Tracey, N., Clark, J., Mander, K., McDermid, J.: An automated framework for structural test-data generation. In: Proceedings of the International Conference on Automated Software Engineering, Hawaii, USA, pp. 285–288. IEEE Computer Society Press (1998)

94. Turing, A.M.: Computing machinery and intelligence. Mind 49, 433–460 (1950)

95. Wada, H., Champrasert, P., Suzuki, J., Oba, K.: Multiobjective Optimization of SLA-Aware Service Composition. In: Proceedings of IEEE Workshop on Methodologies for Non-functional Properties in Services Computing, Honolulu, HI, USA, July 6-11, pp. 368–375. IEEE (2008)

96. Wang, H., Chan, W.K., Tse, T.H.: On the construction of context-aware test suites. Technical Report TR-2010-01, Hong Kong University (2010)

97. Wegener, J., Baresel, A., Sthamer, H.: Evolutionary test environment for automatic structural testing. Information and Software Technology 43(14), 841–854 (2001)

98. Wen, F., Lin, C.-M.: Multistage Human Resource Allocation for Software Development by Multiobjective Genetic Algorithm. The Open Applied Mathematics Journal 2, 95–103 (2008)

99. White, D.R., Clark, J.A., Jacob, J., Poulding, S.M.: Searching for Resource-Efficient Programs: Low-Power Pseudorandom Number Generators. In: Keijzer, M. (ed.) Proceedings of the 10th Annual Conference on Genetic and Evolutionary Computation (GECCO 2008), Atlanta, GA, USA, July 12-16, pp. 1775–1782. ACM (2008)
100. Whitley, D.: The GENITOR algorithm and selection pressure: Why rank-based allocation of reproductive trials is best. In: Schaffer, J.D. (ed.) Proceedings of the International Conference on Genetic Algorithms, San Mateo, California, USA, pp. 116–121. Morgan Kaufmann (1989)
101. Whitley, D.: A genetic algorithm tutorial. Statistics and Computing 4, 65–85 (1994)
102. Whitley, D.: An overview of evolutionary algorithms: practical issues and common pitfalls. Information and Software Technology 43(14), 817–831 (2001)
103. Whitley, D., Sutton, A.M., Howe, A.E.: Understanding elementary landscapes. In: Proceedings of the 10th Annual Conference on Genetic and Evolutionary Computation (GECCO 2008), pp. 585–592. ACM, New York (2008)
104. Williams, K.P.: Evolutionary Algorithms for Automatic Parallelization. PhD thesis, University of Reading, UK, Department of Computer Science (September 1998)
105. Yoo, S.: A novel mask-coding representation for set cover problems with applications in test suite minimisation. In: Proceedings of the 2nd International Symposium on Search-Based Software Engineering, SSBSE 2010 (2010)
106. Yoo, S., Harman, M.: Pareto efficient multi-objective test case selection. In: International Symposium on Software Testing and Analysis (ISSTA 2007), pp. 140–150. Association for Computer Machinery, London (2007)
107. Yoo, S., Harman, M.: Using hybrid algorithm for pareto efficient multi-objective test suite minimisation. Journal of Systems and Software 83(4), 689–701 (2010)
108. Yoo, S., Harman, M.: Regression testing minimisation, selection and prioritisation: A survey. Journal of Software Testing, Verification and Reliability (to appear, 2011)
109. Yoo, S., Harman, M., Tonella, P., Susi, A.: Clustering test cases to achieve effective and scalable prioritisation incorporating expert knowledge. In: ACM International Conference on Software Testing and Analysis (ISSTA 2009), Chicago, Illinois, USA, July 19-23, pp. 201–212 (2009)
110. Yoo, S., Harman, M., Ur, S.: Highly scalable multi-objective test suite minimisation using graphics card. Rn/11/07, Department of Computer Science, University College London (January 2011)
111. Zhang, Y.-Y., Finkelstein, A., Harman, M.: Search Based Requirements Optimisation: Existing Work and Challenges. In: Rolland, C. (ed.) REFSQ 2008. LNCS, vol. 5025, pp. 88–94. Springer, Heidelberg (2008)
112. Zhang, Y., Harman, M., Finkelstein, A., Mansouri, A.: Comparing the performance of metaheuristics for the analysis of multi-stakeholder tradeoffs in requirements optimisation. Journal of Information and Software Technology (to appear, 2011)
113. Zhang, Y., Harman, M., Mansouri, A.: The multi-objective next release problem. In: GECCO 2007: Proceedings of the 9th Annual Conference on Genetic and Evolutionary Computation, pp. 1129–1137. ACM Press, London (2007)

Replication of Software Engineering Experiments

Natalia Juristo and Omar S. Gómez*

Facultad de Informática,
Universidad Politécnica de Madrid,
Boadilla del Monte 28660, Madrid, España
natalia@fi.upm.es, ogomez@ieee.org

Abstract. Experimentation has played a major role in scientific advancement. Replication is one of the essentials of the experimental methods. In replications, experiments are repeated aiming to check their results. Successful replication increases the validity and reliability of the outcomes observed in an experiment.

There is debate about the best way of running replications of Software Engineering (SE) experiments. Some of the questions that have cropped up in this debate are, "Should replicators reuse the baseline experiment materials? Which is the adequate sort of communication among experimenters and replicators if any? What elements of the experimental structure can be changed and still be considered a replication instead of a new experiment?". A deeper understanding of the concept of replication should help to clarify these issues as well as increase and improve replications in SE experimental practices.

In this chapter, we study the concept of replication in order to gain insight. The chapter starts with an introduction to the importance of replication and the state of replication in ESE. Then we discuss replication from both the statistical and scientific viewpoint. Based on a review of the diverse types of replication used in other scientific disciplines, we identify the different types of replication that are feasible to be run in our discipline. Finally, we present the different purposes that replication can serve in Experimental Software Engineering (ESE).

Keywords: Experimental Replicaction, Types of Replication, Experimental Software Engineering, Empirical Software Engineering.

1 Introduction

Experimentation should be an indispensable part of SE research. As Tichy says [1], "Experimentation can help build a reliable base of knowledge and thus reduce uncertainty about which theories, methods, and tools are adequate". Basili [2] claims that "Experimental SE is necessary, common wisdom, intuition, speculation, and proofs of concepts are not reliable sources of credible knowledge".

* This work has been performed under research grant TIN 2008-00555 of the Spanish Ministry of Science and Innovation, and research grant 206747 of the México's National Council of Science and Technology (CONACyT).

B. Meyer and M. Nordio (Eds.): LASER Summer School 2008-2010, LNCS 7007, pp. 60–88, 2012.

Voices in favour of experimentalism as a way of research about software development have recently grown stronger. DeMarco [3] claims that "The actual software construction isn't necessarily experimental, but its conception is. And this is where our focus ought to be. It's where our focus always ought to have been". Meyer [4, 5] has also joined the line of researchers to point to the importance of experimentation in SE.

A key component of experimentation is replication. To consolidate a body of knowledge built upon experimental results, they have to be extensively verified. This verification is carried out by replicating an experiment to check if its results can be reproducible. If the same results are reproduced in different replications, we can infer that such results are regularities existing in the piece of reality under study. Experimenters acquainted with such regularities can find out mechanisms regulating the observed results or, at least, predict their behaviour.

Most of the events observed through experiments in SE nowadays are isolated. In other words, most SE experiments results have not been reproduced. So there is no way to distinguish the following three situations: the results were produced by chance (the event occurred accidentally); the results are artifactual (the event only occurs in the experiment not in the reality under study), or the results really do conform to a regularity of the piece of reality being examined.

A replication has some elements in common with its baseline experiment. When we start to examine a phenomenon experimentally, most aspects are unknown. Even the tiniest change in a replication can lead to inexplicable differences in the results. In immature experimental disciplines, which experimental conditions should be controlled can be found out by starting off with replications closely following the baseline experiment [6]. In the case of well-known phenomena, the experimental conditions that influence the results can be controlled, and artifactual results are identified by running less similar replications. For example, using different experimental protocols to verify the results correspond to experiment-independent events.

The immaturity of ESE has been an obstacle to replication. As the mechanisms regulating software development and the key experimental conditions for its investigation are yet unknown, even the slightest change in the replication leads to inexplicable differences in the results. However, context differences oblige experimenters to adapt the experiment. These changes can lead to sizeable differences in the replication results that prevent the outcomes of the baseline experiment from being corroborated. In several attempts at combining the results of ESE replications, Hayes [7], Miller [8–10], Hannay et al. [11], Jørgensen [12], Pickard et al. [13], Shull et al. [14] and Juristo et al. [15] reported that the differences between results were so large that they found it impossible to draw any consequences from the results comparison.

ESE stereotype of replication is an experiment that is repeated independently by other researchers at different sites to the baseline experiment. But some of the replications in ESE do not conform to this stereotype: either they are jointly run, or replicators researchers reuse some of the materials employed in the baseline experiment or they are run at the same site [16–25]. How replications should be run has moved a debate in ESE. There are researchers that recommend reusing some of the baseline experiment materials to run replications [2, 26] with the aim of assuring that the replications are similar and results can be compared. There are researches who advise the use of different protocols and materials to those employed in the baseline experiment [10, 27] with the aim of preserving the principle of independence and preventing error propagation in replications that use the same materials. Others suggest using alternative ways of verifying the experimental results [28] with the aim of understanding the problems that replication have had to date in SE experiments. This debate can probably be put down to the fact that replication has still not satisfactorily tailored to ESE.

In this chapter we study the concept of replication with the aim of getting a better understanding of its use in ESE. This chapter is organized as follows. Section 2 describes the statistical perspective of replication. Section 3 discusses replication in science. Section 4 reviews different types of replication accepted in different experimental disciplines. Section 5 discusses the differences between the concepts of replication and reproduction. Section 6 describes adequate variations in replication. Section 7 discusses some types of replications in SE. Section 8 presents the purposes that a replication can serves. Section 9 presents the conclusions. Finally, Annex A lists and describes replication typologies found in other disciplines.

2   Statistical Perspective of Replication

Sample size is an essential element in a controlled experiment. An adequate sample size increases the possibilities of the effect observed in the sample occurring in the real population. The accuracy level of the results grows in proportion to the sample size.

One of the commonly used coefficients for representing effect size observed in an experiment is Cohen's d [29]. This coefficient is used to measure the differences between the treatments studied in the experiment. The effect size indicates how much better one treatment is compared to another. This coefficient is usually used with one-digit accuracy. For example [29], $d=0.2$ represents a small effect, $d=0.5$ indicates a medium effect or $d=0.8$ is a large effect. The sample size required to satisfy a one-digit accuracy level can be calculated from (1): the function in (1) is derived from (2) and (3), where the differences in the confidence intervals (left and right) are equal at the specified accuracy level, in this case 0.1.

$$N = \frac{2 + d^2}{2(0.0255102)^2} \tag{1}$$

$$2 \times 1.96 \times deviation(d) = 0.1 \tag{2}$$

$$deviation(d) = \sqrt{\frac{n1 + n2}{n1n2} + \frac{d^2}{2(n1 + n1)}} \tag{3}$$

For effect sizes $d=0.2$, $d=0.5$ and $d=0.8$, a sample size of $N=1{,}567$, $N=1{,}729$ and $N=2{,}028$ is required, respectively. Fig. 1 shows the graph of the resulting function in (1).

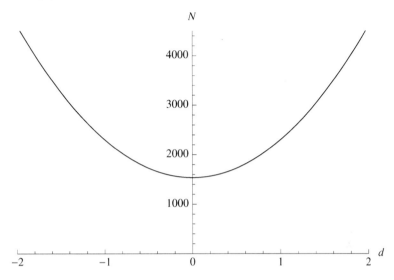

Fig. 1. Sample (N) necessary for a particular effect size (d) with one-digit accuracy

To be able to estimate effect sizes with one-digit accuracy, we need to repeat the same experiment to increase the sample size and reach the required level showed in Fig. 1. In the set of controlled SE experiments examined by Dybå et al. [30], the average sample size of the samples used in these experiments is $N=55$ (55 observations per experiment).

For an average sample size of 50 observations, the same study would have to be repeated 31 times to satisfy the sample size required for an effect size of $d=0.2$; the same study would have to be repeated 34 and 40 times, respectively, to get an effect size of $d=0.5$ and $d=0.8$. Consequently, experiment repetitions have to be equal. For increasing sample size the replications have to measure the independent and dependent variables in exactly the same manner, using exactly the same experimental protocol, and they should all sample the same populations [31].

Since experimental conditions are hard to control in ESE, one option worth considering to satisfy the statistical requirement of identical repetitions is running internal replications (at the same site and by the same experimenters) of SE experiments. Through internal repetitions, the sample comes closer to the interval of observations [1,537; 2,305] required to be confident that the observed effect (from 0, none; to 1^1, very large) occurs not only in the sample used in the experiment but also in the real population.

---

[1] Note that effect size over 1 is possible. In fact Kampenes et al. [32] show that 32% of the experiments published in SE have an effect size greater than 1. The bigger the effect size the bigger the sample.

The results of a single execution of an experiment is threatened by type I error[2]. Having more (internal) replications of the same experiment considerably reduces this type of error. For example, if an experimenter establishes the significance level α of an experiment at 0.05, which represents a 1:20 probability of obtaining a chance result, the likelihood of again obtaining an accidental result drops to 1:400 ($p = 0.05 \times 0.05 = 0.0025$) if the experiment is identically internally repeated again.

The sample size of experiments run in SE is not large enough to accurately estimate the effect size under study. Therefore, identical replications are required to be able to estimate the effect size with any accuracy. However, identical replications are virtually impossible when they are carried out in other sites [25].

3   Replication in Science

In science, replication refers to the repetition of a previously run experiment. Some definitions of replication in science are:

1. "Replication refers to a conscious and systematic repeat of an original study" [33].
2. "Replication is traditionally defined as the duplication of a previously published empirical study" [34].
3. "Replication is a methodological tool based on a repetition procedure that is involved in establishing a fact, truth or piece of knowledge" [35].
4. "Replication – the performance of another study statistically confirming the same hypothesis" [36].
5. "Replication is the repetition of the basic experiment. That is, replication involves repeating an experiment under identical conditions, rather than repeating measurements on the same experimental unit" [37].
6. "The deliberate repetition of research procedures in a second investigation for the purpose of determining if earlier results can be repeated" [38].
7. "Is the process of going back, or re-searching an observation, investigation, or experimentation to compare findings" [39].

The value of replication has been widely recognized in a number of scientific disciplines. Popper [40] claimed that "We do not take even our own observations quite seriously, or accept them as scientific observations, until we have repeated and tested them. Only by such repetitions can we convince ourselves that we are not dealing with a mere isolated 'coincidence', but with events which, on account of their regularity and reproducibility, are in principle inter-subjectively testable". Hempel [41] realized the importance of reckoning with more than one

---

[2] Type I error occurs when the null hypothesis is rejected while it is true, i.e. when there is believed to be a significant difference between the treatments that the experiment compares and there is, in actual fact, no such difference.

study to increase the robustness of the gathered evidence. Campbell and Stanley [42] claim that "The experiments we do today, if successful, will need replication and cross-validation at other times under other conditions before they can become an established part of science, before they can be theoretically interpreted with confidence". Other widely accepted claims about replication are that it "is the Supreme Court of the scientific system" [43], it is considered the cornerstone of science [36], "it is the crucial test whereby theories and experiments in science are judged" [44], and "it is at the heart of (any) experimental science" [35].

From a scientific viewpoint, not having sufficient replications of an experiment can lead to the acceptance of results that are not robust enough. Fahs et al. [45] gave a good example of this problem in an article concerning the retinopathy of prematurity (ROP). Nurses working in neonatal intensive care units (NICUs) tend to place premature babies in incubators or try to somehow protect their eyes from the light, as this practice is believed to reduce the rate of ROP. This practice apparently dates back to a study by Glass et al. [46], concluding that ROP was possibly caused by the bright lighting in NICUs. Years later, however, Ackerman et al. [47] replicated this study and provided evidence contrary to the results published by Glass et al. [46]. Later another two replications of this study were run [48, 49] and corroborated the results reported by Ackerman et al. [47], i.e. NICU lighting is not a factor causing ROP.

Replications of experiments have proven the need to be careful about accepting evidence that has not been subject to strict checks. The evidence provided by a single study or experiment can be weak. Several replications have to be run to strengthen the evidence. In the field of SE, many of the empirical studies published have low statistical power [30]. Failure to replicate these experiments can lead to the belief that there is no significant effect when there probably is.

Even though replication is an important experimental mechanism, we have to be aware of its limits. It is not possible to completely verify a theory based on a finite series of observations. For example, someone observing three black crows at different times cannot conclude that all crows are black. To do this, s/he would have to observe all the crows of all times. Replication is closely related to induction[3], which has been used since ancient times as a way of inferring general rules from repeated past regular observations (instances) [43]. As Restivo [50] says, "replication is the experimental equivalent of induction; what is regularly reproducible is generalizable" or, as Collins [51] argues "experimental replication is the experimental equivalent of inductive inference".

Induction has a catch [40, 52–55] or logical defect, as the general conclusion is reached without individually evaluating all the cases. The problem of proving something inductively is that the gathered knowledge cannot be fully verified. Using probabilistic approaches [56–60], however, we can be somewhat confident about a conclusion reached based on a finite number of observations, that is, a hypothesis can be verified with some level of confidence based on a set of replications.

---

[3] Also known as inductive reasoning or inductive logic.

4   Replication Types in Other Disciplines

With the aim of discovering how to run a replication, we examined several types of replication used in other disciplines. We identified the different types of replication after running Google®, Google scholar®, ScienceDirect® and JSTOR® searches with different keywords (*types of replications, types of experimental replications, typology of replications, replication types, replication typologies, replication types* and *classification of replications*).

After running the searches on the four search engines and examining all the results returned, we located an initial set of 10 replication typologies [31, 35, 61–68]. This initial set of typologies served as a source for locating more replication types. Following the references in this initial set, we were able to locate another 8 [33, 69–75]. This way, we ended up with 18 replication typologies shown in Annex A. Altogether the typologies contain a total of 79 replication types. These typologies belong to the fields of social science (61%), business (33%) and philosophy (6%). Table 1 lists the typologies grouped by field.

Table 1. Typologies grouped by discipline

Area	Number of Typologies	References
(Social Science)		
Psychology	5	Lykken [69]; Hendrick [70]; Hunter [31]; Schmidt [35]; Kantowitz et al. [65]
Sociology	3	Finifter [71]; La Sorte [33]; Bahr et al. [62]
Economics	1	Mittelstaedt and Zorn [67]
Human Communication	1	Kelly et al. [72]
Human Development	1	Van IJzendoorn [63]
(Business)		
Marketing	3	Leone and Schultz [73]; Easley et al. [61]; Monroe [74]
Accounting	1	Lindsay and Ehrenberg [68]
Management	1	Tsang and Kwan [66]
Forecasting	1	Evanschitzky and Armstrong [64]
(Philosophy)		
Philosophy of Science	1	Radder [75]
TOTAL	18	

Lykken's [69] is the most often cited typology, followed by Hendrick's [70]. Lykken's [69], Hendrick's [70] and Bahr et al.'s [62] typologies have been referenced not only within their disciplines, but also in some business areas. We have counted citations where the author somehow uses the typology rather than referring to other questions that the above articles address.

In most typologies, the authors give the replication types an original name. They tend, therefore, to use their own terms to refer to a replication type. There are some exceptions, like Kelly et al. [72], who use the same terms as are applied in Lykken's [69] typology. In the identified typologies, we also find that there is no intra- or inter-disciplinary standardization for naming replication types.

The identified typologies were found to have two purposes: 1) some authors developed the typology to classify existing sets of replications; 2) other authors generated the typology for no particular purpose. Within this purpose, some authors illustrate the replication types using a number of existing replications, whereas others develop the typology and use examples to describe the replication types. Table 2 shows the possible usage of typologies.

Table 2. Typologies usage

Typologies generated to classify existing sets of replications	Typologies generated for understanding replication types	
	With examples of real replications	With imaginary examples
Bahr et al. [62]	Lindsay and Ehrenberg [68]	Hendrick [70]
Kelly et al. [72]	Tsang and Kwan [66]	Monroe [74]
Leone and Schultz [73]	Kantowitz et al. [65]	Radder [75]
Evanschitzky and Armstrong [64]	Lykken [69]	Easley et al. [61]
	Hendrick [70]	Hunter [31]
	La Sorte [33]	Schmidt [35]
	Van IJzendoorn [63]	Finifter [71]
		Mittelstaedt and Zorn [67]

Examining the typologies, we found that experiment results were not always verified by running the experiment over again. Neither did the replication always repeat the experimental protocol of the baseline experiment. We have identified three major groups of methods for verifying findings:

1. Follow the **same experimental protocol** used in the baseline experiment. The degree of similarity between the replication and the baseline experiment vary. For verification purpose some of the elements of the baseline experiment can be changed or modified in the replication. For example, Tsang and Kwan [66] use the term *empirical generalization* when the study is repeated on different populations. Monroe [74] uses the term *independent replication* when the study is repeated by different researchers.

   This type of replication is used for different purposes. According to Lykken [69], for example, the purpose of *operational replication* is to check that the experimental recipe produces the same results with another researcher. Tsang and Kwan's [66] *empirical generalization* purpose is to test the extent to which the study results are generalizable to other populations.

Most researchers use the term *replication* accompanied by an adjective to refer to this method of verification, e.g. *real replication, strict replication, close replication.* The adjective denotes the degree of change made to the structure of the experiment. Table 3 shows the replication types in this category.

Table 3. Using the same experimental protocol

Term	Author(s)
Close Replication	Lindsay and Ehrenberg [68]
Conceptual Replication	Hunter [31]; Monroe [74]
Demonstrated Replication	Monroe [74]
Differentiated Replication	Lindsay and Ehrenberg [68]
Direct Replication	Schmidt [35]; Kantowitz et al. [65]
Empirical Generalization	Tsang and Kwan [66]
Exact Replicarion	Van IJzendoorn [63]; Tsang and Kwan [66]
Experimental Replication	Leone and Schultz [73]
Generalization and Extension	Tsang and Kwan [66]
Independent Replication	La Sorte [33]; Monroe [74]
Instrumental Replication	Kelly et al. [72]
Literal Replication	Lykken [69]; Kelly et al. [72]
Nonexperimental Replication	Leone and Schultz [73]
Nonindependend Replication	Monroe [74]
Operational Replication	Lykken [69]; Kelly et al. [72]
Partial Replication	Hendrick [70]; Monroe [74]
Real Replications	Evanschitzky and Armstrong [64]
Reproducibility of an experiment under a fixed theoretical interpretation	Radder [75]
Reproducibility of the material realization of an experiment	Radder [75]
Retest Replication	La Sorte [33]
Scientific Replication	Hunter [31]
Sequential Replication	Monroe [74]
Statistical Replication	Hunter [31]
Strict Replication	Hendrick [70]; Monroe [74]
Systematic Replication	Kantowitz et al. [65]; Finifter [71]
Types 0, I, II	Easley et al. [61]
Types A..H	Bahr et al. [62]
Varied Replication	Van IJzendoorn [63]
Virtual Replication	Finifter [71]

2. Use a **different experimental protocol** to the baseline experiment. In this type of verification, the only thing the replication has in common with the baseline experiment is that they are both based on the same theoretical structure, i.e. they share the same constructs. This verification is used to corroborate previously observed findings through a different path. Hendrick [70], Schmidt [35] and Kantowitz et al. [65] call this type of verification *conceptual replication*, whereas Finifter [71] names it *systematic replication*. Radder [75], describes it as the *reproducibility of the result of an experiment*. Table 4 shows the replication types that adhere to this kind of verification.

Table 4. Using a different experimental protocol

Replication Type	Author(s)
Conceptual Extension	Tsang and Kwan [66]
Conceptual Replication	Hendrick [70]; Schmidt [35]; Kantowitz et al. [65]
Constructive Replication	Lykken [69]; Kelly et al. [72]
Corroboration	Leone and Schultz [73]
Differentiated Replication	Lindsay and Ehrenberg [68]
Generalization and Extension	Tsang and Kwan [66]
Reproducibility of the result of an experiment	Radder [75]
Systematic Replication	Finifter [71]
Theoretical Replication	La Sorte [33]
Type III	Easley et al. [61]
Types I..P	Bahr et al. [62]

3. Use **existing data sets** from a previous experiment to reanalyse the data employing either the same analysis procedures or others. This modus operandi is useful for verifying whether errors were made during the data analysis stage or whether the outcomes are affected by any particular data analysis technique. Some replication types reanalyse the statistical models instead of the existing study data. Different names are used for this type of verification. For example, La Sorte [33] calls it *internal replication*; Finifter [71] terms it *pseudoreplication*, and Tsang and Kwan [66] describe it as *checking of analysis* and *reanalysis of data*. Table 5 shows the replication types we identified that fall into this category.

Table 5. Reanalyzing existing data

Replication Type	Author(s)
Checking of Analysis	Tsang and Kwan [66]
Complete Secondary Analysis	Van IJzendoorn [63]
Data Re-analyses	Evanschitzky and Armstrong [64]
Internal Replication	La Sorte [33]
Pseudoreplication	Finifter [71]
Reanalysis of Data	Tsang and Kwan [66]
Restricted Secondary Analysis	Van IJzendoorn [63]
Types I, II	Mittelstaedt and Zorn [67]

If we want one term to identify each of the three forms of verification, we would surely refer to the third one as *re-analysis*, because the descriptions clearly allude to this term. However, the naming of the other two forms causes some confusion. Do both forms adhere to the concept of replication, or does each one introduce a different concept? The authors of some of the articles that we consulted to identify the typologies use the terms replication and reproduction indistinctly. This led us to examine whether these two concepts are equivalent or different.

5 Replication vs. Reproduction

According to the typologies we found, most researchers use the term replication to refer to the repetition of an experiment, although some use the term reproduction or reproducibility to describe this repetition. So it seems that many researchers consider the two terms to be synonyms. Likewise, Wikipedia uses these terms indistinctly and defines reproducibility as "one of the main principles of the scientific method, and refers to the ability of a test or experiment to be accurately reproduced, or replicated, by someone else working independently" [76].

Some researchers, however, do make a distinction between the two terms. Cartwright [77], for example, suggests that replicability "doing the same experiment again" should be distinguished from reproducibility "doing a new experiment". For Cartwright [77] the replication of an experiment refers to repeating a new experiment very closely following the experimental protocol used in the previous experiment, whereas reproduction refers re-examining a previously observed result using a different experimental protocol to what was employed in the previous experiment.

According to Cartwright [77], replication does not guarantee that the observed result represents the reality under observation. The result can be artifactual, i.e. a product of the materials or the instruments used in the experiment. To guarantee that the result is consistent with the reality under observation, we have to undertake a reproduction using different experimental protocols to ensure that the observed result is independent of the procedure, materials or instruments used in the experiments that arrived at the result.

When the results are repeatable using the same experimental protocol, the experimenters can be confident that they have observed some sort of phenomenon that is stable enough to be observed more than once. But, as it was observed using the same experimental protocol, there could be a very close relationship between the protocol and the phenomenon. As Radder put it [78], "[this result] does not imply any agreement about what the phenomenon is. Some interpreters may even argue that the phenomenon is an artifact, because, though it is stable, it is not to be attributed to the object under study but to certain features of the apparatus", where the term apparatus refers to the instruments, materials or procedures used, i.e. the experimental protocol. Cartwright [77] claims that "reproducibility, then, is a guard against errors in our instruments" in such a situation. According to Cartwright [77], though, reproduction is not absolutely necessary, as the better designed the instruments (apparatus) are, the less likely it is to have to use reproducibility.

Reproduction can be seen as a sort of triangulation, where the experimenters use different experimental protocols in an attempt to validate or corroborate the findings of the previous experiment [79]. According to Park [80], "These triangulation strategies can be used to support a conceptual finding, but they are not replications of any degree".

In this respect, the concept of replication given by Cartwright [77] would fit the first form of verification described in the previous section, whereas the concept of reproduction adheres to the second form of verification that we identified in the replication typologies.

6 Variation among Replications

Based on the different replication types that we have found, replications appear to fall into three groups:

1. Replications that vary little or not at all with respect to the baseline experiment.
2. Replications that do vary but still follow the same experimental protocol as the baseline experiment.
3. Replications that use different experimental protocol to check the baseline experimental results i.e. reproductions.

Tables 6 and 7 list the replication types that fall into these first two groups. The third group corresponds with the second type of verification presented in section 4 (Use a different experimental protocol to the baseline experiment).

Table 6. Replications with few or no variations that adhere to the baseline experiment

Replication Type	Author(s)
Close Replication	Lindsay and Ehrenberg [68]
Direct Replication	Schmidt [35]; Kantowitz et al. [65]
Exact Replication	Van IJzendoorn [63]; Tsang and Kwan [66]
Experimental Replication	Leone and Schultz [73]
Literal Replication	Lykken [69]; Kelly et al. [72]
Real Replications	Evanschitzky and Armstrong [64]
Reproducibility of the material realization of an experiment	Radder [75]
Sequential Replication	Monroe [74]
Statistical Replication	Hunter [31]
Strict Replication	Hendrick [70]; Monroe [74]
Type 0	Easley et al. [61]
Types A..D	Bahr et al. [62]
Type I	Easley et al. [61]

Based on the descriptions of the replications, it appears that a replication can have different levels of similarity to the baseline experiment. In other words, the elements of the experiment structure do not necessarily have to be the same in the replication. Table 8 shows some experimental elements that, according to the typologies we have found, do not necessarily have to be the same in each replication. Note that the type (or aim) of the replication differs depending on this change.

Table 7. Replications with variations that adhere to the same experimental protocol

Replication Type	Author(s)
Conceptual Replication	Hunter [31]; Monroe [74]
Demonstrated Replication	Monroe [74]
Differentiated Replication	Lindsay and Ehrenberg [68]
Direct Replication	Schmidt [35]
Empirical Generalization	Tsang and Kwan [66]
Generalization and Extension	Tsang and Kwan [66]
Independent Replication	La Sorte [33]; Monroe [74]
Instrumental Replication	Kelly et al. [72]
Nonexperimental Replication	Leone and Schultz [73]
Nonindependent Replication	Monroe [74]
Operational Replication	Lykken [69]; Kelly et al. [72]
Partial Replication	Hendrick [70]; Monroe [74]
Reproducibility of an experiment under a fixed theoretical interpretation	Radder [75]
Retest Replication	La Sorte [33]
Scientific Replication	Hunter [31]
Sequential Replication	Monroe [74]
Systematic Replication	Kantowitz et al. [65]; Finifter [71]
Types E..H	Bahr et al. [62]
Type II	Easley et al. [61]
Varied Replication	Van IJzendoorn [63]
Virtual Replication	Finifter [71]

Table 8. Some identified elements that can vary in the replication

Variable element	Replication Type	Author(s)
Measurement instruments	Differentiated Replication	Lindsay and Ehrenberg [68]
Measures	Operational Replication	Kelly et al. [72]
Method	Conceptual Replication	Schmidt [35]
Place	Types B,F,J,N,D,H,L,P	Bahr et al. [62]
Populations	Empirical Generalization	Tsang and Kwan [66]
Research Design	Retest Replication	La Sorte [33]
Researcher	Independent Replication	Monroe [74]
Sample	Virtual Replication	Finifter [71]

Although the overall objective of a replication is to check an experimental result, we find that different replication types have specific aims or purposes. For example, according to Lykken [69], the purpose of *operational replication* is to check that the experimental recipe outputs the same results with another researcher. However, Finifter's *systematic replication* [71] aims to output new findings using different methods to the baseline experiment.

Each specific aim of a replication type denotes an aspect of the experiment that needs to be verified. The more experimental aspects or elements are verified, the greater the confidence that the observed effect is not artifactual. An effect observed in an experiment may not be observed at sites other than where it was replicated, by other researchers, using other materials or methods or under other conditions. Different replication types should be run to check that the different experiment elements do not bias the observed findings and that the experiment results are real.

Consequently, there are several degrees of similarity between a replication and the baseline experiment. The changes serve different replication purposes. Although the general purpose of a replication is to check a previously observed finding, each replication type has special goals depending on what specific element of the experiment is to be checked.

7   Types of Replications in SE

We did not find any specific research aiming to build a typology or classification of replications in the field of ESE. We did locate, however, three works in our discipline that classified replications as part of the research conducted.

The first piece of research is a master's thesis [81] that set out to study the use of replication of controlled experiments in ESE. Almqvist [81] surveys 44 articles describing 51 controlled experiments and 31 replications. He runs a systematic review as a method for identifying relevant articles. In Chapter 4 of the thesis, Almqvist [81] defines several categories for organizing the identified experiments. In one of the categories, he develops a classification for categorizing the identified replications. Almqvist takes the replication types described by Lindsay and Ehrenberg [68] as a reference and adds *internal* and *external replication*. On this basis, he defines the following four types of replications:

1. Similar-external replications.
2. Improved-internal replications.
3. Similar-internal replications.
4. Differentiated-external replications.

The second classification is found in an article by Basili et al. [2], presenting a framework for organizing sets of related studies. This article describes the different aspects of the framework being one of these aspects a classification of replications composed of three major categories, where two of these categories define several types of replications. Basili et al. [2] illustrate the classification with examples of different replications that they have run. The classification is composed of a total of six replication types:

1. Strict replications.
2. Replications that vary the manner in wich the experiment is run.
3. Replications that vary variables intrinsic to the object of study.
4. Replications that vary variables instrinsic to the focus of the evaluation.

5. Replications that vary context variables in the environment in wich the solution is evaluated.
6. Replications that extend the theory.

The third classification is found in a research conducted by Krein and Knutson [82]. The paper presents a framework for organizing research methods in SE. Krein and Knutson [82] define a replication taxonomy with four types of replications:

1. Strict replication. Which is meant to replicate a prior study as precisely as possible.
2. Differentiated replication. Which intentionally alters aspects of the prior study in order to test the limits of that study's conclusions.
3. Dependent replication. Which is a study that is specifically designed with reference to one or more previous studies, and is, therefore, intended to be a replication study.
4. Independent replication. Which addresses the same questions and/or hypotheses of a previous study, but is conducted without knowledge of, or deference to, that prior study either because the researchers are unaware of the prior work, or because they want to avoid bias.

Other ESE works mention replication types but do not refer to any classification. For example, Brooks et al. [83] and Mendonça et al. [84] mention differences between *internal* and *external replication*. Shull et al. [26] discuss some types of replications (*exact, independent, dependent* and *conceptual replications*) to describe the role that they play in ESE. Finally, Lung et al. [85] mention two types of replication (*literal* and *theoretical replication*) to explain the type of replication that they ran, and Mandić et al. [86] discuss two types of replications, namely, *exact* or *partial replications*, and replications designed to improve the goal of the original experiment.

8   Purposes of Replication in ESE

The elements of an experiment to be replicated vary depending on the purpose of the replication. We have identified five elements that can vary in a replication:

1. *Experimenters.* The experimenters in a replication can be the same people as participated in the baseline experiment, different experimenters or a mixture of both, though some cooperation between the baseline experiment researchers and the replicators.
2. *Site.* The replication can be run at the same site as the baseline experiment or at another place.
3. *Experimental Protocol.* This term refers to the experimental design, instruments, materials, experimental objects, forms and procedures used to run an experiment. The experimental protocol is how these elements are set up for use by the experimenter to observe the effects of the treatments. Different elements of the protocol can be changed in a replication.

4. *Construct Operationalizations.* Operationalizations describe the act of translating a construct into its manifestation. In a controlled experiment we have cause and effect operationalizations. The cause operationalizations represent the primary treatments to be evaluated in the experiment (independent variables) whereas the effect operationalizations represent the response variables (dependent variables) used to measure the effects of the treatments. Both types of operationalization contain elements that can be varied in a replication.

5. *Population Properties.* In SE experiments there are at least two populations that are worth generalizing: the subjects and the experimental objects with which subjects work or interact during the experiment. The generalization takes place when the replication changes the properties of the subject or the experimental objects.

Based on the elements that may vary in a replication, we identify the following purposes of a replication in ESE:

1. *Control for Sampling Error.* If the basic elements of the baseline experiment structure are kept unchanged, the purpose of the replication is to verify that the results output by that experiment are not chance outcomes. This function is useful for verifying that the effect identified in the baseline experiment is not due to a Type-I error.

2. *Control for Experimenters.* If different experimenters run the replication, then it aims is to verify that the experimenters do not influence the results.

3. *Control for Site.* If the replication is run at another site, then it aims is to verify that the results are independent of the site where the experiment is run.

4. *Control for Artifactual Results.* If the experimental protocol is changed, the purpose of the replication is to verify that the observed results are not artifactual, that is, they reflect reality and are not a product of the experimental protocol setup.

5. *Determine Limits for Operationalizations.* If the operationalizations are changed a replication aims to determine the range of variation of the primary treatments (independent variables) and the measures (dependent variables) used to gauge the effects of the treatments.

6. *Determine Limits in the Population Properties.* If the population properties are changed, the purpose of the replication is to determine the types of experimental subject or objects to which the results of the replication hold.

9   Conclusions

Replication plays an important role in scientific progress where facts are at least as important as ideas [31]. Experiments have to be replicated to identify evidences. If we want to build up a SE body of knowledge based on empirical evidence, different types of replications have to be run. In this chapter we have studied the concept of replication as it is used in other scientific disciplines with the aim of getting a better understanding of this mechanism.

Although we identified several replication typologies, replication types are not standardised at either the intra or interdisciplinary level. Some authors use the same replication name, although they each define the replication differently. Also authors use different replication names to refer to equivalent replications types.

Several of the different replication types that we have found describe changes of the structure of the experiment to be replicated. That is, replication can have different levels of similarity to the baseline experiment. The changes to the experiment in a replication are linked with the verification purposes. Although the aim of a replication is to verify the experimental outcomes, a replication has specific purposes depending on which elements in the experiment are varied.

All different replication purposes have to be reached and satisfied in order for an experiment result to be considered verified. A systematic approach where different types of replications are planified can help experimenters to advance step by step in the verification path.

Discovering new conditions influencing the results of the experiments (and thus software development) is an important co-lateral effect of replications. With a better understanding of these conditions, we will be able to assemble the small segments learnt in systematically varied replications to put together a piece of knowledge.

References

1. Tichy, W.: Should Computer Scientists Experiment more? Computer 31(5), 32–40 (1998)
2. Basili, V., Shull, F., Lanubile, F.: Building Knowledge through Families of Experiments. IEEE Transactions on Software Engineering 25(4), 456–473 (1999)
3. DeMarco, T.: Software Engineering: An Idea Whose Time has Come and Gone? IEEE Software 26(4), 95–96 (2009)
4. Meyer, B.: Credible Objective Answers to Fundamental Software Engineering Questions. LASER Summer School on Software Engineering (2010)
5. Meyer, B.: Empirical Research: Questions from Software Engineering. In: 4th International Symposium on Empirical Software Engineering and Measurement (ESEM 2010) (2010)
6. Brinberg, D., McGrath, J.E.: Validity and the Research Process, p. 176. Sage Publications, Inc. (June 1985)
7. Hayes, W.: Research Synthesis in Software Engineering: A Case for Meta-Analysis. In: METRICS 1999: Proceedings of the 6th International Symposium on Software Metrics, p. 143. IEEE Computer Society (1999)
8. Miller, J.: Can Results from Software Engineering Experiments be Safely Combined? In: METRICS 1999: Proceedings of the 6th International Symposium on Software Metrics, p. 152. IEEE Computer Society (1999)
9. Miller, J.: Applying Meta-analytical Procedures to Software Engineering Experiments. J. Syst. Softw. 54(1), 29–39 (2000)
10. Miller, J.: Replicating Software Engineering Experiments: A poisoned Chalice or the Holy Grail. Information and Software Technology 47(4), 233–244 (2005)

11. Hannay, J., Dybå, T., Arisholm, E., Sjøberg, D.: The Effectiveness of Pair Programming: A Meta-analysis. Information and Software Technology, Special Section: Software Engineering for Secure Systems 51(7), 1110–1122 (2009)
12. Jørgensen, M.: A Review of Studies on Expert Estimation of Software Development Effort. Journal of Systems and Software 70(1-2), 37–60 (2004)
13. Pickard, L., Kitchenham, B., Jones, P.: Combining Empirical Results in Software Engineering. Information and Software Technology 40(14), 811–821 (1998)
14. Shull, F., Basili, V., Carver, J., Maldonado, J., Travassos, G., Mendonça, M., Fabbri, S.: Replicating Software Engineering Experiments: Addressing the Tacit Knowledge Problem. In: SESE 2002: Proceedings of the 2002 International Symposium on Empirical Software Engineering, p. 7. IEEE Computer Society (2002)
15. Juristo, N., Moreno, A., Vegas, S.: Reviewing 25 Years of Testing Technique Experiments. Empirical Softw. Engg. 9(1-2), 7–44 (2004)
16. Basili, V., Selby, R.: Comparing the Effectiveness of Software Testing Strategies. IEEE Trans. Softw. Eng. 13(12), 1278–1296 (1987)
17. Porter, A., Votta, L., Basili, V.: Comparing Detection Methods for Software Requirements Inspections: A Replicated Experiment. IEEE Trans. Softw. Eng. 21(6), 563–575 (1995)
18. Fusaro, P., Lanubile, F., Visaggio, G.: A Replicated Experiment to Assess Requirements InspectionTechniques. Empirical Softw. Engg. 2(1), 39–57 (1997)
19. Miller, J., Wood, M., Roper, M.: Further Experiences with Scenarios and Checklists. Empirical Software Engineering 3(1), 37–64 (1998)
20. Sandahl, K., Blomkvist, O., Karlsson, J., Krysander, C., Lindvall, M., Ohlsson, N.: An Extended Replication of an Experiment for Assessing Methods for Software Requirements Inspections. Empirical Software Engineering 3(4), 327–354 (1998)
21. Porter, A., Votta, L.: Comparing Detection Methods For Software Requirements Inspections: A Replication Using Professional Subjects. Empirical Software Engineering 3(4), 355–379 (1998)
22. Wood, M., Roper, M., Brooks, A., Miller, J.: Comparing and Combining Software Defect Detection Techniques: A Replicated Empirical Study. SIGSOFT Softw. Eng. Notes 22(6), 262–277 (1997)
23. Juristo, N., Vegas, S.: Functional Testing, Structural Testing, and Code Reading: What Fault Type Do They Each Detect? ESERNET, 208–232 (2003)
24. Vegas, S., Juristo, N., Moreno, A., Solari, M., Letelier, P.: Analysis of the Influence of Communication between Researchers on Experiment Replication. In: ISESE 2006: Proceedings of the 2006 ACM/IEEE international symposium on Empirical software engineering, pp. 28–37. ACM (2006)
25. Juristo, N., Vegas, S.: Using Differences among Replications of Software Engineering Experiments to Gain Knowledge. In: ESEM 2009: Proceedings of the 2009 3rd International Symposium on Empirical Software Engineering and Measurement, pp. 356–366. IEEE Computer Society (2009)
26. Shull, F., Carver, J., Vegas, S., Juristo, N.: The Role of Replications in Empirical Software Engineering. Empirical Softw. Engg. 13(2), 211–218 (2008)
27. Kitchenham, B.: The Role of Replications in Empirical Software Engineering – A Word of Warning. Empirical Softw. Engg. 13(2), 219–221 (2008)
28. Miller, J.: Triangulation as a Basis for Knowledge Discovery in Software Engineering. Empirical Softw. Engg. 13(2), 223–228 (2008)
29. Cohen, J.: Statistical Power Analysis for the Behavioral Sciences. L. Erlbaum Associates (1988)

30. Dybå, T., Kampenes, V., Sjøberg, D.: A Systematic Review of Statistical Power in Software Engineering Experiments. Information and Software Technology 48(8), 745–755 (2006)
31. Hunter, J.: The Desperate Need for Replications. Journal of Consumer Research 28(1), 149–158 (2001)
32. Kampenes, V., Dybå, T., Hannay, J., Sjøberg, D.: A Systematic Review of Effect Size in Software Engineering Experiments. Information and Software Technology 49(11-12), 1073–1086 (2007)
33. La Sorte, M.A.: Replication as a Verification Technique in Survey Research: A Paradigm. The Sociological Quarterly 13(2), 218–227 (1972)
34. Singh, K., Ang, S.H., Leong, S.M.: Increasing Replication for Knowledge Accumulation in Strategy Research. Journal of Management 29(4), 533–549 (2003)
35. Schmidt, S.: Shall We Really Do It Again? The Powerful Concept of Replication Is Neglected in the Social Sciences. Review of General Psychology 13(2), 90–100 (2009)
36. Moonesinghe, R., Khoury, M.J., Janssens, A.C.: Most Published Research Findings Are False – But a Little Replication Goes a Long Way. PLoS Med. 4(2), 218–221 (2007)
37. Pfleeger, S.L.: Experimental Design and Analysis in Software Engineering: Part 2: how to set up and experiment. SIGSOFT Softw. Eng. Notes 20(1), 22–26 (1995)
38. Polit, D.F., Hungler, B.P.: Nursing Research: Principles and Methods, p. 816. Lippincott Williams & Wilkins (1998)
39. Berthon, P., Pitt, L., Ewing, M., Carr, C.L.: Potential Research Space in MIS: A Framework for Envisioning and Evaluating Research Replication, Extension, and Generation. Info. Sys. Research 13, 416–427 (2002)
40. Popper, K.: The Logic of Scientific Discovery. Hutchinson & Co. (1959)
41. Hempel, C.G.: Philosophy of Natural Science. Prentice-Hall (1962)
42. Campbell, D.T., Stanley, J.C.: Experimental and Quasi-Experimental Designs for Research. Houghton Mifflin Company (June 1963)
43. Collins, H.M.: Changing Order: Replication and Induction in Scientific Practice. Sage Publications (1985)
44. Broad, W., Wade, N.: Betrayers Of The Truth, Fraud and Deceit in the Halls of Science. Simon & Schuster, Inc. (1982)
45. Fahs, P.S., Morgan, L.L., Kalman, M.: A Call for Replication. Journal of Nursing Scholarship 35(1), 67–72 (2003)
46. Glass, P., Avery, G.B., Subramanian, K.N.S., Keys, M.P., Sostek, A.M., Friendly, D.S.: Effect of Bright Light in the Hospital Nursery on the Incidence of Retinopathy of Prematurity. New England Journal of Medicine 313(7), 401–404 (1985)
47. Ackerman, B., Sherwonit, E., Williams, J.: Reduced Incidental Light Exposure: Effect on the Development of Retinopathy of Prematurity in Low Birth Weight Infants. Pediatrics 83(6), 958–962 (1989)
48. Reynolds, J.D., Hardy, R.J., Kennedy, K.A., Spencer, R., van Heuven, W., Fielder, A.R.: Lack of Efficacy of Light Reduction in Preventing Retinopathy of Prematurity. New England Journal of Medicine 338(22), 1572–1576 (1998)
49. Seiberth, V., Linderkamp, O., Knorz, M.C., Liesenhoff, H.: A Controlled Clinical Trial of Light and Retinopathy of Prematurity. Am. J. Ophthalmol. 118(4), 492–495 (1994)
50. Restivo, S.: Science, Technology, and Society: An Encyclopedia, p. 728. Oxford University Press (May 2005)
51. Collins, H.: The Experimenter's Regress as Philosophical Sociology. Studies in History and Philosophy of Science Part A 33, 149–156(8) (2002)

52. Hume, D.: An Enquiry Concerning Human Understanding (1749)
53. Hempel, C.G.: Studies in the Logic of Confirmation (I.). Mind 54(213), 1–26 (1945)
54. Good, I.: The White Shoe Is A Red Herring. British Journal for the Philosophy of Science 17(4), 322 (1967)
55. Goodman, N.: Fact, Fiction, and Forecast. Harvard University Press (1955)
56. Bayes, T.: An Essay towards solving a Problem in the Doctrine of Chances. Philosophical Transactions of the Royal Society of London (1763)
57. Fisher, R.A.: The Design of Experiments. Oliver & Boyd (1935)
58. Neyman, J.: First Course in Probability and Statistics. Henry Holt (1950)
59. Rivadula, A.: Inducción, Deducción y Decisión en las Teorías Estadísticas de la Inferencia Científica. Revista de Filosofía 9, 3–14 (1993)
60. Singh, G.: A Shift from Significance Test to Hypothesis Test trough Power Analysis in Medical Research. Journal of Postgraduate Medicine 52(2), 148–150 (2006)
61. Easley, R., Madden, C., Dunn, M.: Conducting Marketing Science: The Role of Replication in the Research Process. Journal of Business Research 48(1), 83–92 (2000)
62. Bahr, H.M., Caplow, T., Chadwick, B.A.: Middletown III: Problems of Replication, Longitudinal Measurement, and Triangulation. Annu. Rev. Sociol 9(1), 243–264 (1983)
63. Van IJzendoorn, M.H.: A Process Model of Replication Studies: On the Relation between Different Types of Replication. Leiden University Library (1994)
64. Evanschitzky, H., Armstrong, J.S.: Replications of Forecasting Research. International Journal of Forecasting 26(1), 4–8 (2010)
65. Kantowitz, B.H., Roediger III, H.L., Elmes, D.G.: Experimental Psychology, p. 592. Wadsworth Publishing (1984)
66. Tsang, E., Kwan, K.-M.: Replication and Theory Development in Organizational Science: A Critical Realist Perspective. The Academy of Management Review 24(4), 759–780 (1999)
67. Mittelstaedt, R., Zorn, T.: Econometric Replication: Lessons from the Experimental Sciences. Quarterly Journal of Business & Economics 23(1) (1984)
68. Lindsay, R.M., Ehrenberg, A.S.C.: The Design of Replicated Studies. The American Statistician 47(3), 217–228 (1993)
69. Lykken, D.T.: Statistical Significance in Psychological Research. Psychol. Bull. 70(3), 151–159 (1968)
70. Hendrick, C.: Replications, Strict Replications, and Conceptual Replications: Are They Important?, pp. 41–49. Sage, Newbury Park (1990)
71. Finifter, B.: The Generation of Confidence: Evaluating Research Findings by Random Subsample Replication. Sociological Methodology 4, 112–175 (1972)
72. Kelly, C., Chase, L., Tucker, R.: Replication in Experimental Communication Research: an Analysis. Human Communication Research 5(4), 338–342 (1979)
73. Leone, R., Schultz, R.: A Study of Marketing Generalizations. The Journal of Marketing 44(1), 10–18 (1980)
74. Monroe, K.B.: Front Matter. The Journal of Consumer Research 19(1) pp. i–iv (1992)
75. Radder, H.: Experimental Reproducibility and the Experimenters' Regress. PSA: Proceedings of the Biennial Meeting of the Philosophy of Science Association 1, 63–73 (1992)
76. Wikipedia: Reproducibility — Wikipedia, The Free Encyclopedia (2009)
77. Cartwright, N.: Replicability, Reproducibility, and Robustness: Comments on Harry Collins. History of Political Economy 23(1), 143–155 (1991)

78. Radder, H.: In and About the World: Philosophical Studies of Science and Technology, p. 225. State University of New York Press, Albany (1996)
79. Easterbrook, S., Singer, J., Storey, M., Damian, D.: Selecting Empirical Methods for Software Engineering Research. In: Guide to Advanced Empirical Software Engineering, pp. 285–311. Springer, Heidelberg (2008)
80. Park, C.L.: What Is The Value of Replicating other Studies? Research Evaluation 13, 189–195(7) (2004)
81. Almqvist, J.P.F.: Replication of Controlled Experiments in Empirical Software Engineering – A Survey (2006)
82. Krein, J.L., Knutson, C.D.: A Case for Replication: Synthesizing Research Methodologies in Software Engineering. In: 1st International Workshop on Replication in Empirical Software Engineering Research, RESER 2010 (2010)
83. Brooks, A., Daly, J., Miller, J., Roper, M., Wood, M.: Replication of experimental results in software engineering. Number ISERN–96-10 (1996)
84. Mendonça, M., Maldonado, J., de Oliveira, M., Carver, J., Fabbri, S., Shull, F., Travassos, G., Höhn, E., Basili, V.: A Framework for Software Engineering Experimental Replications. In: ICECCS 2008: Proceedings of the 13th IEEE International Conference on Engineering of Complex Computer Systems, pp. 203–212. IEEE Computer Society (2008)
85. Lung, J., Aranda, J., Easterbrook, S., Wilson, G.: On the Difficulty of Replicating Human Subjects Studies in Software Engineering. In: ICSE 2008: Proceedings of the 30th International Conference on Software Engineering, pp. 191–200. ACM (2008)
86. Mandić, V., Markkula, J., Oivo, M.: Towards Multi-Method Research Approach in Empirical Software Engineering. In: Bomarius, F., Oivo, M., Jaring, P., Abrahamsson, P. (eds.) PROFES 2009. LNBIP, vol. 32, pp. 96–110. Springer, Heidelberg (2009)

A   Descriptions of the Replications Typologies

A.1   Bahr et al. [62]

Types A..P. This classification categorizes replications according to four dichotomic properties (equal or different) of a replication. These properties are: time, place, subjects and methods. Based on combinations of these properties, Bahr et al. define 16 replication types.

A.2   Easley et al. [61]

Type 0 (Precise Duplication). This replication is defined as a precise duplication of a prior study. Therefore, Type 0 (precise duplication) studies are those studies in which every nuance of the experimental setting is precisely reproduced; as such, the cause-effect relationship is finite. The ability to conduct a Type 0 replication is limited to experimenters in only some of the natural sciences. As others have stated, it is an impossibility to conduct a Type 0 replication in a social science context because uncontrolled extraneous factors have the potential to interact with the various components in an experimental setting. For example, human subjects cannot be precisely duplicated. A social scientist is limited only to matching subjects as closely as possible.

Type I (Duplication). A type I replication is a faithful duplication of a prior study and, as such, is considered the "purest" form of replication research in the social sciences. It should be mentioned at this point that a Type I replication is the one most closely associated with the term "replication" in the minds of most researches. More over, this is also the type of replication research most criticized for not being creative. This is somewhat ironic, given the apparent receptivity of reviewers to cross-cultural research that, in many cases, is usually the study of the generalizability of findings from a single country or culture to others and, thus, is simply a Type I replication.

Type II (Similar). A type II replication is a close replication is a close replication of a prior study, and a Type III replication is a deliberate modification of a prior study. Type II replications are the most common form of replication research in marketing settings and are useful in testing phenomena in multiple contexts. If effects are shown in a variety of testing contexts, the case for the findings is strengthened. This has been called the process of triangulation.

Type III (Modification). This replication is a deliberate modification of a prior study. In a Type III replication, the threat of extraneous factors inherent to the nature of human subjects, unless explicitly accounted for in theory testing, is not a factor of concern with regard to replicability.

A.3   Evanschitzky and Armstrong [64]

Real Replications. This replication is a duplication of a previously published empirical study that is concerned with assessing whether similar findings can be obtained upon repeating the study. This definition covers what are variously referred to as "exact", "straight" or "direct" replications. Such works duplicate as closely as possible the research design used in the original study by employing the same variable definitions, settings, measurement instruments, analytical techniques, and so on.

Model Comparisons. This replication is an application of a previously published statistical analysis that is concerned with assessing whether a superior goodness-of-fit can be obtained, comparing the original statistical model with at least one other statistical model.

Data Re-analyses. This replication can be defined as an application of previously published data that is concerned with assessing whether similar findings can be obtained using a different methodology with the same data or a sub-sample of the data.

A.4 Finifter [71]

Virtual Replication. The intention is to repeat an original study not identically but "for all practical purposes" to see whether its results hold up against chance and artifact. Virtual replications are also frequently conducted to find out how dependent a result is on the specific research conditions and procedures used in an original study. To answer this question, one or more of the initial methodological conditions is intentionally altered. For example, a survey or experiment might be repeated except for a change in measuring devices, in the samples used, or in research personnel. If the initial result reappears despite changes, faith in the original finding mounts.

Systematic Replication. The emphasis in systematic replication is not on reproducing either the methods or the substance of a previous study. Instead, the objective is to produce new findings (using whatever methods) which are expected by logical implication to follow from the original study being replicated. When such an implication is actually confirmed by systematic replication, confidence is enhanced not only in the initial finding that prompted the replication but also both in the derived finding and in whatever theoretical superstructure was used to generate the confirmed inference.

Pseudoreplication. It can be defined according to three main operational variations: the repetition of a study on certain subsets of an available total body of real data; the repetition of areal data study on artificial data sets which are intended to simulate the real data; and the repeated generation of completely artificial data sets according to an experimental prescription.

A.5 Hendrick [70]

Strict Replication. An exact, or strict, replication is one in which independent variables (treatments) are duplicated as exactly as possible. That is, the physical procedures are reinstituted as closely as possible. It is implicitly assumed that contextual variables are either the same as in the original experiment, or are irrelevant.

Partial Replication. A partial replication is some change (deletion or addition) in part of the procedural variables, while other parts are duplicated as in the original experiment. Usually some aspect of the procedures is considered "unessential", or some small addition is made to expedite data collection.

Conceptual Replication. A conceptual replication is an attempt to convey the same crucial structure of information in the independent variables to subjects, but by a radical transformation of the procedural variables. In addition, specific task variables are often necessarily changed as well.

A.6   Hunter [31]

Statistical Replication. For statistical replications as perfectly replicated studies:

1. All studies measure the independent variable in exactly the same way.
2. All studies measure the dependent variable in exactly the same way.
3. All studies use exactly the same procedure.
4. All studies draw samples from the same population.

Scientific Replication. For scientific replications for simple causal studies:

1. All studies measure the same independent variable X.
2. All studies measure the same dependent variable Y.
3. All studies use essentially the same procedure.
4. All studies should sample from populations that are equivalent in terms of the study question and hence the study outcome. The difference is that statistical replications assume that the word "same" means identical, while scientists interpret the word "same" to mean equivalent.

Conceptual Replication. This replication verifies one of the hypotheses that were not tested in the original study. The researcher of the original study defines control groups to test the most obvious alternative hypotheses against administrative details that are thought to be irrelevant. Any treatment, intervention or manipulation is a set of administrative procedures, which are mostly intrinsic to the active ingredient of the treatment. These replications examine whether the administrative procedures influence the treatments as reflected in the dependent variable.

A.7   Van IJzendoorn [63]

Complete Secondary Analysis. It is a kind of replication in which all parameters except the researcher and the method of data analysis are kept constant. Secondary analysis also is one of the most inexpensive and efficient types of replication, because it is based on existing data sets. One of the main barriers to secondary replication is, however, the accessibility of the original data sets. The complete secondary analysis may include recoding of the original raw data. In this replication, there are two phases of processing the raw data involved: the coding and analyzing of the data.

Restricted Secondary Analysis. In this type, the coding system is not changed but only the methods of analyzing the data, to see whether the original results survive statistical criticism or the application of refined methods of statistical analysis.

Exact Replication. A replication will be called "exact" if it is essentially similar to the original study. This replication is applied to (dis)confirm the doubts, and to check the assumptions of the varied replications. Many scientists feel that exact replications may be carried out, but usually are irrelevant for scientific progress.

Varied Replication. Replications should be carried out in which new data under different conditions are being collected. From the start, the original study will be "trusted" so much that rather significant variations in the design will be applied. Larger variations may lead to more interesting discoveries in addition to the original study, but they will be followed by smaller variations if more global replications fail to produce new "facts". If even modest variations fail to reproduce the results, a more or less exact replication is needed.

A.8   Kantowitz et al. [65]

Direct Replication. This is the attempt to repeat the experiment as closely as is practical, with as few changes as possible in the original method.

Systematic Replication. The experimenter attempts to vary factors believed to be irrelevant to the experimental outcome. If the phenomenon is not illusory, it will survive these changes. If the effect disappears, then the researcher has discovered important boundary conditions on the phenomenon being studied.

Conceptual Replication. One attempts to replicate a phenomenon, but in a way radically different from the original experiment.

A.9   Kelly et al. [72]

Literal Replication. The earlier findings may be reexamined using the same manipulations (independent variables, experimental procedures, etc.) and measures (dependent variables, methods of data analysis, etc.).

Operational Replication. If the experimenter wishes to vary criterion measures, the experiment would be termed an operational replication. In this instance, the dependent variable would represent a different operationalization of the construct; the essential conceptual meaning would remain unchanged.

Instrumental Replication. This replication is carried out when the dependent measures are replicated and the experimental manipulations are varied. Variations in the implementation of experimental procedures which do not go beyond the originally established relationship would be included in this category.

Constructive Replication. A constructive replication attempt may be identified when both manipulations and measures are varied. This replication involves the attempt to achieve equivalent results using an entirely original methods recipe.

A.10   La Sorte [33]

Retest Replication. In its general form retest replication is a repeat of an original study with few if any significant changes in the research design. The retest has two major purposes: 1) it acts as a reliability check of the original study, and 2) inconsistencies and errors in procedure and analysis can be uncovered in the repeat. Although the retest increases one's confidence that the findings are not artifactual, it does not eliminate the possibility of error in process, especially when the same investigator conducts both studies.

Internal Replication. The differences between the retest and internal replication are mainly procedural. Instead of seeking confirmation of an original study, the internal replication is built into the original study design. So the data, part of which are used for the replication, are gathered simultaneously by the same investigator using a common set of research operations. One finds variations in the procedures for selecting the samples. Two of these procedures are: 1) drawing two or more independent samples, and 2) taking a single sample and later dividing it into subsamples for purposes of analysis and comparison. The internal replication provides an additional data supply which acts to cross-check the reliability of the observed relationships. Thus it is methodologically superior to the single study where the hypothesis is tested only once by one body of data.

Independent Replication. Independent replication is the basic procedure for verifying an empirical generalization. It does this by introducing significant modifications into the original research design in order to answer questions about the empirical generalization that go beyond those of reliability and confirmation. The essential modifications include independent samples drawn from related or different universes by different investigators. These replications differ in design and purpose. They can, however, be broadly categorized into three problem areas. First, is the empirical generalization valid? Second, does further investigation extend it to other social situations or subgroups outside the scope of the original study? Or, third, is the empirical generalization limited by the conditions of particular social situations or specific subgroups?

Theoretical Replication. It involves the inductive process of examining the feasibility of fitting empirical findings into a general theoretical framework. These replications seek to verify theoretical generalizations. In these replications, empirical variables, which have concrete anchoring points are abstracted and conceptualized to a higher theoretical plane, it is necessary to sample a variety of groups using different indicators of the same concepts.

A.11   Leone and Schultz [73]

Experimental Replication. The same experiment is conduced more than once, although there can be (especially with social systems) no perfect replications. It involves the same method and the same situation.

Nonexperimental Replication. The same method is applied to different situations.

Corroboration. It involves different method and same situation, or different method and different situation.

A.12   Lindsay and Ehrenberg [68]

Close Replication. This replication attempts to keep almost all the know conditions of the study much the same or at least very similar (for example, the population or populations in question, the sampling procedure, the measuring techniques, the background conditions, and the methods of analysis). A close replication is particularly suitable early in a program of research to establish quickly and relatively easily and cheaply whether a new result can be repeated at all.

Differentiated Replication. It involves deliberate, or at least known, variations in fairly major aspects of the conditions of the study. The aim is to extend the range of conditions under which the result still holds. Exploring a result with deliberate variations in the conditions of observation is the essence of generalization. According to the authors, there are three reasons for running a differentiated replication:

1. Use different methods (different measuring instruments, analysis procedures, experimental setups, and/or investigators) to reach the same result (triangulation),
2. Extended the scope of the results,
3. Define the conditions under which the generalization no longer holds.

A.13   Lykken [69]

Literal Replication. This involves exact duplication of the first investigator's sampling procedure, experimental conditions, measuring techniques, and methods of analysis.

Operational Replication. One strives to duplicate exactly just the sampling and experimental procedures given in the first author's report. The purpose of operational replication is to test whether the investigator's "experimental recipe" the conditions and procedures he considered salient enough to be listed in the "Methods" section of his report will in other hands produce the results that he obtained.

Constructive Replication. One deliberately avoids imitation of the first author's methods. To obtain an ideal constructive replication, one would provide a competent investigator with nothing more than a clear statement of the empirical "fact" which the first author would claim to have established.

A.14   Mittelstaedt and Zorn [67]

Type I. The replicating researcher uses the same data sources, models, proxy variables and statistical methods as the original researcher.

Type II. The replicating researcher uses the same data sources, but employs different models, proxy variables and/or statistical methods.

Type III. The replicating researcher uses the same models, proxy variables and statistical methods, but applies them to different data than those used by the original researcher.

Type IV. In this replication, different models, proxy variables and statistical methods are applied to different data.

A.15   Monroe [74]

Simultaneous Replication. Does the same researcher in the same study investigate consumer reactions to more than one product, or to more than one advertisement?

Sequential Replication. Does the researcher or another researcher repeat the study using the same or different stimuli at another point in time?

Nonindependent Replication. The replication is conducted by the same researcher.

Independent Replication. The replication is conducted by different researcher.

Assumed Replication. For example, a researcher using both males and females simultaneously in a study and finding no gender covariate effect assumes replication across gender.

Demonstrated Replication. What is preferable is separate gender conditions wherein the effect has or has not been obtained separately for males an females, that is, demonstrated.

Strict Replication. The replication is a faithful reproduction of the original study.

Partial Replication. The replication is a faithful reproduction of some aspects of the original study.

Conceptual Replication. The replication uses a similar conceptual structure but incorporates changes in procedures and independent variables.

A.16   Radder [75]

Reproducibility of the material realization of an experiment. In this type of reproduction, the replicator correctly performs all the experimental actions following instructions given by the experimenter who ran the previous experiment. This reproduction is based on a division of labour, where other previously instructed people can run the replication without being acquainted with the theory underlying the experiment. As in this reproduction it is possible to follow the same procedure to verify the outcome without detailed knowledge of the theory, there may be differences in the theoretical interpretations of the experiment.

Reproducibility of an experiment under a fixed theoretical interpretation. This reproduction implies that the conditions of the previous experiment can be intentionally altered in the replications, provided that the variations are irrelevant to the theoretical interpretation of the experiment.

Reproducibility of the results of an experiment. This type of reproduction refers to when it is possible to achieve the same result as a previous experiment using different methods. This category excludes a reproduction of the same material operationalization.

A.17   Schmidt [35]

Direct Replication. This involves repeating the procedure of a previous experiment. In this replication, the context variables, the dependent variable or subject selection are open to modification.

Conceptual Replication. This is the use of different methods to retest the hypothesis or result of a previous experiment.

A.18   Tsang and Kwan [66]

Checking of Analysis. In this type of replication, the researcher employs exactly the same procedures used in a past study to analyze the latter's data set. Its purpose is to check whether investigators of the original study have committed any errors in the process of analyzing the data.

Reanalysis of Data. Unlike the checking of analysis, in this type of replication, the researcher uses different procedures to reanalyze the data of a previous study. The aim is to assess whether and how the results are affected by problems of definition, as well as by the particular techniques of analysis. Quite often the replication involves using more powerful statistical thecniques that were not available when the original study was conducted.

Exact Replication. This is the case where a previous study is repeated on the same population by using basically the same procedures. The objective is to keep the contingent conditions as similar as possible to those of the previous study. The researcher usually uses a different sample of the subjects. The main purpose is to assess whether the findings of a past study are reproducible.

Conceptual Extension. A conceptual extension involves employing procedures different from those of the original study and drawing a sample from the same population. The differences may lie in the way of measuring constructs, structuring the relationships among constructs, analyzing data, and so forth. In spite of these differences, the replication is based on the same theory as the original study. The findings may lead to a revision of the theory.

Empirical Generalization. In this replication, a previous study is repeated on different populations. The researcher runs an empirical generalization to test the extent to which the study results can be generalized to other populations. It follows the original experimental procedures as closely as possible.

Generalization and Extension. The researcher employs different research procedures and draws a sample from a different population of subjects. The more imprecise the replication, the greater the benefit to the external validity of the original finding, if its results support the finding. However, if the result fail to support the original finding, it is difficult to tell whether that lack of support stems from the instability of the finding or from the imprecision of the replication.

A Formal Reference for SCOOP

Benjamin Morandi, Sebastian Nanz, and Bertrand Meyer

Chair of Software Engineering, ETH Zurich, Switzerland
firstname.lastname@inf.ethz.ch
http://se.inf.ethz.ch/

Abstract. Operational semantics is a flexible but rigorous means to describe the meaning of programming languages. Small semantics are often preferred, for example to facilitate model checking. However, omitting too many details in a semantics limits results to a core language only, leaving a wide gap towards real implementations. In this paper we present a comprehensive semantics of the concurrent programming model SCOOP (Simple Concurrent Object-Oriented Programming). The semantics has been found detailed enough to guide an implementation of the SCOOP compiler and runtime system, and to detect and correct a variety of errors and ambiguities in the original informal specification and prototype implementation. In our formal specification, we use abstract data types with preconditions and axioms to describe the state, and introduce a number of special operations to model the runtime system with our inference rules. This approach makes our large formal specification manageable, providing a first step towards reference documents for specifying concurrent object-oriented languages based on operational semantics.

1 Introduction

Concurrent programming has become an important part of mainstream software development, caused by the widespread use of multicore processors. The notorious difficulty of writing concurrent programs correctly has on the other hand spawned work into novel language abstractions to express concurrency and synchronization. One such language is SCOOP [21,25], an object-oriented programming model for concurrency based on the idea of contracts.

The main idea of SCOOP is to simplify the writing of correct concurrent programs for developers, who can use familiar concepts from object-oriented programming but are protected by the model from common concurrency errors such as data races. This is achieved by a runtime system that automatically takes care of operations such as obtaining and releasing of necessary locks, without the need for explicit program statements. While being based on conceptually simple ideas, the semantics of the language concepts and runtime system turns out to be very complex.

The question is therefore how the semantics can be properly documented. The initial version of SCOOP has been defined in [21], where all the main concepts are outlined but implementation aspects are neglected for the most part. A first prototype implementation was then introduced in [25], where the semantics was described only informally, with the exception of a formalization of the type system. In this paper we provide a full

B. Meyer and M. Nordio (Eds.): LASER Summer School 2008-2010, LNCS 7007, pp. 89–157, 2012.
© Springer-Verlag Berlin Heidelberg 2012

formalization of the operational behavior of SCOOP, specified by a structural operational semantics. The main contributions of the paper are:

- A formal specification of SCOOP that treats all important language elements.
- Clarification and correction of the informal specification in [25].

This work does not provide a formal completeness and soundness proof with respect to an axiomatic semantics. Sec. 6 discusses this possibility as part of future work. This work focuses on a formal reference for a concurrent programming language. We argue that this formal reference reflects and corrects the informal description by following a systematic approach.

This article is a condensed version of our technical report [24] on the same subject. This paper is structured as follows. The remainder of this introduction gives a brief overview of the main ideas of the SCOOP model to provide a basic intuition for the main part of the paper. Sec. 2 gives an overview of related work. Sec. 3 gives an overview of the considered language. The two following chapters contain the main parts of the formalization: Sec. 4 describes the state formalization and Sec. 5 the formalization of computations. Sec. 6 concludes and discusses future applications of the formalization.

1.1   An Informal Overview of SCOOP

The starting idea of SCOOP is that every object is associated for its lifetime with a processor, called its *handler*. A *processor* is an autonomous thread of control capable of executing actions (features) on objects. A processor can be a hardware CPU, but it can also be implemented in software, for example as a process or as a thread; any mechanism that can execute instructions sequentially is suitable as a processor.

A reference variable belonging to a processor (for example, a field of an object handled by that processor) can point to an object with the same handler, or to an object on another processor. In the second case the reference is said to be *separate*. The semantics of a call *x.f* depends on this distinction: if *x* is not separate (as always in sequential programming), the call is synchronous; if *x* is separate, meaning that it points to an object handled by a different processor, that processor will execute the call asynchronously. This possibility of asynchronous calls is the main source of concurrent execution.

The producer-consumer problem serves as a simple illustration of these ideas. A root class defines the entities *producer* and *consumer*. The keyword **separate** specifies that these entities may be handled by a processor different from the current one. A creation instruction on a separate entity such as *producer* and *consumer* will create an object on another processor; by default the instruction also creates that processor.

producer: **separate** *PRODUCER*
        — — The producer.
consumer: **separate** *CONSUMER*
        — — The consumer.

Both the producer and the consumer access an unbounded buffer:

buffer: **separate** *BUFFER* [*INTEGER*]
       — — The data structure for exchanging objects between the producer and the
       consumer.

Both the producer and the consumer need to access the buffer, in calls such as *buffer.put*
(*x*) and *buffer.item*. The basic SCOOP rule to ensure mutual exclusion and guarantee
the absence of data races is that any target that is declared as separate, such as *buffer*,
must be an argument of an enclosing routine, which in turn guarantees that this routine
has exclusive access to the corresponding separate object for the duration of its execution. The SCOOP scheduler locks the processors handling all objects corresponding to
these *controlled* arguments. This rule prevents any data races on the group of controlled
objects. For example, in a call *consume* (*buffer*), the buffer is controlled; the call gets
exclusive access to its handler.

Condition synchronization relies on preconditions (after the **require** keyword) to
express wait conditions. Any precondition of the form *x.some_condition* will make the
execution of the routine wait until the condition is true. For example, the precondition
of the *consume* routine ensures that the routine will wait until the buffer is not empty.

consume (*buffer*: **separate** *BUFFER* [*INTEGER*])
          — — Consume an item from the buffer.
     require
          not (*buffer.count* = 0)
     local
          consumed_item: *INTEGER*
     do
          consumed_item := *buffer.item*
     end

During a feature call, the consumer processor could pass its locks to the buffer processor
if it has a lock that the buffer processor requires. This mechanism is known as *lock
passing*. In such a case, the consumer processor would have to wait for the passed locks
to return. For the feature call *buffer.item*, the buffer processor does not require any
locks from the consumer processor. Hence, the consumer processor does not have to
wait due to lock passing. However, the runtime system ensures that the result of the call
buffer.item is properly assigned to the entity *consumed_item* using a mechanism called
wait by necessity: while the consumer processor usually does not have to wait for an
asynchronous call to finish, it will do so if it needs the result of this call.

As the buffer is unbounded, the corresponding producer routine does not need a wait
condition; mutual exclusion will be ensured as before:

produce (*buffer*: **separate** *BUFFER* [*INTEGER*])
          — — Produce an item and put it into the buffer.

```
local
    produced_item: INTEGER
do
    produced_item := new_item
    buffer.put (produced_item)
end
```

The asynchronous nature of separate calls such as *buffer.put* (*x*) implies a distinction between the notion of *feature call* and *feature application*. In sequential programming, executing a call means executing the corresponding feature immediately. With asynchronous calls, the client processor logs the call with the supplier processor (feature call) and moves on. Only at some later time will the supplier processor actually execute the body (feature application).

The main part of the paper defines formally the implementation that gives rise to the behavior outlined above. It also introduces advanced concepts and additional language elements, which cannot be covered in a brief overview, and shows how these give rise to a complexity which can only be dealt with satisfactorily with a formal specification.

2   Related Work

The discussion is divided into work on SCOOP and work on other languages.

2.1   Approaches for SCOOP

In his dissertation, Nienaltowski [25] worked out the details of an implementation of SCOOP as suggested by Meyer [21], and provided a prototype implementation. The language semantics is described informally only, with the exception of the type system which is defined using an inference system. The informal description and the prototype contain various ambiguities and omissions, which we are able to clarify.

Torshizi et al. [33] have defined and implemented JSCOOP, a version of the SCOOP model for the Java language. Only the most important language elements are considered, and no attempt at formalization is made. In contrast, our specification and implementation [31] on top of Eiffel considers all language elements. We believe that our specification could help to extend JSCOOP to a full treatment of the language concepts.

Brooke, Paige and Jacob [5] have used CSP [13] to give a semantics to SCOOP as described by Meyer [21]. Their initial hope was to use tools for analyzing CSP specifications, such as FDR, to automatically check for deadlock in SCOOP programs, but found the size of the specification prohibitive. A benefit of their approach is that CSP provides the machinery needed to express concurrency and synchronization, leading to a relatively concise model. Our goal is to provide formal descriptions close to an actual implementation, and therefore prefer to design an own operational semantics, rather than going through the indirection of another process algebra.

Structural operational semantics, introduced by Plotkin [29], is a flavor of operational semantics that has been used with great success to define various concurrent systems. Our specification uses this style of semantics as well. To model SCOOP we also make use of established modeling concepts from process algebra, such as the notion of channels, which is present in most calculi such as CSP [13] or the π-calculus [23]. We use the theory of abstract data types (ADT) [18] to model the elements of a program text and to model the state of a SCOOP program.

Ostroff et al. [28] describe a structural operational semantics for SCOOP in the refined version by Nienaltowski [25]. This operational semantics inspired our work, and we have attempted to stay close to their modeling ideas where possible, so that [28] can be viewed as a reduced version of the semantics we describe in this paper. While [28] covers some of the most significant aspects of SCOOP, it falls short of describing a number of other critical language concepts: in their reduced model, a query routine handled by some processor p must not make calls to a processor other than p; lock passing, expanded objects and the import mechanism, once routines, evaluation of (asynchronous) postconditions and invariants, and explicit processor tags are not considered. We clarify these aspects in this paper. Furthermore, [28] have pursued the goal to check temporal logic properties of SCOOP programs using their semantics and the SPIN model checker, but were limited to small programs by state space explosion. We have the different goal of providing a reference document for SCOOP, and thus don't have to sacrifice coverage of the language for keeping the specification small.

2.2 Approaches for Other Concurrent Programming Languages

Axum [22] is a concurrent programming language based on the actor model. In Axum, actors are called agents. An agent is an isolated runtime component that executes in parallel with other agents. The agents communicate with each other by sending messages through channels. Each channel has input ports, output ports, and a protocol. The ports are queues of messages. The protocol is a state machine that defines how the channel behaves. Schemas define the structure of messages. Besides message passing, Axum also provides domains – shared state between groups of actors. Erlang [10] and Scala [27] are further examples of actor-based programming languages.

Cω [3] is an extension of C# that integrates elements of the Join Calculus [11]. Cω allows computations to be spawned off into different threads using asynchronous methods: while for synchronous methods the caller must wait until a routine completes, asynchronous methods return immediately while their body is scheduled for execution in another thread. Cω supports so-called chords, which associate the body of a routine with more than one method; the body is executed only if all methods have been called.

Another language is Cilk [4], which extends C with concurrency concepts. A method marked with the cilk keyword can be asynchronously spawned with the spawn keyword. The sync keyword requires the current method to wait for all previously spawned tasks to complete. An inlet function within a parent method receives the result of a spawned child method; the inlet functions of a parent method are guaranteed to execute atomically. Within an inlet function, the abort keyword tells the scheduler that any other child method spawned by the parent method can be aborted. Cilk also implements a work stealing mechanism to achieve high performance by dividing method executions efficiently among processors.

Ada [14] defines tasks – units that can run in parallel. A task is declared within a procedure; it consists of a specification and an implementation. The task is activated when the procedure starts executing. The task specification can define a number of entry points with parameters; an entry point specifies an action the task can synchronize on. An accept statement within the task body indicates the point where the rendezvous can take place. Another task calls the entry point to take part in the rendezvous. With a select statement, one can wait for multiple entry points; alternatives may be guarded with boolean expressions. Ada defines protected objects – a monitor-like construct with guards instead of conditional variables. A protected object is declared within a procedure; it has a specification and an implementation.

The occam programming language [32] builds on the CSP process algebra [13]. A parallel construct defines a number of processes that execute concurrently; the parallel construct terminates when all spawned processes terminated. Processes communicate with each other through named channels. The alternation construct defines a number of processes, where only one of them gets executed; a guard defines when a process can be executed.

X10 [7], Fortress [2], and Chapel [15] are based on the Partitioned Global Address Space (PGAS) model. PGAS uses a global shared memory. It defines portions on the global shared memory and associates them to specific processors to improve performance and scalability. X10 provides important abstractions such as places, asynchronous methods, future invocations, and barriers. However, it places a considerable burden on programmers. Fortress offers implicit parallelization of loops and operations on data structures. Chapel provides a higher-level multithreaded parallel programming model with abstractions for data parallelism, task parallelism, and nested parallelism.

Linda [12] is a coordination language to connect concurrent components; the components can be written in different programming languages. The coordination is based on a tuple space, which holds data tuples that can be stored and retrieved by the processes. Pattern matching is used to read and remove tuples; the operations block until a matching tuple is found. The eval construct creates a new process to evaluate an expression; the new process writes the evaluation result into the tuple space. Implementations of Linda can be found in several programming languages such as Java and C.

For the related languages mentioned above, we are not aware of rigorous behavioral specifications, with the exception of Cω and occam, which use the Join Calculus respectively CSP as the underlying model. For multi-threaded Java however, such formalizations have been attempted.

Ábrahám, de Boer, de Roever, and Steffen [1] present an operational semantics for a subset of multi-threaded Java. They focus on the most important multi-threaded aspects, i.e., dynamic thread creation, thread termination, and re-entrant monitors. The semantics consists of two components: the semantics for isolated objects and the semantics for interacting objects. The authors want to use the semantics to develop a proof system that is based on an existing proof-system for isolated objects. A configuration is a set of instance configurations. An instance configuration contains the attribute values of one object. It also contains the local environment and the expression of each thread that is concurrently executing within the object. In modeling the state of a program, our semantics strictly separates the actions to be executed from the data. This makes it easier to derive implementations from the semantics because an implementation is likely to keep the program text and data separate. Ábrahám et al. use transition labels to synchronize inference rules. The labels allow an external observer to follow the transitions. Our semantics is a pure reduction semantics without labels because we do not require observable transitions.

Cenciarelli, Knapp, Reus, and Wirsing [6] also describe an operational semantics for a larger subset of multi-threaded Java. They cover a larger number of multi-threaded aspects than [1]. In particular they formalize Java's notification mechanism and the working memory. A configuration consists of a function that maps each thread to its expression and its local environments. The configuration also has a container with the objects and the static typing information. Lastly, the configuration consists of an event space. The event space is a partially ordered set of events that have been executed by the threads. The ordering reflects the order in which the events took place. An event space serves two purposes. First, it contains certain aspects of the state. For example, the lock and unlock actions tell us which thread owns which lock. Second, it records the history. A number of constraints state when an event space is valid. Hence, the event space indicates which further actions can take place. The authors use two different validity constraints for both Java's non-prescient semantics and its prescient semantics. Using this, they show that any prescient execution of a properly synchronized program can be simulated by a non-prescient execution. Compared to our semantics, there is no clean division between program text and the state and there is no clean division between the state and the typing information.

Lochbihler [19] suggest a different operational semantics for a large subset of multi-threaded Java. Just like [6], he covers the notification mechanism, but he does not formalize the working memory. He defines an instantiating semantics based on an extension of Jinja [17]. Jinja is an operational semantics for a subset of single-threaded Java. The instantiating semantics is used for the sequential case. Lochbihler defines a generic formal framework to lift the instantiating semantics to the concurrent case. The configuration of the instantiating semantics consists of the expression, a container with the objects, and the local environments. The state of the framework semantics consists of the lock status, the thread information with the thread's expression along with the thread's local environments, a container with the objects, and the wait sets. Lochbihler formalizes the notion of deadlocks, where deadlocks are either based on locks or on wait sets. He then proves that every program that satisfies certain criteria either produces a final value, throws an exception, or deadlocks. He also shows that every such program preserves type safety.

3   Language Overview

SCOOP is a programming language based on Eiffel, an object-oriented programming language, defined in the Eiffel ECMA standard [9]. SCOOP's concurrency model can be applied to other programming languages as well. For this reason, this work does not focus on SCOOP, but on its concurrency model. This section defines a subset of SCOOP, reduced to the parts that are relevant for the concurrency model. It presents the syntax of the subset and a list of simplifications. It then discusses the program representation that this formalization assumes.

3.1 Syntax

The following EBNF grammar defines the set of all considered programs:

program = *class_declaration*∗ *root_procedure_declaration* ;
root_procedure_declaration = {*class_name*}.*routine_name* ;
class_declaration =
  ["**expanded**"] "**class**" *class_name*
    "**inherit**" *class_name*
    ["**create**" *routine_name* {"," *routine_name*}]
    "**feature**" ["{" *class_name* {"," *class_name*} "}"] {*feature_declaration*}
    ["**invariant**" *expression*]
  "**end**" ;

feature_declaration = *routine_declaration* | *attribute_declaration* ;
routine_declaration =
  routine_name ["(" *entity_declaration* {"," *entity_declaration*} ")"] [":" *type*]
    ["**require**" *expression*]
    ["**local**" *entity_declaration* {*entity_declaration*}]
    ("**do**" | "**once**")
      instruction {";" *instruction*}
    ["**ensure**" *expression*]
    "**end**" ;
attribute_declaration = *entity_declaration* ;
entity_declaration = *entity_name* ":" *type* ;

instruction =
  entity_name ":=" *expression* |
  expression "." *feature_name* ["(" *expression* {"," *expression*} ")"] |
  "**create**" *entity_name* "." *routine_name* ["(" *expression* {, *expression*} ")"] |
  "**if**" *expression* "**then**" *instruction* {";" *instruction*} "**else**" *instruction* {";"
      instruction} "**end**" |
  "**until**" *expression* "**loop**" *instruction* {";" *instruction*} "**end**" ;

expression =
  literal |
  entity_name |
  expression "." *feature_name* ["(" *expression* {, *expression*} ")"] ;
literal = *boolean_literal* | *integer_literal* | *character_literal* | *void_literal* ;
boolean_literal = "**True**" | "**False**" ;
integer_literal = ["−"]("**0**" | ... | "**9**") {"**0**" | ... | "**9**"} ;
character_literal = " ' " "**a**" | ... | "**z**" | "**A**" | ... | "**Z**" | "**0**" | ... | "**9**" " ' " ;
void_literal = "**Void**" ;

type =
  [*detachable_tag*]

[”**separate**”] [*explicit_processor_specification*]
   class_name [*actual_generics*] ;
detachable_tag =
   ”**attached**” | ”**detachable**” ;
explicit_processor_specification =
   qualified_explicit_processor_specification |
   unqualified_explicit_processor_specification ;
qualified_explicit_processor_specification =
   ”<” *entity_name* ”.” ”**handler**” ”>” ;
unqualified_explicit_processor_specification =
   ”<” *entity_name* ”>” ;

class_name = *name* ;
feature_name = *routine_name* | *entity_name* ;
routine_name = *name* ;
entity_name = *name* | ”**Result**” | ”**Current**” ;
name = (”**a**” | … | ”**z**” | ”**A**” | … | ”**Z**”) {”**a**” | … | ”**z**” | ”**A**” | … | ”**Z**”};

A *class* consists of a number of features. A *feature* is either a *routine* – a sequence of instructions – or an *attribute* – a data storage. If a routine returns a result, then it is called a *function*; otherwise, it is called a *procedure*. If a routine is marked as a once routine (**once** keyword), then the routine gets executed only once in a given context. Functions and attributes are also called *queries*; routines are also called *commands*. A routine can define a *precondition* (**require** keyword) and a *postcondition* (**ensure** keyword). The enclosing class can define an *invariant* (**invariant** keyword). Each feature can be exported to a list of classes, so that only these classes can use the feature. A number of procedures are dedicated *creation procedures*. These procedures can be used in creation expression (**create** keyword) to create new objects. A class can be marked as an *expanded class* (**expanded** keyword). Objects of expanded classes get copied when they get passed around; objects of non-expanded classes get aliased.

    Formally, a type t is a triple (d, p, c). The component d is the *detachable tag*, p is the *processor tag*, and c is the *class type*. The detachable tag d captures detachability. An entity of attached type (**attached** keyword), i.e., $d = !$, is statically guaranteed to store a value, i.e., to be non-void. An entity of detachable type (**detachable** keyword), i.e., $d = ?$, can be void. As discussed later, the detachable tag is also used for the selective locking mechanism to prevent a request queue from being locked. The processor tag p captures the locality of objects accessed by an entity of the type t. The processor tag p can be separate (**separate** keyword without explicit processor specification), i.e., $p = \top$. The object attached to the entity of the type t is potentially handled by a different processor than the current processor. The processor tag p can be explicit (**separate** keyword with explicit processor specification), i.e., $p = \alpha$. The object attached to the entity of the type t is handled by the processor specified by α. The processor tag p can be non-separate (no **separate** keyword), i.e. $p = \bullet$. The object attached to the entity of the type t is handled by the current processor. The processor tag p can denote no processor, i.e., $p = \bot$. It is used in the type of the void reference. The explicit processor tag either has an unqualified or a qualified specification. An *unqualified explicit processor specification*, i.e., $< p >$, is based on a processor attribute p. The processor attribute p must have the type $(!, \bullet, PROCESSOR)$ and it must be declared in the same class as the explicit processor specification or in one of the ancestors. The processor denoted by this explicit processor specification is the processor stored in p. A *qualified explicit processor specification*, i.e., $< e.handler >$, relies on an entity e occurring in the same class as the explicit processor specification or in one of the ancestors. The entity e must be a non-writable entity of attached type and the type of e must not have a qualified explicit processor tag. The processor denoted by this explicit processor specification is the same processor as the one of the object referenced by e. Explicit processor tags support precise reasoning about object locality. Entities declared with the same processor tag represent objects handled by the same processor. The absence of both the keywords is treated as if there was an **attached** keyword.

3.2 Simplifications

This work makes the following simplifications:

- It does not consider unqualified feature calls. It expects all feature calls to be in the qualified form. This includes accesses to attributes of the current object in expressions.
- It does not consider infix feature calls. It expects all feature calls in the non-infix form. For example, an expression $x > y$ must be transformed into the equivalent form $x.is\_greater(y)$.
- It simplifies the automatic initialization of entities. All entities, except for the current object entity, are initialized with the void reference.
- It neglects exception handling. The exception handling mechanism for SCOOP is still under development.
- It does not consider garbage collection because garbage collection is not refined in the SCOOP model.
- It does not consider agents. From this work's point of view, agents are normal objects.

3.3 Intermediate Representation

For the purpose of the formalization, this work assumes that a program is given in an enriched intermediate representation, where the syntactical elements are replaced with instances of abstract data types. In particular, it assumes ADTs for class types, features, expressions, and instructions. Fig. 1 summarizes these ADTs. The instances of **CLASS_TYPE** are all possible class types, i.e., the types directly defined by all non-generic classes and all possible generic derivations of all possible generic classes. Sec. 4.1 discusses how to get these instances. The ADT **CLASS_TYPE** defines a name query *name*. Each class type can either be a reference class type or an expanded class type. The queries *is_ref* and *is_exp* provide this information. Each class type defines a number of features. These features can be divided into attributes, functions, and procedures. An attribute of an object stores a value. A function performs a computation and

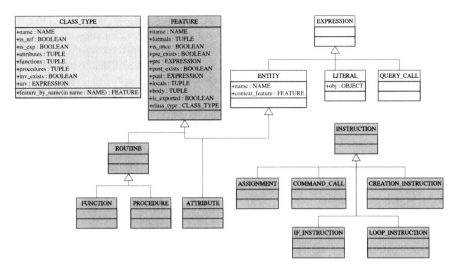

Fig. 1. ADTs for the intermediate representation

returns the result. This computation must not modify the state. A procedure performs a computation that modifies the state. Functions and procedures are also known as routines. For each of these categories, **CLASS_TYPE** defines a query that returns a tuple of features. The query *attributes* returns a tuple of attributes, the query *functions* returns a tuple of functions, and the query *procedures* returns a tuple of procedures. If the name of a feature is known, then the query *feature_by_name* can be used to get the feature with that name. Each class type can have an invariant. The query *inv_exists* indicates whether such an invariant exists. In case an invariant exists, it can be accessed with the query *inv* as an expression. One of the instances of **CLASS_TYPE** is *BOOLEAN*. This class type is expanded and it has an attribute with name *item*. The value of this attribute is the represented boolean value, i.e., an instance of **BOOLEAN**.

In this formalization, a feature is an instance of **FEATURE**. The name of the feature can be retrieved with the query *name* and the formal arguments are given by the query *formals* that returns a tuple with the formal arguments as entities. Whether or not the feature is a once feature can be determined using the query *is_once*. The queries *pre* and *post* return an expression for the precondition respectively the postcondition, provided that the queries *pre_exists* and *post_exists* indicate that the assertions exist. Next, there is the query *locals* that gives the locals of the feature as entities. The query *body* returns the body of the feature as a tuple of instructions. Each feature is either exported or not. A non-exported feature is only available in calls on the current object within the class that declared the feature. An exported feature can be called by other clients as well. The query *exported* returns whether a feature is exported or not. Lastly, each feature has a link to the class it belongs to. This is given by the query *class_type*. This can be used for example to retrieve the invariant that must be preserved by a feature. For each feature category, there is an ADT that inherits from the **FEATURE** ADT.

Expressions can either be entities, literals, or query calls. Every expression is an instance of **EXPRESSION**. For each form of expression, there is one ADT that inherits from the **EXPRESSION** ADT. For entities there is an ADT with a query *name* that returns the name of an entity. A query *context_feature* links an entity to the feature in which the entity is declared. A literal is a character sequence that represents a constant value. As such, literals count as manifest expressions - programming constructs whose values can be deduced by the compiler statically. Literals are instances of an ADT **LITERAL**. This ADT has instances for booleans, integers, characters, and the void literal. Each literal except the void literal can be translated into an object with the query *obj*. This object matches the literal in both type and value. The following notation describes instances of **EXPRESSION**:

$$e \triangleq w \mid b \mid e.f(e, \ldots, e)$$

Here, w is an element of **LITERAL**, b is an instance of **ENTITY**, and f is an instance of **FEATURE**. For instructions, there is an ADT **INSTRUCTION** and an ADT for each kind of instruction. The following notation describes such instances:

$h \triangleq$
    $b := e \mid$
    $e.f(e, \ldots, e) \mid$
    create $b.f(e, \ldots, e) \mid$
    if e **then** $[s\{;s\}*]$ **else** $[s\{;s\}*]$ **end** $\mid$
    until e **loop** $[s\{;s\}*]$ **end**

Here, s stands either for an instance of **INSTRUCTION** or an operation. Instructions are actions that occur in the intermediate representation (user syntax). Operations are actions that do not explicitly occur in the intermediate representation (run-time syntax).

    This work builds on an existing type system formalization. It assumes the existence of a typing environment that can be queried for type information.

4   State Formalization

This section provides a formalization of the state of a SCOOP program. This is necessary to describe the effect of SCOOP constructs on the state. The discussion starts with the general approach and continues with the description of the state.

4.1   General Approach

This work considers the state of a SCOOP program to be a data structure that can be created, modified, and queried through features. For the specification of the state, this work uses Liskov's ADT theory [18]. The discussion begins with a justification and the consequences of this choice. The discussion finishes with an explanation on how to get types for elements in the intermediate representation.

Abstract data types. Meyer's work on a three-level approach to the description of data structure [20] defines three levels on which a data structure can be described: functional, constructive, and physical. The functional specification is an algebraic approach that uses an implicit characterization of the data structure. The constructive specification provides a means to construct instances of the data structure. The instances constructed like this are mathematical entities. A physical description describes the layout of instances in memory. The constructive specification can be derived from the functional specification and the physical description can be derived from the constructive description.

This work models the state as an ADT instance, on the functional level in the hierarchy described above. This has several reasons. First of all, ADT theory allows us to describe the state on an abstract level without dealing with aspects of the implementation. The constructive and the physical level can be derived from the ADTs on the functional level. Second, ADT theory allows us to modularize the state. Different concerns of the state can be modeled as individual ADTs, while a single ADT can be used to consolidate the individual ADTs. This improves understandability and maintainability of the state description. Lastly, ADT theory is well established and suitable for the task at hand.

An ADT t consists of queries, commands, and constructors. A query of t provides information about an instance of t. The query takes as a first argument the target of type t, which is the instance to be queried. Next to the target, the query can take further arguments with types $t_1, \ldots, t_n$. Finally, the query returns a result of a type t_{n+1}. The declaration of this query is written as $query \colon t \to t_1 \to \ldots \to t_n \to t_{n+1}$. For flexibility reasons, this work uses the curried form (as in Haskell) instead of the equivalent Cartesian form $query \colon t \times t_1 \times \ldots \times t_n \to t_{n+1}$. A command of t returns an updated instance according to the command's semantics. The declaration of a command looks much like the one of a query. However, the result of the command is an instance of t. To simplify the discussions, the following terminology is used: an *update of an ADT instance* is the act of calling a command on the instance; the *updated instance* is the result of the command. A constructor of t creates a new instance of t. In contrast to queries and commands, a constructor does not take the target as the first argument because its purpose is to create a new instance.

To describe an instance of an ADT, one can build an expression that starts with a constructor call. This expression can then be used as the first actual argument of a command call. The resulting expression can then be used as the first actual argument of the next command. This leads to a nested expression, in which the first feature call is in the root of the expression and the last feature call is on the outside of the expression. The instance described in such a way can then be queried. We find this functional notation hard to read. Therefore we use an equivalent object-oriented notation in which the first feature call is on the left and the last feature call is on the right. The main idea is not to write targets as arguments, but to write a target in front of the feature name and to use a dot to separate the two parts from each other. This leads to the following translation between the functional notation and the object-oriented notation:

- The query expression $query(e_0, e_1, \ldots, e_n)$ written in functional notation is equivalent to the expression $e_0.query(e_1, \ldots, e_n)$ written in object-oriented notation.
- The command expression $command(e_0, e_1, \ldots, e_n)$ written in functional notation is equivalent to the expression $e_0.command(e_1, \ldots, e_n)$ written in object-oriented notation.
- The creation expression $constructor(e_1, \ldots, e_n)$ for an instance of an ADT t written in functional notation is equivalent to the expression $new \ t.constructor(e_1, \ldots, e_n)$ written in object-oriented notation.

The identity of an ADT instance is given by its query values. Hence, the following holds for all ADTs t: $new\ t.constructor(e_1,\ldots,e_n) = new\ t.constructor(e_1,\ldots,e_n)$.

Example 1 (Functional notation versus object-oriented notation). The expression in functional notation *is_empty(pop(push(new* **STACK**[**PROC**]*.make,p)))* can be written in object-oriented notation as *new* **STACK**[**PROC**]*.make.push(p).pop.is_empty*.

Each feature can have a precondition that must be satisfied before the feature gets called. A precondition is expressed as a number of assertions on the target and the arguments. A feature with a precondition is a partial feature. A partial feature is a feature whose domain is restricted. Such a partial feature is indicated with a crossed arrow $\nrightarrow$ after the type of each formal argument that got restricted by the feature's precondition. Non-restricted formal arguments are indicated with a normal arrow $\rightarrow$. The effect of an ADT command is described in a number of axioms. This work deviates from the practice of bundling all axioms for a specific ADT. Instead, all the axioms for a specific feature occur in the feature's declaration. Note that this work does not aspire a sufficiently complete ADT because this would lead to rule explosion. An ADT is sufficiently complete if its axioms make it possible to reduce any query expression to a form that does not involve an instance of the ADT. This requires that the axioms describe the effect of each command on each query. This work follows the practice to describe the effect of each command of an ADT on all the queries of the ADT that have been changed by the command. Unmentioned queries are unchanged.

Example 2 (Command declaration). The following declaration shows a command to set the value of an attribute f of an object o to the value v. The value can either be a reference or a processor. The command takes the object as the target and returns an updated object whose attribute value is set.

set_att_val: **OBJ** $\rightarrow$ **FEATURE** $\nrightarrow$ **REF** $\cup$ **PROC** $\rightarrow$ **OBJ**
$\quad o.set\_att\_val(f,v)$ **require**
$\quad\quad o.class\_type.attributes.has(f)$
$\quad$ **axioms**
$\quad\quad o.set\_att\_val(f,v).att\_val(f) = v$

The command states in its precondition that the class type of the target object o must have an attribute f. This is expressed as an assertion after the require keyword. The part in front of the require keyword gives names to the target and the arguments. Note that the precondition makes the command partial. The updated object has the value of its attribute f set to v. This is stated as an axiom after the ensure keyword.

So far the discussion covered queries, commands, and constructors for ADTs. This work extends the ADT theory with the notion of auxiliary features. Auxiliary features are convenience features that are not essential for the definition of the ADT, but nevertheless useful.

The remainder of this work declares various ADTs to model the state of a SCOOP program. Unless it would create confusion, it uses the same name for an instance of an ADT and the corresponding domain element. For example, the instance of the ADT **OBJ** is called an object.

Identifier management. This formalization models objects, references, and processors. All of these domain elements have an identity. These identities are automatically managed by the runtime system. The work by Khoshafian and Copeland [16] on different levels of object identity provides good reasons for this decision. They introduce a scale that starts with identities given by the value, goes on with user-supplied identities, and ends with built-in identities. Built-in identities have the advantage that the identities are preserved in case of modifications. According to this hierarchy, our domain elements have a built-in identity. One straightforward way to reflect this, is to model each domain element as an instance of an ADT. However, this direct approach does not properly capture the identities of the domain elements because the identity of an ADT instance is not built-in, but based on the query values. This section describes a way to introduce built-in identities for ADT instances.

To model domain elements with built-in identities, one can define an ADT with an identifier query. A number of ADT instances represent a single domain element over time. Each of the ADT instances has the same value for the identifier query. A modification of the domain element can then be modeled as a new ADT instance where the value of the identity query is preserved and all other queries modulo the modification are preserved.

For this to work, the formalization ensures that no two ADT instances that model different domain elements have the same identity. This is ensured with a fresh identifier for each ADT instance that models a new domain element. For this purpose, the universal stateful query *new_id* returns a fresh identifier. The formalization then preserves the identifier in every modification.

Typing environment. Nienaltowski [25] presents a formalization of the SCOOP type system for a core of SCOOP called SCOOP_C. The type system formalization is part of the base for this work. The *typing environment* Γ contains the class hierarchy of a SCOOP program along with all the type definitions of all features and entities. Type rules allow us to derive conclusions.

The notation $\Gamma \vdash e : t$ denotes that expression e is of type t. Based on this derivation, the function $type\_of(\Gamma, e)$ denotes the type of expression e in the typing environment Γ. The type rules can be used to check whether an expression is controlled or not. In a SCOOP program, each processor p that wants to apply a feature f must make sure that all the processors $(q_1, \ldots, q_n)$ of all attached actual arguments of f are exclusively available on behalf of processor p. This guarantees exclusive access on all objects handled by processors $\{p, q_1, \ldots, q_n\}$. Note that processor p is in this set too because p can exclusively access its objects during a feature execution. For safety, the type system only allows feature calls in f on expressions, where the type system can derive that the value of the expression is a reference to an object and this object is handled by one of the processors $\{p, q_1, \ldots, q_n\}$. Such an expression is called *controlled*. Whether or not an expression is controlled can be determined through the context in which the expression appears and the type of the expression. The context can either be the enclosing class, in case of expressions in invariants, or it can be the enclosing feature, in case of all other expressions. To be more precise, an expression e of type $t = (d, p, c)$ is controlled if and only if t is attached, i.e., $d = \text{!}$, and t satisfies at least one of the following conditions:

- The expression e is non-separate, i.e., $p = \bullet$.
- The expression e appears in a routine f that has an attached formal argument w with the same handler as e, i.e., $p = w.handler$.

The second condition is satisfied if and only if at least one of the following conditions is true:

- The expression e appears as an attached formal argument of f.
- The expression e has a qualified explicit processor specification $w.handler$ and w is an attached formal argument of f.
- The expression e has an unqualified explicit processor specification p, and some attached formal argument of f has p as its unqualified explicit processor specification.

The notation $\Gamma \vdash controlled(t)$ denotes that an expression e of type t is controlled. To establish the derivation $\Gamma \vdash controlled(t)$ one has to find an attached formal argument w in the enclosing routine such that the types suggest that w and e are handled by the same processor or one has the establish that the type t is non-separate. One can therefore be sure that whenever an expression e is controlled, either a matching formal argument exists or its type is non-separate. For the first case, the formal argument is the *controlling entity* for e. For the second case, the current entity is the controlling entity. Although not present in Nienaltowski's formalization of the type system, this work introduces a new derivation $\Gamma \vdash y = controlling\_entity(e)$ that returns the controlling entity y for an expression e as an instance of **ENTITY**. This notion is essential to determine the handler of any controlled expression without evaluating the expression. One can simply determine the controlling entity and then determine the handler of the controlling entity.

4.2   Components of the State

The state is divided into three parts: the regions, the heap, and the store. The main purpose of the heap is to keep track of objects and to maintain the mapping of references to objects. It also maintains the once status of once routines, i.e., whether a once routine is fresh on a processor. The regions manage the association between objects and processors. Objects that are handled by the same processor form a region. The regions are also concerned with locking. The store is a map of names to references. It maps names of formal argument, names of local variables, the name of the current object entity, and the name of the result entity to references. A state ADT models the state with one query for each of the three parts.

regions: **STATE** → **REG**

heap: **STATE** → **HEAP**

store: **STATE** → **STORE**

The next few sections introduce ADTs for each of the parts. A later section presents the state ADT.

4.3   Heap ADT

The *heap* keeps track of the objects and the references associated to them. It also keeps track of the status of once routines. This section first defines an ADT for objects and references. Then it introduces an ADT for the heap.

Objects and references.   There are two kinds of class types in the SCOOP type system: reference class types and expanded class types. The main difference lies in the semantics of using an instance of the types as the source of an attachment, such as assignment or argument passing. If an object of *reference class type* is the source of an attachment, then the reference to the object gets copied over to the destination of the attachment. The object is then accessible both through the source of the attachment as well as through the destination of the attachment. If an object of *expanded class type* is the source of an attachment, then a copy of the object gets attached to the destination of the attachment. The details can be found in Sec. 7.4 of the Eiffel ECMA standard [9].

  This formalization takes a unified view on objects and references that is compatible with the semantics described in the Eiffel ECMA standard. It does not consider objects of expanded class type as sub-objects in other objects or in an environment. Instead it locates expanded objects on the heap, just like objects of reference class type. For each object there is exactly one reference. Assigning references to objects of expanded type has one major advantage for the formalization. If an ADT instance x that models an object gets updated, then one gets a new ADT instance y. If one would model expanded objects as sub-objects stored in other objects or in environments, then such an update might trigger a cascade of ADT instance updates: each ADT instance that has x as a query value would have to be updated with y, and so on. A consequent usage of references avoids this issue. To do the update, one simply alters the reference to x so that it points to y from now on.

  The ADT **REF** models references with an identity query *id* and a constructor *make*. The constructor uses the query *new_id* to create a fresh identifier for the newly created reference. The void reference *void* is an instance of this ADT.

  The ADT **OBJ** models objects. Each object has a query *id* for its identifier, a query *class_type* for its class type, and a query *att_val* for its attribute values. An object can only have attribute values for attributes that are defined in its class type.

  The attribute values of an object can be modified with the command *set_att_val*. Only the attribute values for attributes that are defined in the class type can be modified. The result is an updated object where the attribute value of f is set to v. Note that the value can either be a reference or a processor. Processor values are necessary to support processor attributes.

set_att_val: $\textbf{OBJ} \rightarrow \textbf{FEATURE} \nrightarrow \textbf{REF} \cup \textbf{PROC} \rightarrow \textbf{OBJ}$
  $o.set\_att\_val(f,v)$ **require**
    $o.class\_type.attributes.has(f)$
  axioms
    $o.set\_att\_val(f,v).att\_val(f) = v$

The constructor *make* can be used to create a new object. It creates a new object with the given class type. The new object has a new identifier that is given by the query *new_id*. The constructor initializes all the attribute values of the new object with the void reference.

$make:$ **CLASS_TYPE** $\rightarrow$ **OBJ**
> **axioms**
>> $make(c).id = new\_id$
>> $make(c).class\_type = c$
>> $\forall i \in \{1,\ldots,n\}: make(c).att\_val(a_i) = void$
>> **where**
>>> $\{a_1,\ldots,a_n\} \stackrel{def}{=} c.attributes$

An object can also be copied with the auxiliary query *copy*. This is important for expanded objects with copy semantics. The copied object has the same class type and the same attribute values as the original object, but it has a new identity. The new identity comes from the call to the constructor *make*.

$copy:$ **OBJ** $\rightarrow$ **OBJ**
> **axioms**
>> $o.copy = make(o.class\_type)$
>>> $.set\_att\_val(a_1, o.att\_val(a_1))$
>>> $.\ldots$
>>> $.set\_att\_val(a_n, o.att\_val(a_n))$
>> **where**
>>> $n \stackrel{def}{=} o.class\_type.attributes.count$
>>> $\{a_1,\ldots,a_n\} \stackrel{def}{=} o.class\_type.attributes$

Mapping from references to objects. The ADT **HEAP** makes use of **OBJ** and **REF** to model the mapping from references to objects. For this purpose, it declares the query *objs* to store all the objects on the heap and it declares the query *refs* to get all the references to these objects. The reference *void* is not part of the reference set. The query *ref_obj* defines the actual mapping. For each reference in *refs* an object in *objs* gets returned. The ADT also declares the query *last_added_obj* to keep track of the last object that has been added to the heap. It uses this query to define the effect of adding an object to the heap.

$objs:$ **HEAP** $\rightarrow$ **SET[OBJ]**

$refs:$ **HEAP** $\rightarrow$ **SET[REF]**

$ref\_obj:$ **HEAP** $\rightarrow$ **REF** $\nrightarrow$ **OBJ**
> $h.ref\_obj(r)$ **require**
>> $h.refs.has(r)$

$last\_added\_obj:$ **HEAP** $\rightarrow$ **OBJ**
> $h.last\_added\_obj$ **require**
>> $\neg h.objs.is\_empty$

A number of commands are responsible for adding objects and for altering the mapping of references to objects. The command *add_obj* takes an object o and adds it to the heap. The result of the command is a new heap with the object o and a new reference that points to o. The newly added object is indicated in the query *last_added_obj*. Note that this command does not create a new object. It simply adds an object that has been provided as an argument. The command requires that the object is not yet part of the heap.

add_obj: **HEAP** $\rightarrow$ **OBJ** $\nrightarrow$ **HEAP**
> $h.add\_obj(o)$ **require**
>> $\forall u \in h.objs\colon u.id \neq o.id$
>> $\forall a \in o.class\_type.attributes\colon$
>>> $o.att\_val(a) \in$ **REF** $\rightarrow (o.att\_val(a) = void \vee h.refs.has(o.att\_val(a)))$
>
> **axioms**
>> $h.add\_obj(o).objs = h.objs \cup \{o\}$
>> $h.add\_obj(o).refs = h.refs \cup \{r\}$
>> $h.add\_obj(o).ref\_obj(r) = o$
>> $h.add\_obj(o).last\_added\_obj = o$
>>
>> **where**
>>> $r \stackrel{def}{=} new$ **REF**.*make*

If an object that is already part of the heap gets updated, then it is necessary to update the mapping from the reference to the object on the heap. This can be done with the command *update_ref* that takes a reference r and an updated object o and returns a heap where the reference r points to o. The command requires that r is a valid reference and that o is an updated version of the original object. Because the remaining part of the state only deals with references rather than objects directly, a reference update does not require an update of these parts.

$update\_ref$: **HEAP** $\rightarrow$ **REF** $\nrightarrow$ **OBJ** $\nrightarrow$ **HEAP**
> $h.update\_ref(r,o)$ **require**
>> $h.refs.has(r)$
>> $o.id = h.ref\_obj(r).id$
>> $\forall a \in o.class\_type.attributes\colon$
>>> $o.att\_val(a) \in$ **REF** $\rightarrow (o.att\_val(a) = void \vee h.refs.has(o.att\_val(a)))$
>
> **axioms**
>> $h.update\_ref(r,o).objs.has(o)$
>> $o \neq h.ref\_obj(r) \rightarrow \neg h.update\_ref(r,o).objs.has(h.ref\_obj(r))$
>> $h.update\_ref(r,o).ref\_obj(r) = o$
>> $h.last\_added\_obj = h.ref\_obj(r) \rightarrow h.update\_ref(r,o).last\_added\_obj = o$

So far **HEAP** covers the mapping from references to objects. Occasionally it is necessary to have the inverse mapping. The commands *add_obj* and *update_ref* ensure that there is exactly one reference for each object on the heap. Thus it is possible to define the inverse query *ref* as an auxiliary query.

ref: **HEAP** $\rightarrow$ **OBJ** $\nrightarrow$ **REF**
> $h.ref(o)$ **require**
>> $h.objs.has(o)$
>
> **axioms**
>> $h.ref\_obj(h.ref(o)) = o$

Once routines. A *once routine* can either be a once function or a once procedure. A once routine gets executed at most once in a certain context. If a once routine has been executed in the context, then it is called *non-fresh* in the context. Otherwise it is called *fresh* in the context. The context is either the set of all processors in the system or a single processor. The heap remembers which once routines are fresh. For this purpose, **HEAP** declares the queries *is_fresh* and *once_result*. For any processor p and any once routine f, the query *is_fresh* states whether f is fresh on p or not. For a once function f that is not fresh on a processor p, the query *once_result* returns the result of f on p.

Two commands change the once status of a fresh once routine to non-fresh. One version works for once functions and the other one for once procedures. Both commands take the once routine f and the processor p. The version for once functions also takes a once result r. The two commands implement the semantics for once routines: a once routine has either a once per system or a once per processor semantics. Once functions declared as separate with or without an explicit processor specification have the once per system semantics. In this case, the command *set_once_func_not_fresh* defines f as non-fresh on all processors. Once functions with a non-separate result type have the once per processor semantics. In this case, the command *set_once_func_not_fresh* sets f as non-fresh on p with the once result r. Once procedures have the once per processor semantics. In this case, the command *set_once_proc_not_fresh* sets f as non-fresh on p.

set_once_func_not_fresh: **HEAP** $\rightarrow$ **PROC** $\rightarrow$ **FEATURE** $\nrightarrow$ **REF** $\nrightarrow$ **HEAP**
  $h.set\_once\_func\_not\_fresh(p, f, r)$ **require**
    $f \in$ **FUNCTION** $\wedge f.is\_once$
    $r \neq void \rightarrow h.refs.has(r)$
  axioms
    $(\exists d, c \colon \Gamma \vdash f \colon (d, \bullet, c)) \rightarrow$
      $\neg h.set\_once\_func\_not\_fresh(p, f, r).is\_fresh(p, f) \wedge$
      $h.set\_once\_func\_not\_fresh(p, f, r).once\_result(p, f) = r$
    $(\exists d, c \colon \Gamma \vdash f \colon (d, p, c) \wedge p \neq \bullet) \rightarrow \forall q \in$ **PROC**:
      $\neg h.set\_once\_func\_not\_fresh(p, f, r).is\_fresh(q, f) \wedge$
      $h.set\_once\_func\_not\_fresh(p, f, r).once\_result(q, f) = r$

set_once_proc_not_fresh: **HEAP** $\rightarrow$ **PROC** $\rightarrow$ **FEATURE** $\nrightarrow$ **HEAP**
  $h.set\_once\_proc\_not\_fresh(p, f)$ **require**
    $f \in$ **PROCEDURE** $\wedge f.is\_once$
  axioms
    $\neg h.set\_once\_proc\_not\_fresh(p, f).is\_fresh(p, f)$

Creation. A new heap can be created with the constructor *make*. A new heap has no objects and no references. All once routines are marked as fresh on all processors.

make: **HEAP**
  axioms
    $make.objs.is\_empty$
    $make.refs.is\_empty$
    $\forall p \in$ **PROC**, $f \in$ **FEATURE**: $f.is\_once \rightarrow make.is\_fresh(p, f)$

4.4   Regions ADT

The heap is partitioned into disjoint *regions*, and each region is assigned to exactly one processor. This concept relates to the concept of a ken in Schmidt's work [30]. The processor of a region is the handler of all the objects in the region. Regions are also used to maintain locks. The following discussion first describes an ADT for processor and then describes an ADT for regions.

Processors. A *processor* is an autonomous thread of control capable of executing features on objects. Each processor is responsible for a set of objects. As such a processor is called the *handler* of its associated objects. Each object is assigned to exactly one processor that is the authority of feature executions on this object. If a processor q wants to call a feature on an object handled by a different processor p, then q needs to send a feature request to processor p. This is where the request queue of processor p comes into place. The *request queue* keeps track of features to be executed on behalf of other processors. Processor q can add a request to this queue and processor p will execute the request as soon as it executed all previous requests in the request queue. Processor p uses its *call stack* to execute the feature request at the beginning of the request queue. The call stack is responsible for the order of feature executions on the same processor. In a situation of a non-separate call, the call stack ensures that the calling feature execution resumes once the called feature execution terminated. The interaction between the call stack and the request queue is best described with the following loop through which each processor goes:

1. Idle wait. If both the call stack and the request queue are empty, then wait for new requests to be enqueued.
2. Request scheduling. If the call stack is empty but the request queue is not empty, then dequeue an item and push it onto the call stack.
3. Request processing. If there is an item on the call stack, then pop the item from the call stack and process it. If the item is a feature request, then apply the feature. If the item is an operation, then execute the operation.

For each processor there is a *request queue lock* and a *call stack lock*. A lock on the request queue grants permission to add a feature request to the end of the request queue. A lock on the call stack grants permission to add a feature request to the top of the call stack. Before processor q can add a request to p's request queue, it must have a lock on this request queue. Otherwise another processor could intervene. Once processor q is done with the request queue of processor p it can add an unlock operation to the end of the request queue. This makes sure that the request queue lock of p will be released after all the previous feature requests have been executed. Similarly, processor p must have a lock on its call stack to add features to its call stack. Initially, each processor has a lock on its own call stack and its request queue is not locked.

Processor q could also make a synchronous call to p. However q might be in possession of some locks that are necessary for the execution of the resulting feature request on p. In such a situation, q is waiting for the synchronous call to terminate and p is waiting for locks to be available. According to the conditions given by Coffman et al. [8] a deadlock occurred. This can be avoided if q temporarily passes its locks to the p. This allows p to finish the execution and hence q can continue.

Clarification 1 (Request queue locks and call stack locks). The notion of request queue locks and call stack locks was not present in Nienaltowski's [25] definition of SCOOP. He defines one lock for each processor. A lock on a processor means exclusive access to the whole processor. This lock model is not sufficient to describe SCOOP. In particular, this lock model creates a contradiction with respect to separate callbacks. A separate callback is a feature call in which processor q made a direct or indirect call to processor

p and now p is calling back processor q. The separate callback is only possible if p has a lock on q. However, p does not necessarily have this lock because the lock might be in possession of the processor that locked q in the first place. Request queue locks and call stack locks allow us to clarify the situation. Thus we propose a new lock model with request queue locks and call stack locks.

The lock model used in Nienaltowski's work [25] is an abstraction of the new lock model. The abstraction works under the assumption that no processor passes its locks. Under this assumption each processor keeps its call stack lock. In this abstraction, the request queue lock on a processor p is called the lock on p. As long as the call stack lock on a processor p is in possession of p, a request queue lock on p in possession of a processor q means that processor p will be executing new feature requests in the request queue exclusively on behalf of q. This means that a request queue lock grants exclusive access to all the objects handled by p. Transferring this insight to the abstraction, a lock on processor p denotes exclusive access to the objects handled by p. □

The formalization defines the ADT **PROC** for processors. A processor has an identifier stored in the query *id*.

The constructor *make* returns a new processor with a fresh identifier. The fresh identifier is defined through the query *new_id*.

make: **PROC**
  axioms
    make.id = new_id

The ADT **PROC** is very simple. It neither takes care of the mapping from processors to the handled objects nor does it take care of the locks. These aspects are taken care of by the ADT for regions.

Mapping of processors to objects and locking. This section introduces the ADT **REG** for regions. This ADT declares a query *procs* that keeps track of all the processors in the system. The query *handled_objs* defines a set of handled objects for each processor in *procs*. Finally, the query *last_added_proc* denotes the last processor that has been added to *procs*.

procs: **REG** → **SET[PROC]**

handled_objs: **REG** → **PROC** ↛ **SET[OBJ]**
  k.handled_objs(p) **require**
    k.procs.has(p)

last_added_proc: **REG** ↛ **PROC**
  k.last_added_proc **require**
    ¬*k.procs.is_empty*

Next to the queries that are concerned with the mapping from processors to objects, there are a number of queries that deal with locking. The feature *rq_locked* states whether the request queue of a processor in *procs* is locked or not. Similarly, the feature *cs_locked* states whether the call stack is locked.

The remaining queries specify the owners of the locks. For this, the formalization distinguishes between *obtained* and *retrieved* locks. Obtained locks are locks that got acquired by a processor. Retrieved locks are locks that got passed from another processor.

The query *obtained_rq_locks* returns a stack of obtained processor sets for a processor. A stack of sets models the way processors acquire locks: they go through a nested series of feature applications and each feature application requires a set of locks before the feature can be executed. For each feature application the executing processor adds a new set on top of its stack. As soon as the feature application finished, the processor removes the top set from its stack. The query *obtained_cs_lock* returns the acquired call stack lock of a processor. Initially each processor starts with a lock on its own call stack and this call stack lock never changes. Thus this query is only declared for reasons of completeness. If a processor appears in a set of request queue locks, then the processor denotes its request queue lock. If a processor appears in a set of call stack locks, then the processor denotes its call stack lock.

A processor can pass its locks to another processor. There are several queries to formalize this aspect. The features *retrieved_rq_locks* and *retrieved_cs_locks* return the retrieved locks of a processor. Both of these queries return a stack of sets. The stack keeps track of the set of retrieved locks for each feature application. These two stacks grow and shrink in parallel to the stack *obtained_rq_locks*. Once a processor passed its locks, it cannot use them anymore until the locks are revoked. The query *locks_passed* returns whether a processor passed some or all of its locks or not.

The following discussion first goes through the list of commands that add processors and commands that change the association of processors to objects. It then proceeds with the commands that handle locks. The command *add_proc* updates the regions with a new processor. Note that the processor must have been created beforehand. The axioms state that the new processor will be included in *procs* and that it will be stored in *last_added_proc*. The axioms also state how the new processor is initialized. The new processor's request queue is unlocked and its call stack is locked. Apart from the initial lock on the call stack there are no obtained or retrieved locks and hence the processor did not pass its locks.

add_proc: **REG** $\rightarrow$ **PROC** $\rightarrow$ **REG**
    $k.add\_proc(p)$ **require**
      $\neg k.procs.has(p)$
  axioms
    $k.add\_proc(p).procs.has(p)$
    $k.add\_proc(p).last\_added\_proc = p$
    $k.add\_proc(p).handled\_objs(p).is\_empty$
    $\neg k.add\_proc(p).rq\_locked(p)$
    $k.add\_proc(p).cs\_locked(p)$
    $k.add\_proc(p).obtained\_rq\_locks(p).is\_empty$
    $k.add\_proc(p).obtained\_cs\_lock(p) = p$
    $k.add\_proc(p).retrieved\_rq\_locks(p).is\_empty$
    $k.add\_proc(p).retrieved\_cs\_locks(p).is\_empty$
    $\neg k.add\_proc(p).locks\_passed(p)$

The command *add_obj* takes a processor p in *procs* and an object o that is not handled by a processor in *procs* yet. It returns the updated regions in which o is handled by p.

$add\_obj\colon \mathbf{REG} \to \mathbf{PROC} \nrightarrow \mathbf{OBJ} \nrightarrow \mathbf{REG}$
   $k.add\_obj(p,o)$ **require**
      $k.procs.has(p)$
      $\forall q \in k.procs, u \in k.handled\_objs(q)\colon u.id \neq o.id$
   axioms
      $k.add\_obj(p,o).handled\_objs(p).has(o)$

In the opposite direction, the command *remove_obj* removes an object that is handled by a processor in *procs* from the regions.

$remove\_obj\colon \mathbf{REG} \to \mathbf{OBJ} \nrightarrow \mathbf{REG}$
   $k.remove\_obj(o)$ **require**
      $\exists p \in k.procs\colon k.handled\_objs(p).has(o)$
   axioms
      $\neg \exists p \in k.procs\colon k.remove\_obj(o).handled\_objs(p).has(o)$

The following part discusses the commands that deal with the locking aspects of the regions. The command *lock_rqs* locks the request queues of a set of processors $\bar{q}$ on behalf of a processor p. None of these request queues must be locked beforehand.

$lock\_rqs\colon \mathbf{REG} \to \mathbf{PROC} \nrightarrow \mathbf{SET[PROC]} \nrightarrow \mathbf{REG}$
   $k.lock\_rqs(p,\bar{l})$ **require**
      $k.procs.has(p)$
      $\forall x \in \bar{l}\colon k.procs.has(x)$
      $\forall x \in \bar{l}\colon \neg k.rq\_locked(x)$
   axioms
      $k.lock\_rqs(p,\bar{l}).obtained\_rq\_locks(p) = k.obtained\_rq\_locks(p).push(\bar{l})$
      $\forall x \in \bar{l}\colon k.lock\_rqs(p,\bar{l}).rq\_locked(x)$

At some point, processor p will not require the obtained request queue locks anymore because p made sure to enqueue all necessary features requests. Processor p uses the command *pop_obtained_rq_locks* to remove his claims on the obtained request queue locks. This requires that processor p is in possession of these locks, i.e., that p did not pass its locks.

$pop\_obtained\_rq\_locks\colon \mathbf{REG} \to \mathbf{PROC} \nrightarrow \mathbf{REG}$
   $k.pop\_obtained\_rq\_locks(p)$ **require**
      $k.procs.has(p)$
      $\neg k.obtained\_rq\_locks(p).is\_empty$
      $\neg k.locks\_passed(p)$
   axioms
      $k.pop\_obtained\_rq\_locks(p).obtained\_rq\_locks(p) = k.obtained\_rq\_locks(p).pop$

Removing the locks from p's obtained request queue locks stack does not mean that these request queues are unlocked. It just means that the request queue locks are not claimed by p anymore and therefore p will not enqueue further feature requests on the respective processors. The request queues remain locked until they get unlocked with a call to the command *unlock_rq*. This happens after the processors whose request queues got locked by p finished all the requested feature applications. The precondition of the command states that a request queue can only be unlocked if it is not claimed by any other processor. This precondition guarantees that the request queue can only be unlocked when it is not used as an obtained or retrieved lock by any other processor anymore. Note that there is no unlock command for call stack locks because the call stack never gets unlocked.

$unlock\_rq$: **REG** $\rightarrow$ **PROC** $\nrightarrow$ **REG**
   $k.unlock\_rq(p)$ **require**
      $k.procs.has(p)$
      $k.rq\_locked(p)$
      $\forall q \in k\colon \neg k.obtained\_rq\_locks(q).flat.has(p)$
   axioms
      $\neg k.unlock\_rq(p).rq\_locked(p)$

The request queues remain locked until explicitly unlocked with a call to $unlock\_rq$. Between the call to $pop\_obtained\_rq\_locks$ and the call to $unlock\_rq$, the owner of these locks is undefined. In some situations this is not satisfactory. A different solution must be found if another processor wants to claim the locks until they are unlocked. The command $delegate\_obtained\_rq\_locks$ serves this purpose. It takes a processor p and a number of processors $\bar{l}$ and makes p the owner of the request queue locks of all processors in $\bar{l}$ by adding these locks to the obtained request queue locks stack of p. This can only work if there is no current owner and the request queues are indeed locked.

$delegate\_obtained\_rq\_locks$: **REG** $\rightarrow$ **PROC** $\nrightarrow$ **SET[PROC]** $\nrightarrow$ **REG**
   $k.delegate\_obtained\_rq\_locks(p,\bar{l})$ **require**
      $k.procs.has(p)$
      $\forall x \in \bar{l}\colon k.procs.has(x)$
      $\forall x \in \bar{l}\colon \neg \exists y \in k.procs\colon k.obtained\_rq\_locks(y).flat.has(x)$
      $\forall x \in \bar{l}\colon k.rq\_locked(x)$
   axioms
      $k.delegate\_obtained\_rq\_locks(p,\bar{l}).obtained\_rq\_locks(p) = k.obtained\_rq\_locks(p).push(\bar{l})$

Delegation is different from lock passing: *delegation* is the permanent transfer of ownership and *lock passing* is the temporary transfer of the right to use the locks. The following discussion looks at the commands to pass and revoke locks. The command $pass\_locks$ takes a processor p and a processor q as well as a set of request queue locks $\bar{l}_r$ along with a set of call stack locks $\bar{l}_c$. The result is an updated instance of **REG** in which $\bar{l}_r$ and $\bar{l}_c$ have been passed from p to q. As a precondition for this task, processor p must be in possession of all these locks. This means that all the locks in $\bar{l}_r$ and $\bar{l}_c$ must be obtained or retrieved locks of p and the locks must not be passed. The updated result must reflect that some or all of p's locks have been passed. However, because the two sets of locks can potentially be empty, p's locks must only be marked as passed if at least one of the two sets of locks is non-empty. Lastly, the command must take care of one special case of the lock passing operation. If a processor q different from processor p passed its locks in a previous lock passing operation and now the command passes these locks back to q, then the command has to mark the locks of processor q as not passed. This case is important to handle separate callbacks.

pass_locks: $\mathbf{REG} \to \mathbf{PROC} \nrightarrow \mathbf{PROC} \nrightarrow \mathbf{TUPLE}[\mathbf{SET}[\mathbf{PROC}], \mathbf{SET}[\mathbf{PROC}]] \nrightarrow \mathbf{REG}$

$k.pass\_locks(p, q, (\overline{l_r}, \overline{l_c}))$ **require**

$\quad k.procs.has(p) \wedge k.procs.has(q)$

$\quad \forall x \in \overline{l_r}: k.procs.has(x) \wedge \forall x \in \overline{l_c}: k.procs.has(x)$

$\quad \forall x \in \overline{l_r}: k.obtained\_rq\_locks(p).flat.has(x) \vee k.retrieved\_rq\_locks(p).flat.has(x)$

$\quad \forall x \in \overline{l_c}: x = k.obtained\_cs\_lock(p) \vee k.retrieved\_cs\_locks(p).flat.has(x)$

$\quad \neg k.locks\_passed(p)$

axioms

$$k.pass\_locks(p, q, (\overline{l_r}, \overline{l_c})).locks\_passed(p) = \begin{cases} true & if \neg \overline{l_r}.is\_empty \vee \neg \overline{l_c}.is\_empty \\ false & otherwise \end{cases}$$

$$k.pass\_locks(p, q, (\overline{l_r}, \overline{l_c})).retrieved\_rq\_locks(q) = k.retrieved\_rq\_locks(q).push(\overline{l_r})$$

$$k.pass\_locks(p, q, (\overline{l_r}, \overline{l_c})).retrieved\_cs\_locks(q) = k.retrieved\_cs\_locks(q).push(\overline{l_c})$$

$$\begin{pmatrix} p \neq q \wedge \\ k.locks\_passed(q) \wedge \\ k.obtained\_rq\_locks(q).flat \subseteq \overline{l_r} \wedge \\ k.retrieved\_rq\_locks(q).flat \subseteq \overline{l_r} \wedge \\ k.obtained\_cs\_lock(q) \in \overline{l_c} \wedge \\ k.retrieved\_cs\_locks(q).flat \subseteq \overline{l_c} \end{pmatrix} \to \neg k.pass\_locks(p, q, (\overline{l_r}, \overline{l_c})).locks\_passed(q)$$

The command *revoke_locks* takes a processor p and a processor q. It reverses the effect of a lock passing operation from a processor p to q and returns an updated instance of **REG**. This is only allowed if processor p passed locks to q in a preceding lock passing operation. Note that the lock passing operation from p to q potentially marked the locks of q as not passed. Revoking the locks from q to p requires the reverse action. If p has retrieved locks in common with the locks of q, even after the retrieved locks from p have been removed from q, then q's locks must be marked as passed because they are now in possession of p.

revoke_locks: $\mathbf{REG} \to \mathbf{PROC} \nrightarrow \mathbf{PROC} \nrightarrow \mathbf{REG}$

$k.revoke\_locks(p, q)$ **require**

$\quad k.procs.has(p) \wedge k.procs.has(q)$

$\quad \neg k.retrieved\_rq\_locks(q).is\_empty \wedge \neg k.retrieved\_cs\_locks(q).is\_empty$

$\quad k.retrieved\_rq\_locks(q).top \subseteq k.obtained\_rq\_locks(p).flat \cup k.retrieved\_rq\_locks(p).flat$

$\quad k.retrieved\_cs\_locks(q).top \subseteq \{k.obtained\_cs\_lock(p)\} \cup k.retrieved\_cs\_locks(p).flat$

$\quad k.retrieved\_rq\_locks(q).top \cup k.retrieved\_cs\_locks(q).top \neq \{\} \to k.locks\_passed(p)$

$\quad \neg k.locks\_passed(q)$

axioms

$\quad \neg k.revoke\_locks(p, q).locks\_passed(p)$

$\quad k.revoke\_locks(p, q).retrieved\_rq\_locks(q) = k.retrieved\_rq\_locks(q).pop$

$\quad k.revoke\_locks(p, q).retrieved\_cs\_locks(q) = k.retrieved\_cs\_locks(q).pop$

$$\begin{pmatrix} p \neq q \wedge \\ \begin{pmatrix} \exists x \in k.retrieved\_rq\_locks(p).flat: (\\ \quad k.obtained\_rq\_locks(q).flat.has(x) \vee \\ \quad k.retrieved\_rq\_locks(q).pop.flat.has(x) \\ ) \vee \\ \exists x \in k.retrieved\_cs\_locks(p).flat: (\\ \quad x = k.obtained\_cs\_lock(q) \vee \\ \quad k.retrieved\_cs\_locks(q).pop.flat.has(x) \\ ) \end{pmatrix} \end{pmatrix}$$
$$\to k.revoke\_locks(p, q).locks\_passed(q)$$

These commands wrap up the mapping of processors to objects and the locking aspects. The discussion continues with a number of auxiliary queries to simplify access to the presented queries. The command *add_obj* makes sure that a processor is assigned to each object that gets added. This mapping is available through the query *handled_objs*. Thus it is possible to define an auxiliary query *handler* that is inverse to the query *handled_objs*.

handler: **REG** $\rightarrow$ **OBJ** $\nrightarrow$ **PROC**
> *k.handler*(*o*) **require**
>> $\exists p \in k.procs: k.handled\_objs(p).has(o)$
>
> **axioms**
>> $k.handled\_objs(k.handler(o)).has(o)$

There are four different categories of locks that each processor can have. For both the request queue locks and the call stack locks, there are queries for obtained and retrieved locks. In some situations it is easier to just work with request queue locks and call stack locks without splitting them into obtained and retrieved locks. The auxiliary queries *rq_locks* and *cs_locks* serve this purpose. The auxiliary query *rq_locks* returns a set that contains all the obtained and the retrieved request queue locks of a processor *p*. Similarly, the auxiliary query *cs_locks* returns all the call stack locks of a processor *p*.

rq_locks: **REG** $\rightarrow$ **PROC** $\nrightarrow$ **SET[PROC]**
> *k.rq_locks*(*p*) **require**
>> $k.procs.has(p)$
>
> **axioms**
>> $k.rq\_locks(p) = k.obtained\_rq\_locks(p).flat \cup k.retrieved\_rq\_locks(p).flat$

cs_locks: **REG** $\rightarrow$ **PROC** $\nrightarrow$ **SET[PROC]**
> *k.cs_locks*(*p*) **require**
>> $k.procs.has(p)$
>
> **axioms**
>> $k.cs\_locks(p) = \{k.obtained\_cs\_lock(p)\} \cup k.retrieved\_cs\_locks(p).flat$

Creation. The constructor *make* creates a new instance of **REG**. The new instance has no processors.

make: **REG**
> **axioms**
>> $make.procs.is\_empty$

4.5 Store ADT

Each processor in the system has a call stack to execute features. Every time a processor executes a feature, a new call stack frame gets created on top of the call stack. The new call stack frame stores the values of formal arguments, local variables, the current object entity, and the result entity for the current feature execution. The call stack is also responsible for the order of feature executions on the same processor. This formalization separates the two concerns of the call stack. The *store* only models the values in each stack frame. A store has a stack of environments for each processor, where each *environment* maps names to values. This section first presents an ADT for environments and then presents an ADT for the store.

Environments. The ADT **ENV** has a query *names* that stores all the defined names. The query *val* can then be used to get the value for each such name.

names: **ENV** → **SET**[**NAME**]

val: **ENV** → **NAME** ⇸ **REF**∪**PROC**
   e.val(n) **require**
      e.names.has(n)

The command *update* takes a name and a value and returns an updated environment. Note that it does not matter whether the name is already defined in the environment or not. In any case, the name will be defined in the updated environment and the name will be mapped to the value. The value can either be a reference or a processor. Environments with processor values are not strictly needed to describe SCOOP, however they make it possible to have a unified view on attribute values and environment values.

update: **ENV** → **NAME** → **REF**∪**PROC** → **ENV**
   axioms
      $e.update(n,v).names = e.names \cup \{n\}$
      $e.update(n,v).val(n) = v$

The constructor *make* returns an empty environment.

make: **ENV**
   axioms
      make.names.is_empty

Mapping from processors to environments. The ADT **STORE** has a single query *envs* that stores a stack of environments for each processor.

envs: **STORE** → **PROC** → **STACK**[**ENV**]

The command *push_env* pushes a given environment on top a processor's stack of environments. The command *pop_env* pops the top environment from a non-empty stack of environments.

push_env: **STORE** → **PROC** → **ENV** → **STORE**
   axioms
      $s.push\_env(p,e).envs(p) = s.envs(p).push(e)$

pop_env: **STORE** → **PROC** ⇸ **STORE**
   s.pop_env(p) **require**
      ¬*s.envs(p).is_empty*
   axioms
      $s.pop\_env(p).envs(p) = s.envs(p).pop$

The constructor *make* creates an empty store.

make: **STORE**
   axioms
      $\forall p \in \textbf{PROC}: make.envs(p).is\_empty$

4.6   State ADT

The ADT **STATE** models the *state* with three queries to retrieve the different parts of the ADT.

regions: **STATE** → **REG**

heap: **STATE** → **HEAP**

store: **STATE** → **STORE**

The command *set* sets the regions, the heap, and the store at the same time. A precondition specifies consistency criteria between the parts of the state. The first precondition clause states that a processor can handle an object if and only if the object is on the heap. The second precondition clause states that if the heap declares a feature as non-fresh on a processor p, then the regions must know about this processor. The third precondition clause requires that all processors stored in attribute values are known by the regions. Note that **HEAP** already requires that the references stored in attribute values are known. The forth precondition clause states that each non-empty environment in the store must belong to a processor that is known by the regions. The fifth precondition clause states that each value in the store must either be a known reference or a known processor.

set: **STATE** → **REG** ↛ **HEAP** ↛ **STORE** ↛ **STATE**
   $\sigma.set(k,h,s)$ **require**
       $\exists p \in k.procs, \exists o \in \textbf{OBJ}: k.handled\_objs(p).has(o) \leftrightarrow h.objs.has(o)$
       $\exists p \in \textbf{PROC}, f \in \textbf{FEATURE}: \neg h.is\_fresh(p,f) \rightarrow k.procs.has(p)$
       $\forall o \in h.objs, a \in o.class\_type.attributes: o.att\_val(a) \in \textbf{PROC} \rightarrow k.procs.has(o.att\_val(a))$
       $\forall p \in \textbf{PROC}, e \in s.envs(p): \neg e.names.is\_empty \rightarrow k.procs.has(p)$
       $\forall p \in k.procs, e \in s.envs(p), x \in e.names:$
           $(e.val(x) \in \textbf{REF} \rightarrow e.val(x) = void \lor h.refs.has(e.val(x))) \land$
           $(e.val(x) \in \textbf{PROC} \rightarrow k.procs.has(e.val(x)))$
   axioms
       $\sigma.set(k,h,s).regions = k$
       $\sigma.set(k,h,s).heap = h$
       $\sigma.set(k,h,s).store = s$

Creation. To create a state, one has to create the three parts of the state. This is done with the constructor *make*.

make: **STATE**
   axioms
       $make.regions = new \; \textbf{REG}.make$
       $make.heap = new \; \textbf{HEAP}.make$
       $make.store = new \; \textbf{STORE}.make$

Facade. It is too cumbersome to work with **STATE** as it is. For example, the following expression defines a new state σ' in which a new processor has been added to the state σ: $\sigma' \stackrel{def}{=} \sigma.set(\sigma.regions.add\_proc(new \; \textbf{PROC}.make), \sigma.heap, \sigma.store)$. This expression is too long for this simple task, especially if the expression is used multiple times.

It would be easier to have an auxiliary command that does this job for us. The *facade* is an abstraction with auxiliary features that provide easy access to the state functionality. The facade is divided into different aspects. The following discussion dedicates one section to each aspect. It starts with the mapping of processors to objects and the mapping of references to objects. It continues with a section on how to set values, followed by a section on how to get values. It concludes with a section on locking.

Mapping of processors to objects and mapping of references to objects. The regions and the heap manage the references, the objects, the processors, and the mapping between them. The facade unifies all related features in one aspect. This section first defines a number of auxiliary queries for the mapping of processors to objects. Next, it defines auxiliary queries for the mapping of references to objects. It then defines auxiliary commands that work on both aspects.

The two auxiliary queries *procs* and *last_added_proc* give access to all the processors and the last added processor.

The auxiliary query *handler* gives the handler of an object referenced by r. The auxiliary query uses the heap to get the referenced object and then gives this object to the regions to get the handler. In contrast to the corresponding auxiliary query in **REG**, the version here takes a reference instead of an object. The version in **REG** deals directly with objects rather than references because it does not know about the heap and thus the mapping from references to objects is not available. The facade, however, has access to both the regions and the heap and thus it can use the preferred way of identifying objects: references.

The auxiliary query *new_proc* is a shorthand for processor creation. The auxiliary query *last_added_obj* returns the object that has been added last to the heap. The auxiliary query *ref_obj* returns the object that is associated to a given reference. In the other direction, the auxiliary query *ref* returns the reference to a given object. The auxiliary query *new_obj* is a shorthand for object creation; it returns a new object with a given class type.

The discussion continues with the auxiliary commands that modify the mapping of processors to objects and the mapping of references to objects. Before an object can be added to the set of handled objects of a processor, the processor must exist. If the processor does not exist yet, the command *add_proc* can be used to update a state with a new processor.

add_proc : **STATE** $\to$ **PROC** $\nrightarrow$ **STATE**
$\quad \sigma.add\_proc(p)$ **require**
$\quad\quad \neg\sigma.regions.procs.has(p)$
$\quad$ **axioms**
$\quad\quad \sigma.add\_proc(p) = \sigma.set(\sigma.regions.add\_proc(p), \sigma.heap, \sigma.store)$

The auxiliary command *add_obj* can then be used to add an object to the processor and the heap. The auxiliary command takes a processor p and an object o and it returns a state in which object o is part of the heap and handled by processor p.

add_obj: **STATE** $\rightarrow$ **PROC** $\nrightarrow$ **OBJ** $\nrightarrow$ **STATE**

   $\sigma.add\_obj(p,o)$ **require**

      $\sigma.regions.procs.has(p)$

      $\forall u \in \sigma.heap.objs: u.id \neq o.id$

      $\forall a \in o.class\_type.attributes$:

         $(o.att\_val(a) \in \textbf{REF} \rightarrow o.att\_val(a) = void \vee \sigma.heap.refs.has(o.att\_val(a))) \wedge$

         $(o.att\_val(a) \in \textbf{PROC} \rightarrow \sigma.regions.procs.has(o.att\_val(a)))$

  axioms

      $\sigma.add\_obj(p,o) = \sigma.set(\sigma.regions.add\_obj(p,o), \sigma.heap.add\_obj(o), \sigma.store)$

The auxiliary command *update_ref* updates a reference with an updated object. It takes a reference r on the heap and an object o and it returns a state in which o replaced the object u referenced by r on the heap and in the regions. Note that o must indeed be an updated version of the object referenced by r. The auxiliary command first removes u from the set of handled objects and then adds o to the set of handled objects of u's handler. Then it updates the heap with the command *update_ref*, which is declared in **HEAP**.

$update\_ref$: **STATE** $\rightarrow$ **REF** $\nrightarrow$ **OBJ** $\nrightarrow$ **STATE**

   $\sigma.update\_ref(r,o)$ **require**

      $\sigma.heap.refs.has(r)$

      $o.id = \sigma.heap.ref\_obj(r).id$

      $\forall a \in o.class\_type.attributes$:

         $(o.att\_val(a) \in \textbf{REF} \rightarrow o.att\_val(a) = void \vee \sigma.heap.refs.has(o.att\_val(a))) \wedge$

         $(o.att\_val(a) \in \textbf{PROC} \rightarrow \sigma.regions.procs.has(o.att\_val(a)))$

  axioms

      $\sigma.update\_ref(r,o) = \sigma.set(k,h,s)$

    where

      $u \stackrel{def}{=} \sigma.heap.ref\_obj(r)$

      $k \stackrel{def}{=} \sigma.regions.remove\_obj(u).add\_obj(\sigma.regions.handler(u),o)$

      $h \stackrel{def}{=} \sigma.heap.update\_ref(r,o)$

      $s \stackrel{def}{=} \sigma.store$

Setting values. This section takes a look at how to set values. To start, it looks at a prerequisite for this task: the deep import operation. Setting values includes setting values of formal arguments, values of local variables, the value of the current object entity, the value of the result entity, and attribute values of the current object. All of these values can be written and read without a feature call. This section concludes with auxiliary commands to set the status of once routines. The SCOOP validity rules exclude other types of value setting operations.

Deep Import Operation. Expanded objects have a copy semantics: if an object o of expanded class type is the source of an attachment, then a copy u gets attached to the destination of the attachment. However, a shallow copy is not sufficient if o's handler p is different from u's handler q. If o has an attached non-separate entity, then u now has a non-separate entity to which a separate object is attached. This would result in a *traitor* – a non-separate entity that points to a separate object. The SCOOP model, as defined by Nienaltowski [25], introduces the *import operation* to solve this issue. Applied to *o* the import operation creates a copied object structure that mirrors the original object structure in a way that *o* and all the objects reachable from *o* through non-separate references are replaced with copied objects that are handled by *q*. This data structure then gets attached to the destination of the attachment. The import operation computes the non-separate version of an object structure.

Clarification 2 (Deep import operation). The import operation potentially results in a copied object structure that contains both copied and original objects. This can be an issue in case one of the copied objects has an invariant over the identities of objects, as shown in example 3.

Example 3 (Invariant violation as a result of the import operation). Imagine two objects *x* and *y* handled by one processor and another object *z* handled by another processor. Object *x* has a separate entity *a* that points to *z* and a non-separate entity *b* that points to *y*. Object *z* has a separate entity *c* that points to *y*. Object *x* has an invariant with a query $a.c = b$. An import operation on *x* executed by a third processor will result in two new objects x' and y' on the third processor. The reference *a* of object x' will point to the original *z*. The reference *b* of object x' will point to the new object y'. This situation is illustrated in Fig. 2. Now object x' is inconsistent, because $a.c$ and *b* identify different objects, namely *y* and y'.

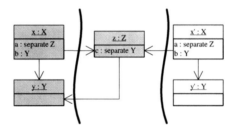

Fig. 2. Invariant violation as a result of the import operation

The *deep import operation* is a variant of the import operation that does not mix the copied and the original objects. □

Instead of copying only the objects that are reachable through non-separate references, the deep import operation makes a full copy of the object structure. The deep importing processor handles all the copies of the objects that are non-separate with respect to the object to be imported. Each other separate object is handled by the processor of the respective original object. The deep import operation does not show the issue with invariants. The drawback of the deep import operation is that more objects must be copied. Nevertheless, we use the deep import operation in our formalization because we cannot tolerate violated invariants. Once routines complicate the deep import operation a bit. Consider a processor *p* that wants to deep import an object *o* handled by a different processor *q*. For each non-separate once function *f* of each copied object the following must be done: if a non-separate once function *f* is fresh on *p* and non-fresh on *q*, then *f* must be marked as non-fresh on p and the value of f on q must be used as the value of f on p. If a once procedure f is fresh on p and non-fresh on q, then f must be marked as non-fresh on p. In all other cases, nothing must be done.

The auxiliary command *deep_import* implements the deep import operation. The command takes an importing processor p and a reference r to be imported. The command returns a state in which the copied object structure exists on the heap and the objects are associated to the respective processors. The copied object structure is accessible through the auxiliary query *last_imported_ref*.

deep_import: **STATE** $\rightarrow$ **PROC** $\nrightarrow$ **REF** $\nrightarrow$ **STATE**
   σ.*deep_import*(p,r) **require**
      σ.*regions.procs.has*(p)
      σ.*heap.refs.has*(r)
  axioms
     σ.*deep_import*$(p,r) = \sigma'$
     σ.*deep_import*(p,r).*last_imported_ref* $= r'$
    where
      $w \stackrel{def}{=}$ new **MAP**[**REF**, **REF**].*make*
      $(r', w', \sigma') \stackrel{def}{=}$ *deep_import_rec_with_map*$(p, \sigma$.*handler*$(r), r, w, \sigma)$

The auxiliary command *deep_import* is based on *deep_import_rec_with_map*. This auxiliary function takes a tuple containing an importing processor p, a processor q that handles the root of the object structure to be imported, a reference r to be deep imported, and a state σ to be modified. Note that the object referenced by r is not necessarily handled by q because this object might be on a different processor than the handler of the root of the object structure to be deep imported. The function returns another tuple with a reference r'' to the copied object structure and an updated state σ''. The auxiliary function *deep_import_rec_with_map* works hand in hand with the auxiliary function *deep_import_rec_without_map*. They have the same signature and together they recursively traverse the object structure and make a deep copy of it. The functions must ensure that no object gets copied twice. For this purpose the functions take as an additional argument a map w that maps references to objects in the input data structure to references in the copied data structure. A mapping from one reference x to another reference y means that the object referenced by y is the copy of the object referenced by x. An updated map is returned as part of the result tuple. The auxiliary command *deep_import* starts the recursion with an empty map. The auxiliary function *deep_import_rec_with_map* uses the map to determine whether the object referenced by r has already been copied. In such a case, the result of the function comes from the map. Otherwise the auxiliary function *deep_import_rec_with_map* returns the result of the auxiliary function *deep_import_rec_without_map*. The auxiliary function *deep_import_rec_without_map* creates a copy of the object referenced by r and handles once routines. Finally, it returns a new reference r', an updated map w' in which r is mapped to r', and an updated state σ'.

$deep\_import\_rec\_with\_map(p,q,r,w,\sigma) = (r'',w'',\sigma'')$

where

$(r',w',\sigma') \overset{def}{=} deep\_import\_rec\_without\_map(p,q,r,w,\sigma)$

$r'' \overset{def}{=} \begin{cases} w.val(r) & if\,w.keys.has(r) \\ r' & if\,\neg w.keys.has(r) \end{cases}$

$w'' \overset{def}{=} \begin{cases} w & if\,w.keys.has(r) \\ w' & if\,\neg w.keys.has(r) \end{cases}$

$\sigma'' \overset{def}{=} \begin{cases} \sigma & if\,w.keys.has(r) \\ \sigma' & if\,\neg w.keys.has(r) \end{cases}$

The auxiliary function *deep_import_rec_without_map* is divided into several steps: a copy step, an attribute values update step, a clients update step, a once status update step, and a result generation step. Each of the steps has several definitions associated to it and each set of definitions depends on the definitions of the previous step. The following discussion goes through each of these steps in more details.

The copy step includes the definitions of o, o_0', σ_0' and w_0'. The definition o is the object referenced by r, and the definition o_0' makes a copy of o. In the next step, the function defines an updated state σ_0' that includes the copy o_0'. There are two cases to be differentiated at this point. If o is handled by q, then o_0' must be handled by p. Otherwise o_0' must be handled by the handler of o. The definition w_0' is the updated map.

The attribute values update step recursively uses *deep_import_rec_with_map* to import all the non-void reference attribute values of o using the updated map. This leads to an updated object with the deep imported values. This step includes the definition of $\{a_1,\ldots,a_n\}$, as well as the definitions of $\{r_1',\ldots,r_n'\}$, $\{w_1',\ldots,w_n'\}$, $\{\sigma_1',\ldots,\sigma_n'\}$, and $\{o_1',\ldots,o_n'\}$. The set $\{a_1,\ldots,a_n\}$ contains each attributes of o whose value is a non-void reference. The function defines (r_i',w_i',σ_i') for $i = 1\ldots n$ as a sequence of tuples. Each of the tuples is responsible for a single recursive deep import operation for one of the attributes in $\{a_1,\ldots,a_n\}$. Each such operation results in an updated map and an updated state that must be used in the next deep import operation. The result of this is an updated map w_n', and updated state σ_n', and references $r_1,\ldots,r_n$ to deep imported data structures. Finally, the function defines a sequence of updated objects $\{o_1',\ldots,o_n'\}$ that ends with the updated object o_n'. The updated object has the values of the attributes $\{a_1,\ldots,a_n\}$ set to the deep imported data structures referenced by $r_1,\ldots,r_n$.

Until now, the function has an updated state σ_n' that contains the initial copy o_0'. In the client update step, the function updates σ_n' such that the reference to o_0' points to the updated object o_n'. This is done in the clients update step. This step includes the definition σ_x'. Note that σ_n' is derived from the state σ_0', which includes the object o_0'.

In a next step, the function takes care of the once routines of the imported object. For this, it defines a new state σ_y' based on the state σ_x'. It defines $\{f_1,\ldots,f_w\}$ as the set of all non-separate once functions of o that are fresh on the processor $\sigma_x'.handler(\sigma_x'.ref(o_n'))$, which handles the copied object, but non-fresh on the processor $\sigma_x'.handler(r)$, which handles the object referenced by r. Note that the two processor can be the same, in which case the set $\{f_1,\ldots,f_w\}$ is empty. Similarly, it defines the set $\{f_{w+1},\ldots,f_m\}$ for once procedures. For each once routine defined in this way, it updates the state σ_x' such that the once status is taken over to the handler of the copied object. These definitions deal with the case where a once routine is fresh on the handler of the copied object, but non-fresh on the handler of the object referenced by r. Note that the remaining cases are implicitly taken care of because no change to the state is necessary. The result is the state σ'_y.

The last step defines the result of the function, based on the definitions of the preceding steps. The result generation step defines the resulting reference r' to the imported object o'_n, the resulting map w', and the resulting state σ'.

$deep\_import\_rec\_without\_map(p,q,r,w,\sigma) = (r',w',\sigma')$
  where

$o \stackrel{def}{=} \sigma.ref\_obj(r)$

$o'_0 \stackrel{def}{=} o.copy$

$\sigma'_0 \stackrel{def}{=} \begin{cases} \sigma.add\_obj(p,o'_0) & if\ \sigma.handler(r) = q \\ \sigma.add\_obj(\sigma.handler(r),o'_0) & otherwise \end{cases}$

$w'_0 \stackrel{def}{=} w.add(r,\sigma'_0.ref(o'_0))$

$\{a_1,\ldots,a_n\} \stackrel{def}{=} \{a \mid o.att\_val(a) \in \mathbf{REF} \wedge o.att\_val(a) \neq void\}$

$\forall i \in \{1,\ldots,n\}: (r'_i,w'_i,\sigma'_i) \stackrel{def}{=} deep\_import\_rec\_with\_map(p,q,o.att\_val(a_i),w'_{i-1},\sigma'_{i-1})$

$\forall i \in \{1,\ldots,n\}: o'_i \stackrel{def}{=} o'_{i-1}.set\_att\_val(a_i,r'_i)$

$\sigma'_x \stackrel{def}{=} \sigma'_n.update\_ref(\sigma'_n.ref(o'_0),o'_n)$

$\sigma'_y \stackrel{def}{=} \sigma'_x$
  $.set\_once\_func\_not\_fresh(\sigma'_x.handler(\sigma'_x.ref(o'_n)),f_1,\sigma'_x.once\_result(\sigma'_x.handler(r),f_1))$
  $.\ .\ .\ .$
  $.set\_once\_func\_not\_fresh(\sigma'_x.handler(\sigma'_x.ref(o'_n)),f_w,\sigma'_x.once\_result(\sigma'_x.handler(r),f_w))$
  $.set\_once\_proc\_not\_fresh(\sigma'_x.handler(\sigma'_x.ref(o'_n)),f_{w+1})$
  $.\ .\ .\ .$
  $.set\_once\_proc\_not\_fresh(\sigma'_x.handler(\sigma'_x.ref(o'_n)),f_m)$
  where

$\{f_1,\ldots,f_w\} \stackrel{def}{=} \begin{cases} \{x \in o.class\_type.functions \mid x.is\_once \wedge \exists c,d: \Gamma \vdash x: (d,\bullet,c) \wedge \\ \quad \sigma'_x.is\_fresh(\sigma'_x.handler(\sigma'_x.ref(o'_n)),x) \wedge \\ \quad \neg\sigma'_x.is\_fresh(\sigma'_x.handler(r),x)\} \end{cases}$

$\{f_{w+1},\ldots,f_m\} \stackrel{def}{=} \begin{cases} \{x \in o.class\_type.procedures \mid x.is\_once \wedge \\ \quad \sigma'_x.is\_fresh(\sigma'_x.handler(\sigma'_x.ref(o'_n)),x) \wedge \\ \quad \neg\sigma'_x.is\_fresh(\sigma'_x.handler(r),x)\} \end{cases}$

$r' \stackrel{def}{=} \sigma'_y.ref(o'_n)$

$w' \stackrel{def}{=} w'_n$

$\sigma' \stackrel{def}{=} \sigma'_y$

Setting values of formal arguments and the value of the current object entity. The deep import operation is used in two ways. It is used when an expanded object handled by one processor gets used as an actual argument for a formal argument on another processor. The deep import operation also gets used when an expanded object handled by one processor gets returned to another processor. This section focuses on the argument passing aspect.

The auxiliary command *push_env_with_feature* defines a state in which a processor p receives a new environment. The new environment is initialized for the execution of the feature f with target reference r_0 and actual argument references $(r_1,\ldots,r_n)$. Actual arguments of expanded type must either be copied or they must be deep imported.

push_env_with_feature: $\textbf{STATE} \rightarrow \textbf{PROC} \nrightarrow \textbf{FEATURE} \rightarrow \textbf{REF} \rightarrow \textbf{TUPLE} \nrightarrow \textbf{STATE}$

$\sigma.push\_env\_with\_feature(p,f,r_0,(r_1,\ldots,r_n))$ **require**

$\quad \sigma.regions.procs.has(p)$

$\quad f.formals.count = n$

$\quad \forall i \in \{0,\ldots,n\}: r_i \neq void \rightarrow \sigma.heap.refs.has(r_i)$

axioms

$\quad \sigma.push\_env\_with\_feature(p,f,r_0,(r_1,\ldots,r_n)) =$

$\qquad \sigma'_n.set(\sigma'_n.regions, \sigma'_n.heap, \sigma'_n.store.push\_env(p,e))$

where

$\quad \sigma'_0 \stackrel{def}{=} \sigma$

$\quad \forall i \in \{1,\ldots,n\}: (\sigma'_i, r'_i) \stackrel{def}{=}$

$$
\begin{cases}
if \exists d,q,c: \Gamma \vdash f.formals(i): (d,q,c) \wedge c.is\_exp \wedge r_i \neq void \wedge \sigma'_{i-1}.handler(r_i) \neq p \\
\quad (\sigma_x, \sigma_x.last\_imported\_ref) \\
\quad \textbf{where} \\
\qquad \sigma_x \stackrel{def}{=} \sigma'_{i-1}.deep\_import(p,r_i) \\
if \exists d,q,c: \Gamma \vdash f.formals(i): (d,q,c) \wedge c.is\_exp \wedge r_i \neq void \wedge \sigma'_{i-1}.handler(r_i) = p \\
\quad (\sigma_x, \sigma_x.last\_added\_obj) \\
\quad \textbf{where} \\
\qquad \sigma_x \stackrel{def}{=} \sigma'_{i-1}.add\_obj(p, \sigma'_{i-1}.heap.ref\_obj(r_i).copy) \\
otherwise \\
\quad (\sigma'_{i-1}, r_i)
\end{cases}
$$

$\quad w \stackrel{def}{=} new\ \textbf{ENV}.make$

$\qquad .update(f.formals(1).name, r'_1)\ \ldots\ .update(f.formals(n).name, r'_n)$

$\qquad .update(f.locals(1).name, void)\ \ldots\ .update(f.locals(f.locals.count).name, void)$

$\qquad .update(\textbf{Current}, r_0)$

$\quad e \stackrel{def}{=} \begin{cases} w & if\ f \in \textbf{PROCEDURE} \\ w.update(\textbf{Result}, void) & if\ f \in \textbf{FUNCTION} \end{cases}$

In a first step, the auxiliary command defines an updated state, in which p gets a new initialized environment e. The updated state is based on an intermediate state σ'_n, which gets defined in a cascade of state updates with the goal of either copying or deep importing the actual arguments of expanded type. The cascade starts with the definition of a starting state σ'_0. For each formal argument, the cascade defines a tuple (σ'_i, r'_i) with an updated state and a reference. If the corresponding actual argument is of reference class type, nothing needs to be done. If the actual argument is of expanded class type and the referenced object is not handled by p, then p must deep import the object structure. This results in an updated state and a new reference to the deep imported object structure. If the actual argument is of expanded class type and the referenced object is handled by p, then the expanded object must be copied. This results in an updated state and a new reference to the copy. The resulting state σ'_n contains all the deep imported and copied objects. The resulting references $r'_1,\ldots,r'_n$ will be used for values of the formal argument names.

In a next step, the command defines the environment w as a new environment that gets updated to map formal argument names, local variable names, the current entity name, and the result entity name to the respective values. The names of the formal arguments get mapped to the references $r'_1,\ldots,r'_n$. Names of local variables are mapped to the void reference. The current entity name is mapped to the target reference.

The environment w is the final environment e in which the result name gets mapped to the void reference. This environment and the updated state σ'_n define the result of the command. The auxiliary command *push_env* pushes e onto p's stack of environments. The auxiliary command *push_env* takes a processor p and an environment e. It returns a state in which e is pushed on top of p's environment stack.

The effect of a call to *push_env_with_feature* or a call to *push_env* can be undone with a call to the auxiliary command *pop_env*. This auxiliary command takes a processor p and removes the top environment from p's stack of environments.

Setting values of local variables and the value of the result entity. The values of local variables and the value of the result entity are maintained in the store. The auxiliary command *set_env_val* sets a value v for the name n in processor p's top environment. For this, it defines an updated environment e in which n is set to v. It then defines an updated store s by first removing the top environment and then adding the updated environment e. The updated store is then used to define an updated state. The updated state becomes the result of the auxiliary command.

Setting attribute values of the current object. The auxiliary command *set_att_val* takes an object o, a name n, and a value v. It returns an updated state in which the attribute with name n of object o is set to the value v. In a first step, the auxiliary command defines an updated object with a call to *set_att_val*. This updated object is then used to update the existing reference to o in the state.

Setting values of local variables, the value of the result entity, and attribute values of the current object in a unified way. The auxiliary command *set_val* attaches a value v to an entity with name n. The entity can either be a local variable or the result entity in the top environment of p. It can also be an attribute of the current object on p. In either case, the update affects an entity on p.

The definition of the resulting state is based on the auxiliary definitions o, σ', and v'. The definition o defines the current object, as defined by the top environment of processor p. The precondition makes sure that there is always such an environment on p where the current object is defined. If v is a reference and the referenced object is an object of reference class type, then v can be attached directly to the entity with name n. If the object is an expanded object handled by processor p, then the referenced object must first be copied. Expanded objects handled by a processor different than p must be deep imported. However, this is done right when the object gets returned from another processor to p. The definitions σ' and v' define a state and a value that are potentially updated according to these rules.

The state σ' must be updated with the value v'. The update can either affect the current object on p or it can affect the top environment of p. Attribute names of the current object, local variable names, and formal argument names are distinct. Therefore it is safe to first check whether the current object o has an attribute with name n, in which case the current object gets updated with a v'. If the current object does not have such an attribute, then it is safe to assume that the top environment contains an entity with name n, in which case the top environment gets updated.

set_val: **STATE** $\rightarrow$ **PROC** $\nrightarrow$ **NAME** $\nrightarrow$ **REF** $\cup$ **PROC** $\nrightarrow$ **STATE**

    σ.*set_val*(p, n, v) **require**

        σ.*regions.procs.has*(p)

        $\neg\sigma$.*store.envs*(p).*is_empty* $\wedge$ σ.*store.envs*(p).*top.names.has*(**Current**)

        $v \in$ **REF** $\wedge v \neq void \rightarrow \sigma$.*heap.refs.has*$(v)$

        $v \in$ **PROC** $\rightarrow \sigma$.*regions.procs.has*(v)

    axioms

$$\sigma.set\_val(p, n, v) = \begin{cases} if \exists a \in o.class\_type.attributes: a.name = n \\ \quad\quad \sigma'.set\_att\_val(o, n, v') \\ otherwise \\ \quad\quad \sigma'.set\_env\_val(p, n, v') \end{cases}$$

      where

$$o \stackrel{def}{=} \sigma.heap.ref\_obj(\sigma.store.envs(p).top.val(\mathbf{Current}))$$

$$(\sigma', v') \stackrel{def}{=}$$
$$\begin{cases} if v \in \mathbf{REF} \wedge v \neq void \wedge \sigma.heap.ref\_obj(v).class\_type.is\_exp \wedge \sigma.handler(v) = p \\ \quad (\sigma_x, \sigma_x.last\_added\_obj) \\ \quad\quad \textbf{where} \\ \quad\quad\quad \sigma_x \stackrel{def}{=} \sigma.add\_obj(p, \sigma.heap.ref\_obj(v).copy) \\ otherwise \\ \quad (\sigma, v) \end{cases}$$

Setting values of once functions. Values can also be stored in the status of once functions. A once function can be fresh or non-fresh. If the once function is non-fresh on a processor p, then there is a once result for the once function on p. A once function is set as non-fresh during the execution of the once function. The following discussion takes a look at how a processor can set the status of once routines in general, i.e., it considers both once functions and once procedures.

    The auxiliary command *set_once_func_not_fresh* takes a processor p, a once function f, and a value r. It returns an updated state in which f is set as non-fresh with the once result r. If f is declared as non-separate, then f is set as non-fresh on p with the once result r. If f is declared as separate with or without an explicit processor specification, then f is set as non-fresh on all processors.

    The auxiliary command *set_once_proc_not_fresh* does the same for once procedures. It takes a processor p and a once procedure f and it returns a state in which f is set as non-fresh on p.

Getting values. This section takes a look at how a processor can read a value that got written with one of the mechanisms from Sec. 4.6.

Getting values of formal arguments, the value of the current object entity, values of local variables, and the value of the result entity. The auxiliary query *envs* takes a processor p and returns the stack of environments for p. The auxiliary query *env_val* is more specialized. It takes a processor p and a name n and it returns the value stored under n in the top environment of p.

Getting attribute values of the current object. The auxiliary query *att_val* takes an object o and a name n and returns the attribute value for the attribute with name n of object o.

Getting values of formal arguments, the value of the current object entity, values of local variables, the value of the result entity, and attribute values of the current object in a unified way. The auxiliary queries *env_val* and *att_val* define a new auxiliary query *val* that deals both with values in the top environment as well as with values stored in attributes of the current object. The auxiliary query *val* takes a processor p and a name n and it returns the value of n in p's current feature execution context. This context consists of the top environment and its reference to the current object. The auxiliary query requires that the execution context of processor p is setup properly, i.e., there is a top environment with a reference to the current object. The precondition also states that either the top environment has the name n registered or the current object has an attribute with name n. In any valid SCOOP program, any environment variable has a name that is distinct from the attribute names of the current object. This allows us to define the result of the auxiliary query in a simple way. If the name exists in the top environment, then the result is the value given by *env_val*. Otherwise the name must be the name of an attribute of the current object, in which case the result is given by *att_val*.

val: $\mathbf{STATE} \rightarrow \mathbf{PROC} \nrightarrow \mathbf{NAME} \nrightarrow \mathbf{REF} \cup \mathbf{PROC}$

$\quad \sigma.val(p, n)$ **require**

$\quad\quad \sigma.regions.procs.has(p)$

$\quad\quad \neg \sigma.store.envs(p).is\_empty$

$\quad\quad e.names.has(\mathbf{Current})$

$\quad\quad e.names.has(n) \vee \exists a \in o.class\_type.attributes: a.name = n$

$\quad\quad$ **where**

$\quad\quad\quad e \overset{def}{=} \sigma.store.envs(p).top$

$\quad\quad\quad o \overset{def}{=} \sigma.heap.ref\_obj(e.val(\mathbf{Current}))$

$\quad$ **axioms**

$$\sigma.val(p, n) = \begin{cases} \begin{aligned} & if\, e.names.has(n) \\ & \quad \sigma.env\_val(p, n) \\ & \textbf{where} \\ & \quad e \overset{def}{=} \sigma.store.envs(p).top \\ & if\, \exists a \in o.class\_type.attributes: a.name = n \\ & \quad \sigma.att\_val(o, n) \\ & \textbf{where} \\ & \quad e \overset{def}{=} \sigma.store.envs(p).top \\ & \quad o \overset{def}{=} \sigma.heap.ref\_obj(e.val(\mathbf{Current})) \end{aligned} \end{cases}$$

Getting values of once functions. The auxiliary query *is_fresh* takes a processor p and a once routine f. It returns whether f is fresh on p or not.

For non-fresh once functions, the auxiliary query *once_result* returns the once result of f on p.

Locking. This section explores the aspect of the facade that deals with locking. The auxiliary query *rq_locked* states whether a processor p's request queue is locked or not. There are no auxiliary queries to distinguish between obtained and retrieved locks. Instead, the auxiliary queries *rq_locks* and *cs_locks* return the set of all request queue locks, respectively the set of all call stack locks of a processor p. These locks are only usable if they are not passed. This information can be retrieved with a call to the auxiliary query *locks_passed*.

The facade provides auxiliary commands for locking request queues, removing obtained request queue locks, unlocking request queues, delegating obtained request queue locks, passing locks, and revoking locks.

5 Formalization of Execution

This section formalizes the execution of a SCOOP program. It explains the general approach, defines the starting point of the execution, and explains the rules that drive the execution. The rules are divided into rules for mechanisms and rules for code elements.

5.1 General Approach

The formalization is based on *structural operational semantics* [29], combined with parts of the terminology from Ostroff et al. [28]. The idea behind a structural operational semantics is to define the behavior of a program in terms of its parts, i.e., the syntactical elements of the program. Such a semantics is intuitive because it talks directly about elements in the code. It is a very powerful semantics because it allows us to apply structural induction as a proof technique.

Computations. A *computation* models the execution of a SCOOP program. It is a sequence of configurations, where each non-initial configuration is derived from a previous configuration through a transition. Each configuration defines a state and a list of statements for each processor. Each transition is described by an inference rule that maps one configuration to another. The transition from one configuration to the next models an atomic step of one processor. The concurrent execution of a SCOOP program is modeled by the interleaved transitions taken by different processors.

Example 4 (Modeling of parallel execution). Suppose there are two processors p and q. Processor p executes the following sequence of statements: $s_{p,1}; s_{p,2}$. In parallel, processor q executes the following sequence of statements: $s_{q,1}$. This execution is modeled by any of the following simplified computations: $s_{p,1}; s_{p,2}; s_{q,1}$ or $s_{p,1}; s_{q,1}; s_{p,2}$ or $s_{q,1}; s_{p,1}; s_{p,2}$.

Configurations. A *configuration* models a snapshot in the execution of a SCOOP program. A configuration consists of a state and a set of processors, each with a queue of statements. The state is an instance of **STATE**. A *schedule* models the processors and the associated queues, called *action queues*. Each processor must execute the statements in its action queue in a FIFO order. The beginning of the action queue contains the statements for the features that are being executed at the moment. The order of these statements models the way the call stack orders feature executions. The tail of the action queue is the request queue of the processor. A call stack lock is the right to add a feature request to the beginning of the action queue and a request queue lock is the right to add a feature request to the end of the action queue. The notation for a configuration with processors $p_1, \ldots, p_n$, respective action queues $s_1, \ldots, s_n$, and state σ is:

$$\langle p_1 :: s_1 \mid \ldots \mid p_n :: s_n, \sigma \rangle$$

The processor separator $|$ is commutative and associative, i.e., $p_1 :: s_1 \mid p_2 :: s_2 = p_2 ::$ $s_2 \mid p_1 :: s_1$ and $p_1 :: s_1 \mid (p_2 :: s_2 \mid p_3 :: s_3) = (p_1 :: s_1 \mid p_2 :: s_2) \mid p_3 :: s_3$. Within an action queue, ; separates statements. The configuration is *well-defined* if and only if $\neg \exists i, j \in \{1, \ldots, n\} : p_i = p_j$.

Statements. A *statement* is an element of the action queue. A statement is either an instruction or an operation. An *instruction* is user syntax, i.e. an action that occurs explicitly in the SCOOP program. An *operation* is run-time syntax, i.e. an action that does not explicitly occur in a SCOOP program. For example, locking of request queues is not an action that is explicit in a SCOOP program. Instead, locking is based on the formal argument list. It is done implicitly before a feature gets executed.

Transitions. A *transition* takes a system in a start configuration and leaves it in a result configuration. The following shows the general form of a transition definition that declares a start configuration $\langle P, \sigma \rangle$ with schedule $P \stackrel{def}{=} p_1 :: s_1 \mid \ldots \mid p_n :: s_n$ and a result configuration $\langle P', \sigma' \rangle$ with schedule $P' \stackrel{def}{=} p'_1 :: s'_1 \mid \ldots \mid p'_m :: s'_m$:

$$\Gamma \vdash \langle P, \sigma \rangle \to \langle P', \sigma' \rangle$$

The typing environment Γ can be used in the transition definition to access static information about the SCOOP program.

Inference rules. An *inference rule* describes the circumstances under which a transition can be used. The inference rule has a premise and a conclusion. The *conclusion* is the transition and the *premise* describes the circumstances under which the transition can be used. The premise consists of a number of transitions and a side condition. The premise is satisfied if all transitions in the premise can be taken and if the side condition is true. In this formalization, most of the rules have no transition in the premise. The following *simplified inference rule template* takes this into account:

Simplified Inference Rule Template

condition
new state σ' *definition*
fresh channels definitions

$$\Gamma \vdash \langle P, \sigma \rangle \to \langle P', \sigma' \rangle$$

The side condition has three parts. The first part defines a *condition* that is based on the typing environment and the start configuration. The second part is the *new state definition* that defines the state of the result configuration. This new state is based on the state in the start configuration. The last part consists of the *fresh channels definitions*. Auxiliary definitions can be used in the condition, the new state definition, and the fresh channels definitions. The side condition can mention features of **STATE**. The preconditions of these features serve as additional conditions in the side condition.

The following inference rule generalizes transitions by adding processors both to the start configuration and to the result configuration. These additional processors run in parallel but do not take any actions during the generalized transition.

Parallelism

$$\frac{\Gamma \vdash \langle P, \sigma \rangle \rightarrow \langle P', \sigma' \rangle}{\Gamma \vdash \langle P \mid Q, \sigma \rangle \rightarrow \langle P' \mid Q, \sigma' \rangle}$$

Scheduling. Before a processor can execute a feature it must acquire locks and it must wait until the wait condition is satisfied. A locking request encapsulates these two requirements; it consists of the requested locks and the wait condition. At every moment, multiple processors can have conflicting locking requests. The scheduler is the arbiter for these conflicts. The scheduler takes locking requests and stores them in a queue. It then approves locking requests according to a certain scheduling algorithm.

The model permits a number of possible scheduling algorithms. The algorithms differ in their level of fairness and their performance. This formalization does not focus on a particular scheduling algorithm. Instead, it uses the conditions of the inference rules to express locking requests. If more than one processor satisfies the conditions, then any of these processors can proceed.

5.2   Initial Configuration

The initial configuration is defined by the SCOOP program. Each SCOOP program defines a root class type c and a root procedure f. The root procedure is a creation procedure of the root class type that has no formal arguments and no precondition.

In the beginning, the runtime generates a bootstrap processor p and root processor q with a root object of the root class type. The request queue of the root processor is locked on behalf of the bootstrap processor. This defines our initial state σ:

$$\sigma_x \stackrel{def}{=} new\ \textbf{STATE}.make$$
$$\sigma_y \stackrel{def}{=} \sigma_x.add\_proc(\sigma_x.new\_proc)$$
$$p \stackrel{def}{=} \sigma_y.last\_added\_proc$$
$$\sigma_z \stackrel{def}{=} \sigma_y.add\_proc(\sigma_y.new\_proc)$$
$$q \stackrel{def}{=} \sigma_z.last\_added\_proc$$
$$\sigma_w \stackrel{def}{=} \sigma_z.add\_obj(q, \sigma_z.new\_obj(c))$$
$$r \stackrel{def}{=} \sigma_w.ref(\sigma_w.last\_added\_obj)$$
$$\sigma \stackrel{def}{=} \sigma_w.lock\_rqs(p, \{q\})$$

The bootstrap processor first asks the root processor to execute the root procedure on the root object and then asks the root processor to unlock its request queue as soon as it finished the execution. The bootstrap processor can do this because it has the request queue lock on the root processor. Finally, the bootstrap processor removes the request queue lock from its stack of obtained request queue locks. This is shown in the following initial configuration:

$$
\begin{aligned}
\langle \\
\quad &p :: \mathtt{call}(r, f, (), ()); \\
\quad &\quad \mathtt{issue}(q, \mathtt{unlock}); \\
\quad &\quad \mathtt{pop\_obtained\_rq\_locks} \mid \\
\quad &q :: \\
, \\
\quad &\sigma \\
\rangle
\end{aligned}
$$

The statements `call`, `issue`, `unlock`, and `pop_obtained_rq_locks` are operations. In a nutshell, the `call`$(r, f, (), ())$ operation asks the handler of the target r to make a call to the feature f on target r. The `unlock` operation unlocks the request queue of the processor that executes the operation. The `issue`$(q, \mathtt{unlock})$ operation adds the `unlock` operation to q's action queue. The `pop_obtained_rq_locks` operation removes the top element from the stack of obtained request queue locks.

5.3 Mechanisms

Mechanisms are the machinery for the execution of code elements. This section studies these mechanisms.

Issuing mechanism. With the issuing mechanism, a processor p can add statements to the action queue of a processor q. It uses the `issue` operation to get a result configuration in which a processor's action queue is extended with the new statements. There are two main cases: p adds the statements to its own action queue, i.e., $p = q$, or p adds the statements to the action queue of a different processor, i.e., $p \neq q$. The first case is the non-separate case and the second one is the separate case.

For the non-separate case p puts the statements to the beginning of q's action queue, which is the same as putting the statements on top of the call stack. This requires that p is in possession of its own call stack lock.

Issue Operation – Non-Separate

$$
\frac{
\begin{array}{c}
q = p \\
\neg \sigma.locks\_passed(p) \\
\sigma.cs\_locks(p).has(q)
\end{array}
}{
\Gamma \vdash \langle p :: \mathtt{issue}(q, s_w); s_p, \sigma \rangle \to \langle p :: s_w; s_p, \sigma \rangle
}
$$

For the separate case there is a difference between a normal and a callback case. In the normal case, p adds the statements to the end of q's action queue. This case requires that p is in possession of q's request queue lock. To distinguish the normal case from the callback case, this case also requires that q does not have a lock on p.

Issue Operation – Separate

$$
\frac{
\begin{array}{c}
q \neq p \\
\neg \sigma.locks\_passed(p) \\
\sigma.rq\_locks(p).has(q) \\
\neg(\sigma.rq\_locks(q).has(p) \vee \sigma.cs\_locks(q).has(p))
\end{array}
}{
\Gamma \vdash \langle p :: \mathtt{issue}(q, s_w); s_p \mid q :: s_q, \sigma \rangle \to \langle p :: s_p \mid q :: s_q; s_w, \sigma \rangle
}
$$

The callback case occurs if q has a lock on p. In this situation, p could issue a statement s_w on q and then wait for q to complete. On the other side, processor q could already be waiting for p to complete. Processor q would be waiting for p to finish and p would be waiting for q to finish. However, since s_w would be at the end of q's action queue and q would be waiting there cannot be any progress. This type of deadlock can be prevented by adding s_w not to the of q's action queue but to the beginning. This will make sure that q can execute the statement right away and hence p can continue. This in return will enable q to continue. As a prerequisite, p must possess q's call stack lock.

Issue Operation – Separate Callback

$$q \neq p$$
$$\neg \sigma.locks\_passed(p)$$
$$\sigma.cs\_locks(p).has(q)$$
$$\sigma.rq\_locks(q).has(p) \vee \sigma.cs\_locks(q).has(p)$$
$$\overline{\Gamma \vdash \langle p :: \mathtt{issue}(q, s_w); s_p \mid q :: s_q, \sigma \rangle \rightarrow \langle p :: s_p \mid q :: s_w; s_q, \sigma \rangle}$$

Delegated execution mechanism. This section discusses how a processor q can delegate the execution of statements to a different processor p. This mechanism is useful for the evaluation of asynchronous postconditions. Processor q must make sure that the statements make sense in the context of processor p. The names that occur in these statements must be defined in the top environment of p and p must have the necessary locks to execute the statements. Statements that fulfill the following conditions can be delegated:

- All names that occur in the statements are defined in q's top environment.
- Their execution only requires the top set of q's stack of obtained request queue locks.

These conditions exclude statements that involve non-separate calls or separate callbacks because such calls require a call stack lock. If these conditions are met, q can transfer its top environment and the top of its obtained request queue locks to p. Given this context, p can then execute the delegated statements instead of q.

The $\mathtt{execute\_delegated}(s_w, x, \{q_1, \ldots, q_m\})$ operation sets up a new context on p with an environment x and obtained request queue locks $\{q_1, \ldots, q_m\}$. To set up the new context, the operation uses a combination of the commands *push_env* and *delegate_obtained_rq_locks*. The command *delegate_obtained_rq_locks* requires that the request queue locks $\{q_1, \ldots, q_m\}$ are not in possession of another processor anymore. It also requires that the request queues of $\{q_1, \ldots, q_m\}$ are locked. Once the context is set up, processor p executes the statements s_w and then gets rid of the context, using the $\mathtt{leave\_delegated}$ operation.

To delegate the execution of the statements s_w, processor q must make sure that its top environment x is set up correctly and it must make sure that the top set of its obtained request queue locks contains all locks $\{q_1, \ldots, q_m\}$ that are necessary for the execution of s_w. Processor q must then issue a $\mathtt{execute\_delegated}(s_w, x, \{q_1, \ldots, q_m\})$ operation to processor p. Processor q must then remove $\{q_1, \ldots, q_m\}$ from its stack of obtained request queue locks so that the *delegate_obtained_rq_locks* operation can take place.

Execute Delegated Operation

$$\forall x \in \{q_1, \ldots, q_m\}: \neg \exists y \in \sigma.procs: \sigma.rq\_locks(y).has(x)$$
$$\forall x \in \{q_1, \ldots, q_m\}: \sigma.rq\_locked(x)$$
$$\sigma' \overset{def}{=} \sigma.push\_env(p,x).delegate\_obtained\_rq\_locks(p, \{q_1, \ldots, q_m\})$$
$$\overline{\Gamma \vdash \langle p :: \texttt{execute\_delegated}(s_w, x, \{q_1, \ldots, q_m\}); s_p, \sigma \rangle \rightarrow}$$
$$\langle p :: s_w; \texttt{leave\_delegated}; s_p, \sigma' \rangle$$

Leave Delegated Execution Operation

$$\neg \sigma.envs(p).is\_empty$$
$$\neg \sigma.obtained\_rq\_locks(p).is\_empty$$
$$\sigma' \overset{def}{=} \sigma.pop\_env(p).pop\_obtained\_rq\_locks(p)$$
$$\overline{\Gamma \vdash \langle p :: \texttt{leave\_delegated}; s_p, \sigma \rangle \rightarrow \langle p :: s_p, \sigma' \rangle}$$

Notification mechanism. Processors can notify each other. A notification can option-ally include a value. The formalization uses channels to describe such communication. Channels are described in Milner's π-calculus [23]. In the π-calculus, the expression $c(x).P$ denotes a process that is waiting for a notification sent on a channel c. Once the notification has been received, the value of the notification is bound to the variable x and the process continues with the expression P. The notification comes from a process that executes $\bar{c}y.Q$ to emit the value y on the channel c before executing Q.

The formalization reuses the channel idea in two flavors: once as a notification mech-anism with a value and once as a notification mechanism without a value. A proces-sor sends a notification with a value r over a channel a as it executes the operation $\texttt{result}(a,r)$. Similarly, the process sends a notification without a value over a channel a by executing the operation $\texttt{notify}(a)$. For both cases, any processor can wait for a notification by executing the operation $\texttt{wait}(a)$. In case a notification on a channel a carries a value, the value can be accessed with $a.data$. This way of accessing the value of a channel is different from the way it is done in the π-calculus. In the π-calculus, each value is bound to a variable. This formalization does not define a new variable for the value. Instead, it uses $a.data$ to identify the value of a channel a.

A number of inference rules describe the interaction between a processor that sent a notification over a channel and a processor that is waiting for a notification over the same channel. Two main cases can be distinguished: either a processor sends a noti-fication to itself or it sends a notification to a different processor. The first case is the non-separate case and the latter case is the separate case. In each of these two main cases, the channel carries a notification with or without a value. For each of these sub cases, there is one inference rule.

In the non-separate case, one processor has a $\texttt{result}(a,r)$ operation or a $\texttt{notify}(a)$ operation at the beginning of its action queue and a $\texttt{wait}(a)$ operation on the same channel later in the action queue. In this case, the $\texttt{wait}(a)$ operation can be removed along with the $\texttt{result}(a,r)$ operation, respectively the $\texttt{notify}(a)$ operation. If the channel carries a value, then the value must be installed on the processor, by substituting all occurrences of $a.data$ with the posted value in all the statements s_p after the $\texttt{wait}(a)$ operation.

Wait and Result Operation – Non-Separate

$$\Gamma \vdash \langle p :: \text{result}(a,r); s_w; \text{wait}(a); s_p, \sigma \rangle \rightarrow \langle p :: s_w; s_p[r/a.data], \sigma \rangle$$

Wait and Notify Operation – Non-Separate

$$\Gamma \vdash \langle p :: \text{notify}(a); s_w; \text{wait}(a); s_p, \sigma \rangle \rightarrow \langle p :: s_w; s_p, \sigma \rangle$$

In the separate case, one processor has a $\text{result}(a,r)$ or a $\text{notify}(a)$ operation at the beginning of its action queue and a different processor has a $\text{wait}(a)$ somewhere in its action queue. In this situation, the $\text{wait}(a)$, $\text{result}(a,r)$, and $\text{notify}(a)$ can be removed from the action queues. In case the notification has a value, the value can be installed in the statements s_p, after the $\text{wait}(a)$ operation.

Wait and Result Operation – Separate

$$\Gamma \vdash \langle p :: s_w; \text{wait}(a); s_p \mid q :: \text{result}(a,r); s_q, \sigma \rangle \rightarrow \langle p :: s_w; s_p[r/a.data] \mid q :: s_q, \sigma \rangle$$

Wait and Notify Operation – Separate

$$\Gamma \vdash \langle p :: s_w; \text{wait}(a); s_p \mid q :: \text{notify}(a); s_q, \sigma \rangle \rightarrow \langle p :: s_w; s_p \mid q :: s_q, \sigma \rangle$$

The operations presented here must be used so that each wait operation can be resolved with exactly one result or notify operation. To define this condition more precisely, we define that one statement s_1 weakly precedes a statement s_2 if and only if s_1 occurs earlier than s_2 in the same action queue or s_1 and s_2 occur in different action queues. One statement s_1 strongly precedes a statement s_1 if and only if s_1 occurs earlier than s_2 in the same action queue. With these definitions, the condition says:

- For each $\text{wait}(a)$ operation there must be either exactly one $\text{result}(a,r)$ or exactly one $\text{notify}(a)$ operation.
- For each $\text{result}(a,r)$ or $\text{notify}(a)$ operation there must be exactly one $\text{wait}(a)$ operation.
- Each $\text{result}(a,r)$ or $\text{notify}(a)$ operation weakly precedes the $\text{wait}(a)$ operation.

Expression evaluation mechanism. An expression can either be a literal, an entity, or a query call. The query call can contain actual arguments that are expressions themselves. This section discusses the general mechanism to evaluate expressions. It focuses on the general approach and defers the evaluation of particular expressions to later sections.

The operation $\text{eval}(a,e)$ takes a channel a and an expression e. Each $\text{eval}(a,e)$ operation determines the value r of the expression e and then sends a notification with value r on channel a. This means that each $\text{eval}(a,e)$ operation creates a $\text{result}(a,r)$ operation in the action queue. It is therefore important to follow each $\text{eval}(a,e)$ operation with exactly one $\text{wait}(a)$ to receive the notification with the value.

Locking and unlocking mechanism. A processor p that wants to execute a feature must first obtain the request queue locks of a number of processors $\{q_1, \ldots, q_n\}$. For this, p adds $\{q_1, \ldots, q_n\}$ on top of its obtained request queue locks stack. Only then can p issue statements to these processors. The $\texttt{lock}(\{q_1, \ldots, q_n\})$ operation serves this purpose. The operation requires that none of the request queues is already locked.

Lock Operation

$$\frac{\neg \exists q_i \in \{q_1, \ldots, q_m\} \colon \sigma.rq\_locked(q_i) \qquad \sigma' \stackrel{def}{=} \sigma.lock\_rqs(p, \{q_1, \ldots, q_m\})}{\Gamma \vdash \langle p :: \texttt{lock}(\{q_1, \ldots, q_m\}); s_p, \sigma \rangle \rightarrow \langle p :: s_p, \sigma' \rangle}$$

Once p is done with the execution of the feature, it asks $\{q_1, \ldots, q_n\}$ to unlock their request queues once they are done with the issued statements. For this purpose, the $\texttt{unlock}$ operation unlocks the request queue. Processor p issues the $\texttt{unlock}$ operation to processors $\{q_1, \ldots, q_n\}$. This operation requires that the request queue is indeed locked and that no processor possesses the request queue lock.

Unlock Operation

$$\frac{\sigma.rq\_locked(p) \qquad \forall q \in \sigma.procs \colon \neg\sigma.rq\_locks(q).has(p) \qquad \sigma' \stackrel{def}{=} \sigma.unlock\_rq(p)}{\Gamma \vdash \langle p :: \texttt{unlock}; s_p, \sigma \rangle \rightarrow \langle p :: s_p, \sigma' \rangle}$$

After p issued the $\texttt{unlock}$ operations, it can remove $\{q_1, \ldots, q_n\}$ from its stack of obtained request queue locks using the $\texttt{pop\_obtained\_rq\_locks}$ operation. This ensures that the $\texttt{unlock}$ operations can proceed.

Pop Obtained Request Queue Locks

$$\frac{\sigma' \stackrel{def}{=} \sigma.pop\_obtained\_rq\_locks(p)}{\Gamma \vdash \langle p :: \texttt{pop\_obtained\_rq\_locks}; s_p, \sigma \rangle \rightarrow \langle p :: s_p, \sigma' \rangle}$$

Brooke, Paige, and Jacob [5] noticed that $\texttt{unlock}$ operations are not optimal. In essence, it could be possible to unlock the request queue of a processor q_i directly after p issued all statements. The request queue lock is important to guarantee exclusive access on q_i's request queue. However, as soon as p issued all statements on q_i, this lock is no longer needed. Unlocking the request queue right away could improve the performance in some situations because q_i's request queue could be locked again earlier and hence another processor that is waiting for this lock could proceed earlier.

Write and read mechanism. A processor p can use the $\texttt{write}(x, v)$ operation to set a value v of an entity with name x. This operation uses the set_val command. Hence, p can both set attribute values of its current object and values of entities in its top environment.

Write Value Operation

$$\frac{\sigma' \stackrel{def}{=} \sigma.set\_val(p, x, v)}{\Gamma \vdash \langle p :: \texttt{write}(x, v); s_p, \sigma \rangle \rightarrow \langle p :: s_p, \sigma' \rangle}$$

Similarly, processor p can execute the $\text{read}(x,a)$ operation to read a value of an entity with name x and send the value over channel a. The read operation does not present its result in a result operation because, unlike an eval operation, a read operation always produces a result for the surrounding action queue. It is easier to do the substitution of the channel access directly. A later section introduces the eval operation for entity expressions. This variant of the eval operation makes use of the read operation and presents the result in a result operation.

Read Value Operation

$$\Gamma \vdash \langle p :: \text{read}(x,a); s_p, \sigma \rangle \rightarrow \langle p :: s_p[\sigma.val(p,x)/a.data], \sigma \rangle$$

Finally, there is the set_not_fresh operation in a variant for once functions and in a variant for once procedures. This operation sets the once status of a once routine. The variant set_not_fresh(f,r) sets the once status of a once function f to non-fresh with value r. If f is of separate type, then the once function becomes non-fresh on all processors in the system. If f has a non-separate type, then f becomes non-fresh only on processor p. The variant set_not_fresh(f) sets the once status of a once procedure f to non-fresh on processor p.

Set Once Routine Not Fresh Operation – Function

$$\frac{f \in \textbf{FUNCTION} \wedge f.is\_once \\ \sigma' \overset{def}{=} \sigma.set\_once\_func\_not\_fresh(p,f,r)}{\Gamma \vdash \langle p :: \text{set\_not\_fresh}(f,r); s_p, \sigma \rangle \rightarrow \langle p :: s_p, \sigma' \rangle}$$

Set Once Routine Not Fresh Operation – Procedure

$$\frac{f \in \textbf{FUNCTION} \wedge f.is\_once \\ \sigma' \overset{def}{=} \sigma.set\_once\_proc\_not\_fresh(p,f)}{\Gamma \vdash \langle p :: \text{set\_not\_fresh}(f); s_p, \sigma \rangle \rightarrow \langle p :: s_p, \sigma' \rangle}$$

Flow control mechanism. In addition to flow control instructions in the user code, there are flow control operations, which implement flow control in the inference rules. This way, fewer inference rules are required because multiple variants can be handled in one inference rule.

The provided x then s_t else s_f end operation takes the condition x as an argument. The operation either executes s_t if x indicates that the condition is true or s_f if x indicates that the condition is false. For each possibility there is one inference rule. The condition x can either be an instance of **BOOLEAN** or it can be a reference that points to an object of class type *BOOLEAN*. To decide which branch to take, the operation must evaluate x. If x is an instance of **BOOLEAN**, then it can determine which instance x is, i.e., *true* or *false*. If x is a reference, then it must get the referenced object and see which boolean value it represents. For this purpose, it evaluates the attribute *item* of the referenced object.

If Operation – True

$$y \stackrel{def}{=} \begin{cases} x & if x \in \textbf{BOOLEAN} \\ \sigma.att\_val(\sigma.ref\_obj(x), item) & if x \in \textbf{REF} \wedge \sigma.ref\_obj(x).class\_type = BOOLEAN \\ false & otherwise \end{cases}$$
$$y = true$$

$$\overline{\Gamma \vdash \langle p :: \text{ provided } x \text{ then } s_t \text{ else } s_f \text{ end}; s_p, \sigma \rangle \rightarrow \langle p :: s_t; s_p, \sigma \rangle}$$

If Operation – False

$$y \stackrel{def}{=} \begin{cases} x & if x \in \textbf{BOOLEAN} \\ \sigma.att\_val(\sigma.ref\_obj(x), item) & if x \in \textbf{REF} \wedge \sigma.ref\_obj(x).class\_type = BOOLEAN \\ true & otherwise \end{cases}$$
$$y = false$$

$$\overline{\Gamma \vdash \langle p :: \text{ provided } x \text{ then } s_t \text{ else } s_f \text{ end}; s_p, \sigma \rangle \rightarrow \langle p :: s_f; s_p, \sigma \rangle}$$

The provided x then s_t else s_f end operation has two branches. Sometimes it is necessary to only have one branch. The nop operation can be executed without an effect. It can be used in the conditional operation to define an empty branch. The nop operation can also be used to indicate that an action queue is empty.

No Operation

$$\overline{\Gamma \vdash \langle p :: \text{nop}; s_p, \sigma \rangle \rightarrow \langle p :: s_p, \sigma \rangle}$$

5.4 Code Elements

This section explains the semantics of code elements: entity expressions, literal expressions, feature calls, feature applications, creation instructions, flow control instructions, and assignment instructions.

Entity expressions. A variant of the eval(a, e) operation evaluates entity expressions. The operation uses the read operation to send a notification with the value of the entity over a new channel a'. It then uses the value of this channel to define the result of the eval operation.

Entity Expression

$$\frac{e \in \textbf{ENTITY} \\ a' \text{ is fresh}}{\Gamma \vdash \langle p :: \text{eval}(a, e); s_p, \sigma \rangle \rightarrow \langle p :: \text{read}(e.name, a'); \text{result}(a, a'.data); s_p, \sigma \rangle}$$

Literal expressions. Another variant of the eval(a, e) operation evaluates literal expressions. To evaluate a non-void literal expression, the operation creates a new object of the literal class type so that the new object represents the literal value. For this purpose, it uses the query *obj* of **LITERAL**. Since the type of every literal is non-separate, it creates the new object on the processor that evaluates the literal expression. The reference r to the new object is the result of the evaluation. To evaluate a void literal, the operation takes the void reference.

Literal Expression

$$e \in \textbf{LITERAL}$$

$$\sigma' \overset{def}{=} \begin{cases} \sigma & if\ e = \textbf{Void} \\ \sigma.add\_obj(p, e.obj) & otherwise \end{cases}$$

$$r \overset{def}{=} \begin{cases} void & if\ e = \textbf{Void} \\ \sigma'.ref(\sigma'.last\_added\_obj) & otherwise \end{cases}$$

$$\Gamma \vdash \langle p :: \texttt{eval}(a, e); s_p, \sigma \rangle \rightarrow \langle p :: \texttt{result}(a, r); s_p, \sigma' \rangle$$

Feature calls. A feature call can occur in two ways. First, a feature call can be a call to a command in a command instruction. Second, a feature call can be a call to a query in an expression. This section studies both variants. A processor p that executes a feature call $e_0.f(e_1, \ldots, e_n)$ goes through the following steps:

1. Target evaluation. Evaluate the target expression e_0 and let q denote the handler of the target.
2. Argument passing. Evaluate the actual arguments expressions $(e_1, \ldots, e_n)$.
3. Lock passing. Determine which locks to pass to q.
   - Take all request queue locks and call stack locks if a controlled actual argument gets attached to an attached formal argument of reference type.
   - Take all request queue locks and call stack locks if the feature call is a separate callback, i.e., q has a lock on p.
   - Otherwise, take no locks.
4. Feature request.
   - Ask q to apply f to the target immediately and wait until the execution terminates if any of the following conditions holds:
     - The feature call is non-separate, i.e., $p = q$.
     - The feature call is a separate callback, i.e., q has a lock on p.
   - Otherwise, ask q to apply f to the target after the previous feature requests.
5. Wait by necessity. If f is a query, then wait for the result.
6. Lock revocation. If lock passing happened, then wait for the locks to come back.

A command instruction is a statement in the action queue. A query is an expression on the right hand side of an assignment, a condition in a flow control instruction, or an actual argument in a feature call. Whenever a query occurs in one of these constructs, the inference rule of the construct encloses the query in an `eval` operation. To handle feature calls, there is an inference rule for command instructions and a variant of the `eval` operation for query calls.

In each case, the statement first evaluates the target expression and all actual argument expressions e_i, it uses one `eval`(a_{e_i}, e_i) operation and a corresponding `wait`(a_{e_i}) operation with a fresh channel a_{e_i}. Each of the channel values gets used in the subsequent `call` operation. With this, the statement handled the target evaluation and the argument passing step. It defers the attachment of the actual arguments to the formal arguments to the point where the called feature gets applied. The reason for this is simple: at this point the context for the feature application does not exist yet.

The `call` operation takes care of the remaining steps. The operation exists in two variants, one for command instructions and one for queries. The variant for queries takes a channel a' and uses it for the result of the query. Since a call to a command does not produce a result, such a channel is not required for command instructions. Both call variants take the reference to the target a_{e_0}, the feature f to be called, the references to the actual arguments $(a_{e_1}.data, \ldots, a_{e_n}.data)$, and the actual argument expressions $(e_1, \ldots, e_n)$. The actual argument expressions are used to check whether there is a controlled actual argument. This information determines whether the locks should be passed.

Command Instruction

$$\frac{\forall i \in \{0, \ldots, n\} : a_{e_i} \text{ is fresh}}{\begin{aligned} \Gamma \vdash \langle p :: e_0.f(e_1, \ldots, e_n); s_p, \sigma \rangle \to \\ \langle p :: \texttt{eval}(a_{e_0}, e_0); \texttt{eval}(a_{e_1}, e_1); \ldots; \texttt{eval}(a_{e_n}, e_n); \\ \texttt{wait}(a_{e_0}); \texttt{wait}(a_{e_1}); \ldots; \texttt{wait}(a_{e_n}); \\ \texttt{call}(a_{e_0}.data, f, (a_{e_1}.data, \ldots, a_{e_n}.data), (e_1, \ldots, e_n)); \\ s_p, \sigma \rangle \end{aligned}}$$

Query Expression

$$\frac{\begin{array}{c} \forall i \in \{0, \ldots, n\} : a_{e_i} \text{ is fresh} \\ a' \text{ is fresh} \end{array}}{\begin{aligned} \Gamma \vdash \langle p :: \texttt{eval}(a, e_0.f(e_1, \ldots, e_n)); s_p, \sigma \rangle \to \\ \langle p :: \texttt{eval}(a_{e_0}, e_0); \texttt{eval}(a_{e_1}, e_1); \ldots; \texttt{eval}(a_{e_n}, e_n); \\ \texttt{wait}(a_{e_0}); \texttt{wait}(a_{e_1}); \ldots; \texttt{wait}(a_{e_n}); \\ \texttt{call}(a', a_{e_0}.data, f, (a_{e_1}.data, \ldots, a_{e_n}.data), (e_1, \ldots, e_n)); \\ \texttt{result}(a, a'.data); \\ s_p, \sigma \rangle \end{aligned}}$$

Both variants of the call operation take the reference to the target r_o, the feature f to be called, the references to the actual arguments $(r_1, \ldots, r_n)$, and the actual argument expressions $(e_1, \ldots, e_n)$. The variant for queries takes an additional channel a to be used for the result of the query. In a first step, the operation must evaluate the handler q of the target. The handler is used in an issue operation to issue a feature request on the responsible processor. The feature request comes in the form of an apply operation. The apply operation takes a channel a for the communication between p and q, the target reference r_0, the called feature f, the references to the actual arguments $(r_1, \ldots, r_n)$, the caller processor p, and the passed locks $\bar{l}$.

Clarification 3 (Lock passing). Processor p passes all its request queue locks and all its call stack locks either if there is a controlled actual argument that will get attached to an attached formal argument of reference type or if the feature call is a separate callback. An attached formal argument of reference type means that the request queue lock or the call stack lock on the actual argument's handler is required during the application of f. A controlled actual argument means that p has a request queue lock or a call stack lock on the handler of the actual argument. In short, p has a lock that is required by q and thus p has to pass the locks. A separate callback occurs if q has a lock on p. In this situation, p can issue a statement to q and then wait for q to complete. However, processor q could already be waiting for p to complete. To handle this case, the issue operation in the call operation triggers an immediate execution by adding the apply to the beginning of q's action queue. The issue operation requires that p has the call stack lock of q. To enable q to perform an immediate execution, p has to give back q's call stack lock.

In both cases, p has to wait for the locks to come back. Thus it does not hurt to pass all the locks in both cases. In contrast to Nienaltowski's [25] description of SCOOP, p only passes the locks that it really has. In particular, p does not pass its own request queue lock in situations where p does not possess this lock, such as when the processor that called p possesses p's request queue lock.   □

In the cases where the operation passes the locks, $\bar{l}$ is $(\sigma.rq\_locks(p), \sigma.cs\_locks(p))$. In all other cases there is no lock passing and thus $\bar{l} = (\{\}, \{\})$. The operation just determines which locks to pass. The actual lock passing action will be executed by q. Similarly, the actual lock revocation action will be executed by q.

For command calls, lock passing is the only reason to wait. In this case, the operation creates a fresh channel a to wait for a notification from q. The notification arrives when q is ready to return the locks. For query calls, the operation has to wait for the result. The operation uses the given channel a to wait for the result. This has the advantage that once the result arrives, it will be substituted after the `call` operation, i.e. in the `result` operation of the `eval` operation.

Call Operation – Command

$q \stackrel{def}{=} \sigma.handler(r_0)$

$\bar{l} \stackrel{def}{=} \begin{cases} if \\ \quad q \neq p \wedge \exists i \in \{1,\ldots,n\} : \Gamma \vdash e_i : t \wedge controlled(t) \wedge \Gamma \vdash f.formals(i) : (!,g,c) \wedge c.is\_ref \\ then \\ \quad (\sigma.rq\_locks(p), \sigma.cs\_locks(p)) \\ if \\ \quad q \neq p \wedge (\sigma.rq\_locks(q).has(p) \vee \sigma.cs\_locks(q).has(p)) \\ then \\ \quad (\sigma.rq\_locks(p), \sigma.cs\_locks(p)) \\ otherwise \\ \quad (\{\}, \{\}) \end{cases}$

$a\ is\ fresh$

$\Gamma \vdash \langle p :: \mathtt{call}(r_0, f, (r_1,\ldots,r_n), (e_1,\ldots,e_n)); s_p, \sigma \rangle \rightarrow$
$\qquad \langle p :: \mathtt{issue}(q, \mathtt{apply}(a, r_0, f, (r_1,\ldots,r_n), p, \bar{l}));$
$\qquad\qquad \mathtt{provided}\ \bar{l} \neq (\{\}, \{\})\ \mathtt{then\ wait}(a)\ \mathtt{else\ nop\ end};$
$\qquad\qquad s_p, \sigma \rangle$

Call Operation – Query

$q \stackrel{def}{=} \sigma.handler(r_0)$

$\bar{l} \stackrel{def}{=} \begin{cases} if \\ \quad q \neq p \wedge \exists i \in \{1,\ldots,n\} : \Gamma \vdash e_i : t \wedge controlled(t) \wedge \Gamma \vdash f.formals(i) : (!,g,c) \wedge c.is\_ref \\ then \\ \quad (\sigma.rq\_locks(p), \sigma.cs\_locks(p)) \\ if \\ \quad q \neq p \wedge (\sigma.rq\_locks(q).has(p) \vee \sigma.cs\_locks(q).has(p)) \\ then \\ \quad (\sigma.rq\_locks(p), \sigma.cs\_locks(p)) \\ otherwise \\ \quad (\{\}, \{\}) \end{cases}$

$\Gamma \vdash \langle p :: \mathtt{call}(a, r_0, f, (r_1,\ldots,r_n), (e_1,\ldots,e_n)); s_p, \sigma \rangle \rightarrow$
$\qquad \langle p :: \mathtt{issue}(q, \mathtt{apply}(a, r_0, f, (r_1,\ldots,r_n), p, \bar{l})); \mathtt{wait}(a); s_p, \sigma \rangle$

Feature applications. A feature call by a client processor q results in a feature request for a supplier processor p. A *feature application* is the serving of the feature request. This section discusses how p applies a feature f on a target referenced by r_0. Processor p takes the following steps:

1. Once status update. If f is a once routine, then set its status to non-fresh.
2. Lock passing. Pass the locks from q to p.
3. Argument passing. Bind the actual arguments to the formal arguments. Arguments of expanded type that are handled by a different processor than p must be deep imported by p.
4. Synchronization. Involve the scheduler to wait until the following synchronization conditions are satisfied atomically:

   – Processor p owns the request queue lock of each processor q such that:

     • Processor q handles an actual argument of f and the corresponding formal argument has an attached reference type.
     • Processor p and processor q are different.
     • Processor p does not have q's request queue lock.
     • Processor q does not have p's request queue lock.

   – The precondition of f holds.

5. Execution.

   – If f is a non-once routine or a fresh once routine, then run its body.
   – If f is a non-fresh procedure, then do nothing. If f is a non-fresh function, then take its once value as the result.
   – If f is an attribute, then evaluate it.

6. Postcondition evaluation. Evaluate the postcondition if any of the following conditions is satisfied:

   – A feature call in the postcondition requires a lock that was not obtained in the synchronization step.
   – The evaluation of the postcondition involves lock passing.

   Otherwise ask any processor whose request queue lock was obtained in the synchronization step to evaluate the postcondition.
7. Lock releasing. Ask each processor whose request queue has been locked in the synchronization step to unlock its request queue after it is done with the feature requests issued by p.
8. Invariant evaluation. If f is a routine, then evaluate the invariant.

9. Result returning. If f is a query, then return the result to q. If the result is of expanded type and $p \neq q$, then the result must be deep imported by q.
10. Lock revocation. Return the passed locks from p to q.

Each feature application starts with an operation $\mathtt{apply}(a, r_0, f, (r_1, \ldots, r_n), q, \bar{l})$ in the action queue of processor p. The channel a is used to communicate with the client processor q. If the called feature f is a procedure and the caller processor q passed some locks, then a is used to signal that the locks returned. If f is query, then a is used to return the value. The reference r_0 points to the target of the call. The references $(r_1, \ldots, r_n)$ point to the actual arguments. The tuple $\bar{l}$ contains the locks to be passed from q to p.

If one takes a look at the execution step, one can differentiate three cases:

- The feature f is a non-once routine or a fresh once routine.
- The feature f is a non-fresh once routine.
- The feature f is an attribute.

For each of these cases, there is one inference rule. Each inference rule covers one variant of the $\mathtt{apply}$ operation. The discussion continues with the most involved case: the feature f is a non-once routine or a fresh once routine.

The condition of the inference rule states that each processor can only apply a feature on one of its own objects. The condition also states the p must not have passed its locks. This part of the condition is always given because p waits whenever it passes its locks. In a first step, the operation defines an updated state σ' to set f's once status to nonfresh, in case f is a once routine. The operation does this before deep importing the actual arguments to avoid the following contradiction.

Clarification 4 (When to change the status of a fresh once routine). Assume f is either a once procedure or a non-separate once routine. The feature f was fresh at the beginning of the $\mathtt{apply}$ operation. Assume that the caller passed an expanded actual argument that is handled by a processor $g \neq p$. Therefore p has to deep import the actual argument. Assume furthermore that the class type of the actual argument has the once routine f and that f is non-fresh on g. If the operation would deep import before setting f as non-fresh on p, then the deep import operation would take over the once status of f from processor g to processor p. But then the $\mathtt{apply}$ operation on p would not make much sense anymore because f would now be non-fresh on p. If the operation sets f as non-fresh at the beginning of the $\mathtt{apply}$ operation, then the deep import operation does not take over the once status from g because f is already non-fresh on p.   □

The operation defines an updated state σ'' in which the locks are passed from q to p and in which there is a new environment with the actual arguments $(r_1, \ldots, r_n)$. The call to the *push_env_with_feature* feature takes care of copying and deep importing actual arguments of expanded type. The caller processor q can also pass an empty tuple $(\{\}, \{\})$ which simply means that q did not pass any locks.

Application Operation – Non-Once Routine or Fresh Once Routine

$f \in \textbf{ROUTINE} \wedge f.is\_once \rightarrow \sigma.is\_fresh(p,f)$
$\sigma.handler(r_0) = p$
$\neg \sigma.locks\_passed(p)$
$\sigma' \stackrel{def}{=} \begin{cases} \sigma.set\_once\_func\_not\_fresh(p,f,void) & if f \in \textbf{FUNCTION} \wedge f.is\_once \\ \sigma.set\_once\_proc\_not\_fresh(p,f) & if f \in \textbf{PROCEDURE} \wedge f.is\_once \\ \sigma & otherwise \end{cases}$
$\sigma'' \stackrel{def}{=} \sigma'.pass\_locks(q,p,\bar{l}).push\_env\_with\_feature(p,f,r_0,(r_1,\ldots,r_n))$
$\overline{g}_{required\_locks} \stackrel{def}{=} \{p\} \cup$
    $\{x \in \textbf{PROC} \mid \exists i \in \{1,\ldots,n\},g,c\colon \Gamma \vdash f.formals(i)\colon (!,g,c) \wedge c.is\_ref \wedge x = \sigma''.handler(r_i)\}$
$\overline{g}_{required\_cs\_locks} \stackrel{def}{=}$
    $\{x \in \overline{g}_{required\_locks} \mid x = p \vee (x \neq p \wedge (\sigma''.rq\_locks(x).has(p) \vee \sigma''.cs\_locks(x).has(p)))\}$
$\overline{g}_{required\_rq\_locks} \stackrel{def}{=} \overline{g}_{required\_locks} \setminus \overline{g}_{required\_cs\_locks}$
$\overline{g}_{missing\_rq\_locks} \stackrel{def}{=} \{x \in \overline{g}_{required\_rq\_locks} \mid \neg \sigma''.rq\_locks(p).has(x)\}$
$\forall x \in \overline{g}_{required\_cs\_locks}\colon \sigma''.cs\_locks(p).has(x)$
$a_{inv}\ is\ fresh \wedge a'\ is\ fresh$

$\Gamma \vdash \langle p :: \texttt{apply}(a,r_0,f,(r_1,\ldots,r_n),q,\bar{l}); s_p, \sigma \rangle \rightarrow$
    $\langle p :: \texttt{check\_pre\_and\_lock\_rqs}(\overline{g}_{missing\_rq\_locks},f);$
        provided $f \in \textbf{FUNCTION} \wedge f.is\_once$ then
            $f.body$
                $[result := y; \texttt{read}(\textbf{Result},a_r); \texttt{set\_not\_fresh}(f,a_r.data)$ **where** $a_r\ is\ fresh/$
                    $result := y]$
                $[\textbf{create}\ result.y; \texttt{read}(\textbf{Result},a_r); \texttt{set\_not\_fresh}(f,a_r.data)$ **where** $a_r\ is\ fresh/$
                    $\textbf{create}\ result.y]$
        else
            $f.body$
        end;
        $\texttt{check\_post\_and\_unlock\_rqs}(\overline{g}_{missing\_rq\_locks},f);$
        provided $f.class\_type.inv\_exists \wedge f.exported$ then
            $\texttt{eval}(a_{inv}, f.class\_type.inv); \texttt{wait}(a_{inv})$
        else
            nop
        end;
        provided $f \in \textbf{FUNCTION}$ then
            $\texttt{read}(\textbf{Result},a'); \texttt{return}(a,a'.data,q)$
        else
            $\texttt{return}(a,q)$
        end;
        $s_p, \sigma'' \rangle$

In the next step, the operation synchronizes. For each target expressions in the body of f, the operation can get the controlling entity. Each of these controlling entities is mapped to an object and each of these objects is handled by a processor. For each of these processors the operation must either get a request queue lock or a call stack lock. There are three types of calls: non-separate calls, separate calls, and separate callback. Non-separate calls and separate callbacks require a call stack lock. Separate calls require a request queue lock. This leads to two sets of required locks: one set with required request queue locks and another set with required call stack locks. The set of required call stack locks is composed of p that will lead to a non-separate call and all the processors that will lead to separate callbacks. The set of required request queue locks is composed of the processors that will lead to separate calls. The operation defines two sets for these two categories: $\overline{g}_{required\_cs\_locks}$ and $\overline{g}_{required\_rq\_locks}$.

Each processor initially has its own call stack lock as its obtained call stack lock. This call stack never gets unlocked. This means that other call stack locks cannot be obtained; they must be retrieved through lock passing. The condition of the inference rule expresses this: $\forall x \in \overline{g}_{required\_cs\_locks} : \sigma''.cs\_locks(p).has(x)$. The operation can be assured that p did not pass its own call stack lock because otherwise p would be waiting. The remaining required call stack locks are the ones for the processors that will lead to separate callbacks. Note that the lock passing conditions are not sufficient to guarantee that the call stack locks for separate callbacks are always available.

As for the request queue locks, the operation calculates $\overline{g}_{missing\_rq\_locks}$ as the required request queue locks minus the already owned request queue locks. The already owned request queue locks are the previously obtained request queue locks and the retrieved request queue locks. In the synchronization step, the operation must obtain the difference. If this is not possible because some of the missing request queue locks are not available, then the operation must wait. The check_pre_and_lock_rqs operation takes care of this; it takes $\overline{g}_{missing\_rq\_locks}$ and the feature f. Once the execution succeeds, p has the request queue locks of $\overline{g}_{missing\_rq\_locks}$ and the precondition of f holds.

The apply operation can be assured that each processor g, whose obtained request queue lock the operation got in the synchronization step, must be in possession of its call stack lock. If g was not in possession of its call stack lock, it must have passed its locks. This means that g is executing a feature call and still waiting for the locks to return. In order to execute the feature call, there must have been a lock on g's request queue lock so that its action queue can contain the feature call. The request queue must still be locked because g is still executing the feature call. Hence, it would not have been possible to obtain g's request queue lock. The only exception is the bootstrap processor. However this processor only plays a role in the system setup and it never passes its own call stack lock.

Once the operation got all the required locks, it can execute the body. For once functions it must update the once status whenever it writes to the result entity as part of an assignment instruction or as part of a creation instruction. For this purpose it adds a read operation and a set_not_fresh operation after each assignment instruction or creation instruction. For each assignment instruction or creation instruction it has to use a fresh channel.

After the execution of the body, the operation has to evaluate the postcondition and it has to make sure that the locked request queues get unlocked at the right time. These two steps are performed by another operation check_post_and_unlock_rqs that takes the missing request queue locks $\overline{g}_{missing\_rq\_locks}$ and the feature f. This operation evaluates the postcondition either synchronously or asynchronously. After the evaluation of the postcondition, the operation enqueues an unlock operation to each request queue in $\overline{g}_{missing\_rq\_locks}$.

SCOOP relies on the Eiffel invariant mechanism. This mechanism is described in Sec. 7.5 and Sec. 8.9.16 of the Eiffel ECMA standard [9]. On one hand, Sec. 7.5 describes the semantics of invariants: invariants must be satisfied after the execution of every exported routine and after the execution of every creation procedure. On the other hand, Sec. 8.9.16 describes the runtime monitoring of invariants: invariants get evaluated on both start and termination of a qualified call to a routine and after every call to a creation procedure. We had to decide whether to rely on the semantics of invariants or on the runtime monitoring of invariants. We decided to rely on the semantics of invariants for two reasons. First, the runtime invariant monitoring mechanism is only one possible implementation of the invariant semantics. Second, the runtime invariant monitoring mechanism relies on the notion of unqualified calls. However, for simplicity this work assumes feature calls to be in the canonical qualified form. The `apply` operation reflects this decision: the operation evaluates the invariant whenever f is exported. Note that the invariant can only contain non-separate target expressions. Hence, each call in the invariant will only require p's call stack lock.

Finally, the operation has to return the locks and it has to return the result if f is a function. The `return` operation takes care of this. It comes in a variant for queries and in a variant for commands. Both variants take the channel a and the caller processor q in order to communicate with q. The variant for queries additionally takes the value to be returned to q.

Before explaining the variants of the `apply` operation for non-fresh once routines and attributes, the discussion continues with the operations that have not been discussed in details so far, namely `check_pre_and_lock_rqs`, `check_post_and_unlock_rqs`, and `return`.

Check Precondition and Lock Request Queues Operation

$$\frac{a \text{ is } fresh}{}$$

$\Gamma \vdash \langle p :: \texttt{check\_pre\_and\_lock\_rqs}(\{q_1, \ldots, q_m\}, f); s_p, \sigma \rangle \rightarrow$
$\quad \langle p :: \texttt{lock}(\{q_1, \ldots, q_m\});$
$\qquad \texttt{provided } f.pre\_exists \texttt{ then}$
$\qquad\quad \texttt{eval}(a, f.pre);$
$\qquad\quad \texttt{wait}(a)$
$\qquad \texttt{else}$
$\qquad\quad \texttt{nop}$
$\qquad \texttt{end};$
$\qquad \texttt{provided } \neg f.pre\_exists \vee a.data \texttt{ then}$
$\qquad\quad \texttt{nop}$
$\qquad \texttt{else}$
$\qquad\quad \texttt{issue}(q_1, \texttt{unlock});$
$\qquad\quad \ldots$
$\qquad\quad \texttt{issue}(q_m, \texttt{unlock});$
$\qquad\quad \texttt{pop\_obtained\_rq\_locks};$
$\qquad\quad \texttt{check\_pre\_and\_lock\_rqs}(\{q_1, \ldots, q_m\}, f)$
$\qquad \texttt{end};$
$\qquad s_p, \sigma \rangle$

The `check_pre_and_lock_rqs`$(\{q_1, \ldots, q_m\}, f)$ operation, executed by processor p, takes a processor set $\{q_1, \ldots, q_m\}$ whose request queues must be locked on behalf of p and it takes a feature f whose precondition must be satisfied. The operation treats the precondition as a wait condition. It goes through a number of iterations. Each iteration obtains the request queue locks and then evaluates the precondition. If the precondition is satisfied, then the `check_pre_and_lock_rqs` operation finishes. Otherwise it unlocks the request queues and then starts a new iteration. If the `check_pre_and_lock_rqs` operation finishes, p can be assured that it obtained all the request queue locks and the precondition holds.

Check Postcondition and Unlock Request Queues Operation

$$\bar{q} \overset{def}{=} \{q_1, \ldots, q_m\}$$
$$p \notin \bar{q}$$
$$targets(e) \overset{def}{=} \begin{cases} \{e_0\} \cup \bigcup_{i=0\ldots n} targets(e_i) & \text{if } e = e_0.w(e_1, \ldots, e_n) \\ \{\} & \text{otherwise} \end{cases}$$
$$args(e) \overset{def}{=} \begin{cases} \bigcup_{i=1\ldots n} \{(e_i, w, i)\} \cup args(e_i) & \text{if } e = e_0.w(e_1, \ldots, e_n) \\ \{\} & \text{otherwise} \end{cases}$$

$$g_0 \overset{def}{\in} \begin{cases} if \\ \quad \bar{q} \neq \{\} \wedge \\ \quad \forall x \in targets(f.post) : (\Gamma \vdash \sigma.handler(\sigma.val(p, controlling\_entity(x).name)) \in \bar{q}) \wedge \\ \quad \neg \exists (x, y, z) \in args(f.post), t, h, c : \\ \quad \quad (\Gamma \vdash x : t \wedge controlled(t) \wedge y.formals(z) : (!, h, c) \wedge c.is\_ref) \\ then \\ \quad \bar{q} \\ otherwise \\ \quad \{p\} \end{cases}$$

$$\{g_1, \ldots, g_j\} \overset{def}{=} \bar{q} \setminus g_0$$
$$a \text{ is fresh}$$

$$\Gamma \vdash \langle p :: \text{check\_post\_and\_unlock\_rqs}(\{q_1, \ldots, q_m\}, f); s_p, \sigma \rangle \rightarrow$$

```
        ⟨p :: provided f.post_exists ∧ g₀ ≠ p then
                issue(
                    g₀,
                    execute_delegated(
                            eval(a, f.post); wait(a);
                            issue(g₁, unlock); ...; issue(gⱼ, unlock)

                        ,
                            σ.envs(p).top, {q₁, ..., qₘ}
                    );
                    unlock
                );
                pop_obtained_rq_locks
            else
                provided f.post_exists then
                    eval(a, f.post); wait(a)
                else
                    nop
                end;
                issue(q₁, unlock); ...; issue(qₘ, unlock);
                pop_obtained_rq_locks
            end;
            sₚ, σ⟩
```

The `check_post_and_unlock_rqs` operation also takes a processor set $\{q_1,\ldots,q_m\}$ and a feature f. The processor set is the same as for the `check_pre_and_lock_rqs` operation, i.e., the set of processors whose request queues got locked in the synchronization step. The operation first determines whether the postcondition should be evaluated synchronously or asynchronously. Then the operation starts the evaluation. Finally, the operation enqueues an `unlock` operation to each request queue in $\{q_1,\ldots,q_m\}$.

Clarification 5 (Asynchronous postcondition evaluation). The postcondition can be evaluated asynchronously if every feature call in the postcondition only requires a request queue lock that was obtained in the synchronization step and if the postcondition does not involve lock passing. If the postcondition has a feature call that requires a lock different from the obtained request queue locks, then p cannot delegate its obtained request queue lock and then continue because the required lock would be required in another feature execution context as well. Hence the postcondition must be evaluated synchronously in this case. If the postcondition involves lock passing, then one of p's lock might be necessary for the evaluation of the postcondition. Hence, p must pass its locks and cannot proceed until the postcondition is evaluated and the passed locks returned. Once again, the postcondition must be evaluated synchronously. In Nienaltowski's description of SCOOP [25] a postcondition can be evaluated asynchronously if the current processor is not involved in the postcondition evaluation. This rule permits configurations in which the evaluating processor does not have the necessary locks for the evaluation. □

If the postcondition can be evaluated asynchronously, then the operation can take one of the processors in $\{q_1,\ldots,q_m\}$. This set does not contain processor p because processor p never obtains its own request queue lock. Each processor in this set is exclusively available in the current execution context and can thus be used to evaluate the postcondition asynchronously. The `check_post_and_unlock_rqs` operation defines g_0 to be the evaluating processor according to the rule just presented. It also defines $\{g_1,\ldots,g_j\}$ to be the set $\{q_1,\ldots,q_m\}$ minus the request queue lock of g_0. If p is the evaluating processor, then this set is the same as $\{q_1,\ldots,q_m\}$. As a result of these definitions, the postcondition can be evaluated asynchronously if $g_0 \neq p$. Otherwise, the postcondition must be evaluated synchronously.

In the synchronous case, processor p evaluates the postcondition, enqueues `unlock` operations to each request queue in $\{q_1,\ldots,q_m\}$, and then removes the corresponding locks from its stack of obtained request queue locks. The `unlock` operations will not proceed until the locks have been removed from p's stack of obtained request queue locks. In the asynchronous case, processor p must delegate the postcondition evaluation to processor g_0. For this purpose, p enqueues an `execute_delegated` operation to g_0. The workload involves the postcondition evaluation along with the subsequent issuing of `unlock` operations to all processor in $\{g_1,\ldots,g_j\}$. Processor g_0 unlocks its own request queue after the delegated execution. The evaluation of the postcondition on g_0 requires the environment that defines the values of the entities in the postcondition. Furthermore, the evaluation requires the request queue locks $\{q_1,\ldots,q_m\}$. These locks are sufficient because the postcondition only gets evaluated asynchronously if the evaluation only requires these locks. To satisfy these two requirements, p gives its top environment and $\{q_1, \ldots, q_m\}$ to g_0. After g_0 performed the delegated execution, it can unlock its own request queue. In the meantime, processor p removes $\{q_1, \ldots, q_m\}$ from its obtained request queue locks to enable g_0 to proceed with the delegated execution.

The return operation comes in two variants: one for queries and one for commands.

Return Operation – Query

$$(\sigma', r') \stackrel{def}{=} \begin{cases} if\, r \neq void \wedge \sigma.ref\_obj(r).class\_type.is\_exp \wedge \sigma.handler(r) \neq q \\ \quad (\sigma_x, \sigma_x.last\_imported\_ref) \\ \quad \textbf{where} \\ \qquad \sigma_x \stackrel{def}{=} \sigma.deep\_import(q, r) \\ otherwise \\ \quad (\sigma, r) \end{cases}$$

$$\sigma'' \stackrel{def}{=} \sigma'.pop\_env(p).revoke\_locks(q, p)$$

$$\overline{\Gamma \vdash \langle p :: return(a, r, q); s_p, \sigma \rangle \rightarrow \langle p :: result(a, r'); s_p, \sigma'' \rangle}$$

Return Operation – Command

$$\sigma' \stackrel{def}{=} \sigma.pop\_env(p).revoke\_locks(q, p)$$

$$\overline{\Gamma \vdash \langle p :: return(a, q); s_p, \sigma \rangle \rightarrow}$$
$$\langle p :: \text{provided } \sigma.locks\_passed(q) \text{ then } notify(a) \text{ else nop end}; s_p, \sigma' \rangle$$

The variant for queries returns the result and the locks. The variant for commands only returns the locks. Both variants take a channel a and the caller processor q. For queries, the channel is used to return the result. For this purpose, the operation takes a reference r that points to the result. Processor q is waiting for this result on channel a. This can be seen in the call operation, which issues an apply operation and a subsequent wait(a) operation. The apply operation calls the return operation with the same channel a. To return the result to q, processor p executes a result on a. The value to be returned is not always r directly. If r points to an object of expanded class type and $q \neq p$, then q must deep import the object. In all other cases, q can take r as the return value. An explanation why the deep import operation is necessary can be found in Sec. 4.6. For commands, the channel is used to signal to q that the locks have been returned in case q passed its locks. This can be determined by looking at the state: $\sigma.locks\_passed(q)$. In both variants of the return operation, p removes the passed locks from the stacks of retrieved locks. In case q did not pass any locks, the removed entries might be the empty set. Processor p also removes its top environment because this environment is no longer needed. In case of an asynchronous postcondition evaluation, this environment temporarily gets delegated to the evaluating processor.

Until now, the discussion left out the non-fresh once routines and the attributes. Non-fresh once functions already have a result. The apply operation just needs to get this result from the state and return it. For non-fresh once procedures it does not even have to do this. The only obligation is the evaluation of the invariant. The evaluation of the invariant requires the call stack lock of p. This lock is given if the condition $\neg\sigma.locks\_passed(p)$ holds. For attributes, note that an instance of **ATTRIBUTE** is also an instance of **EXPRESSION**. Hence, the operation evaluates the attribute expression and returns the result of the evaluation. The invariant does not have to be evaluated in this case.

Application Operation – Non-Fresh Once Routine

$f \in \textbf{ROUTINE} \wedge f.is\_once \wedge \neg \sigma.is\_fresh(p,f)$
$\sigma.handler(r_0) = p$
$\neg \sigma.locks\_passed(p)$
$\sigma' \overset{def}{=} \sigma.pass\_locks(q,p,\overline{l}).push\_env\_with\_feature(p,f,r_0,(r_1,\ldots,r_n))$
a is fresh

$\Gamma \vdash \langle p :: \texttt{apply}(a,r_0,f,(r_1,\ldots,r_n),q,\overline{l}); s_p, \sigma \rangle \rightarrow$
   $\langle p :: \texttt{provided } f.class\_type.inv\_exists \wedge f.exported \texttt{ then}$
     $\texttt{eval}(a, f.class\_type.inv); \texttt{wait}(a)$
   $\texttt{else}$
     $\texttt{nop}$
   $\texttt{end};$
   $\texttt{provided } f \in \textbf{FUNCTION} \texttt{ then}$
     $\texttt{return}(a, \sigma'.once\_result(p,f), q)$
   $\texttt{else}$
     $\texttt{return}(a,q)$
   $\texttt{end};$
   $s_p, \sigma' \rangle$

Application Operation – Attribute

$f \in \textbf{ATTRIBUTE}$
$\sigma.handler(r_0) = p$
$\neg \sigma.locks\_passed(p)$
$\sigma' \overset{def}{=} \sigma.pass\_locks(q,p,\overline{l}).push\_env\_with\_feature(p,f,r_0,())$
a' is fresh

$\Gamma \vdash \langle p :: \texttt{apply}(a,r_0,f,(),q,\overline{l}); s_p, \sigma \rangle \rightarrow$
   $\langle p :: \texttt{eval}(a',f);$
     $\texttt{wait}(a');$
     $\texttt{return}(a, a'.data, q);$
     $s_p, \sigma' \rangle$

Creation instructions. A creation instruction has the form **create** $b.f(e_1,\ldots,e_n)$ where b is the target entity, f is the creation procedure, and $e_1,\ldots,e_n$ are the actual arguments. Assume that b is of type (d,g,c). A processor p that executes this instruction takes the following steps:

1. Processor q creation.
   - If b is separate, i.e., $g = \top$, then create a new processor.
   - If b has an explicit processor specification, i.e., $g = \alpha$, then
     - take the processor denoted by α if it already exists.
     - create a new processor if the processor denoted by α does not exist yet.
   - If b is non-separate, i.e., $g = \bullet$, then take p.
2. Locking. Lock the request queue of q if the following conditions hold:
   - Processor p and processor q are different.
   - Processor p does not have q's request queue lock.
   - Processor q does not have p's request queue lock.

3. Object creation. Ask q to create a new instance with class type c using the creation procedure f. Attach the newly created object to b.
4. Invariant evaluation. If f is not exported, then ask q to evaluate the invariant.
5. Lock releasing. If q's request queue has been locked in the locking step, then ask q to unlock its request queue after it is done with the feature request.

There are four cases in the processor creation step:

- The entity b has a separate type.
- The entity b has an explicit processor specification and the denoted processor already exists.
- The entity b has an explicit processor specification and the denoted processor does not yet exist.
- The entity b has a non-separate type.

For each of these cases, there is one inference rule. The discussion starts with the variant where b has a separate type. In this case, the instruction defines q as a new processor and o as a new object of class type c. The reference r points to this object. First the instruction acquires a request queue lock on the new processor q so that it can issue statements on q. Next, it writes the value r into the entity b. To make a call to the creation procedure, it executes a command instruction. Once this is done, it checks whether there is an invariant to evaluate. If f is exported, then the invariant will be evaluated as part of f's feature application. In this case the instruction does nothing. However, if f is not exported, then it must issue the invariant evaluation to q. After this step, it can issue an unlock operation to q and remove the request queue lock from p's obtained request queue locks.

Create Instruction – Top

$$(d,h,c) \overset{def}{=} type\_of(\Gamma,b)$$
$$h = \top$$
$$q \overset{def}{=} \sigma.new\_proc$$
$$o \overset{def}{=} \sigma.new\_obj(c)$$
$$\sigma' \overset{def}{=} \sigma.add\_proc(q).add\_obj(q,o)$$
$$r \overset{def}{=} \sigma'.ref(o)$$
$$a \text{ is fresh}$$

$$\Gamma \vdash \langle p :: \text{create } b.f(e_1,\ldots,e_n); s_p, \sigma \rangle \rightarrow$$
$$\langle p :: \text{lock}(\{q\});$$
$$\quad \text{write}(b.name, r);$$
$$\quad b.f(e_1,\ldots,e_n);$$
$$\quad \text{provided } \neg f.class\_type.inv\_exists \vee f.exported \text{ then}$$
$$\qquad \text{nop}$$
$$\quad \text{else}$$
$$\qquad \text{issue}(q, \text{eval}(a, f.class\_type.inv); \text{wait}(a))$$
$$\quad \text{end};$$
$$\quad \text{issue}(q, \text{unlock});$$
$$\quad \text{pop\_obtained\_rq\_locks};$$
$$\quad s_p \mid q :: \text{nop}, \sigma' \rangle$$

The following discussion looks at the two variants for the cases where b has an explicit processor specification. There are two forms of explicit processor specifications: unqualified and qualified. An unqualified explicit processor specification, i.e., $<x>$, is based on a processor attribute x with an attached type. The processor denoted by this explicit processor specification is the processor stored in x. A qualified explicit processor specification, i.e., $<y.handler>$, is based on a non-writable entity y of attached type. The processor denoted by this explicit processor specification is the same processor as the one handling the object referenced by y. A qualified explicit processor specification always denotes an existing processor because this specification is based on an attached entity. This means that there is already an object attached to this entity and thus its handler must exist. This insight helps to write the conditions for the two inference rule variants.

Create Instruction – Existing Explicit Processor

$$(d,h,c) \stackrel{def}{=} type\_of(\Gamma, b)$$
$$h = <x> \vee h = <y.handler>$$
$$q \stackrel{def}{=} \begin{cases} \sigma.val(p,x) & if\, t = (d, <x>, c) \\ \sigma.handler(\sigma.val(p,y)) & if\, t = (d, <y.handler>, c) \end{cases}$$
$$\sigma.procs.has(q)$$
$$\overline{g}_{required\_cs\_locks} \stackrel{def}{=} \begin{cases} \{q\} & if\, q \neq p \wedge (\sigma.rq\_locks(q).has(p) \vee \sigma.cs\_locks(q).has(p)) \\ \{\} & otherwise \end{cases}$$
$$\forall x \in \overline{g}_{required\_cs\_locks} : \neg\sigma.locks\_passed(p) \wedge \sigma.cs\_locks(p).has(x)$$
$$o \stackrel{def}{=} \sigma.new\_obj(c)$$
$$\sigma' \stackrel{def}{=} \sigma.add\_obj(q,o)$$
$$r \stackrel{def}{=} \sigma'.ref(o)$$
$$a\ is\ fresh$$

$\Gamma \vdash \langle p :: \mathbf{create}\ b.f(e_1,\ldots,e_n); s_p, \sigma \rangle \rightarrow$
  $\langle p :: \mathtt{provided}\ q \neq p \wedge \neg\sigma'.rq\_locks(p).has(q) \wedge \neg\sigma'.rq\_locks(q).has(p)\ \mathtt{then}$
       $\mathtt{lock}(\{q\})$
    $\mathtt{else}$
       $\mathtt{nop}$
    $\mathtt{end};$
    $\mathtt{write}(b.name, r);$
    $b.f(e_1,\ldots,e_n);$
    $\mathtt{provided}\ \neg f.class\_type.inv\_exists \vee f.exported\ \mathtt{then}$
       $\mathtt{nop}$
    $\mathtt{else}$
       $\mathtt{issue}(q, \mathtt{eval}(a, f.class\_type.inv); \mathtt{wait}(a))$
    $\mathtt{end};$
    $\mathtt{provided}\ q \neq p \wedge \neg\sigma'.rq\_locks(p).has(q) \wedge \neg\sigma'.rq\_locks(q).has(p)\ \mathtt{then}$
       $\mathtt{issue}(q, \mathtt{unlock});$
       $\mathtt{pop\_obtained\_rq\_locks}$
    $\mathtt{else}$
       $\mathtt{nop}$
    $\mathtt{end};$
    $s_p, \sigma' \rangle$

The variant that handles existing processors states that the specified processor must exist. To check this, one must consider both the qualified and the unqualified possibility.

For the qualified option, one can simply lookup the value of the attribute x. For the unqualified option, one first looks up the value of the entity y and then determines the handler of the referenced object. In either case, the result q is either the denoted processor or the void value. One then checks whether q is in the set of processors of our system. The overall idea of this inference rule is the same as in the case where b has a separate type. The difference is in the processor creation, locking, and lock releasing steps. Instead of creating a new processor, the instruction takes the existing processor q. If $q = p$, then the call to the creation procedure will be a non-separate call. In this case, the instruction requires p's call stack lock. This lock is given because otherwise p would be waiting. If $p \neq q$ and q has a lock on p, then the call to the creation procedure will be a separate callback. In this case, the instruction requires q's call stack lock. This is expressed in the condition with the help of the set $\overline{g}_{required\_cs\_locks}$. If $p \neq q$ and q does not have p's request queue lock, then the call to the creation procedure will be a separate call. In this case, the instruction must obtain q's request queue lock, provided it does not already have this lock. Only when it obtained q's request queue lock, does the instruction have to issue an `unlock` operation and remove q from p's stack of obtained request queue locks.

Create Instruction – Non-Existing Explicit Processor

$$(d, h, c) \stackrel{def}{=} type\_of(\Gamma, b)$$
$$h = <x>$$
$$\neg \sigma.procs.has(\sigma.val(p, x))$$
$$q \stackrel{def}{=} \sigma.new\_proc$$
$$o \stackrel{def}{=} \sigma.new\_obj(c)$$
$$\sigma' \stackrel{def}{=} \sigma.add\_proc(q).add\_obj(q, o)$$
$$r \stackrel{def}{=} \sigma'.ref(o)$$
$$a \text{ is fresh}$$

$\Gamma \vdash \langle p :: \textbf{create } b.f(e_1, \ldots, e_n); s_p, \sigma \rangle \rightarrow$
    $\langle p :: \texttt{write}(x.name, q);$
        $\texttt{lock}(\{q\});$
        $\texttt{write}(b.name, r);$
        $b.f(e_1, \ldots, e_n);$
        $\textbf{provided } \neg f.class\_type.inv\_exists \vee f.exported \textbf{ then}$
            $\texttt{nop}$
        $\textbf{else}$
            $\texttt{issue}(q, \texttt{eval}(a, f.class\_type.inv); \texttt{wait}(a))$
        $\textbf{end};$
        $\texttt{issue}(q, \texttt{unlock});$
        $\texttt{pop\_obtained\_rq\_locks};$
        $s_p \mid q :: \texttt{nop}, \sigma' \rangle$

For the variant that handles non-existing processors, one has to verify that the specified processor does not exist. To do so, one considers only unqualified processor specifications. In this case, the instruction creates a new processor q with a new object o and reference r. The steps in this variant are similar to those in the variant where b has a separate type. However, the instruction has to set the value of the processor attribute x to the newly created processor. This ensures that the denoted processor will be found to exist in the future.

Lastly, there is a variant for the case where b has a non-separate type. In this case, the instruction creates the object on p. Processor creation, locking, and lock releasing is not necessary. The required call stack lock on p is given because otherwise p would be waiting.

Create Instruction – Non-Separate

$$\frac{\begin{array}{l} (d,h,c) \stackrel{def}{=} type\_of\,(\Gamma,b) \\ h = \bullet \\ o \stackrel{def}{=} \sigma.new\_obj(c) \\ \sigma' \stackrel{def}{=} \sigma.add\_obj(p,o) \\ r \stackrel{def}{=} \sigma'.ref\,(o) \\ a \ is \ fresh \end{array}}{\begin{array}{l} \Gamma \vdash \langle p :: \textbf{create } b.f(e_1,\ldots,e_n);s_p,\sigma\rangle \rightarrow \\ \quad \langle p :: \texttt{write}(b.name,r); \\ \qquad b.f(e_1,\ldots,e_n); \\ \qquad \texttt{provided } \neg f.class\_type.inv\_exists \vee f.exported \texttt{ then} \\ \qquad\quad \texttt{nop} \\ \qquad \texttt{else} \\ \qquad\quad \texttt{eval}(a,f.class\_type.inv);\texttt{wait}(a) \\ \qquad \texttt{end}; \\ \qquad s_p,\sigma'\rangle \end{array}}$$

Flow control instructions. The **if** e **then** s_t **else** s_f **end** instruction executes s_t if the expression e evaluates to true. Otherwise the instruction executes s_f. There is one inference rule for this instruction. In a first step, the instruction evaluates the expression e using a fresh channel a and then waits for a notification on a. In a second step, it uses the provided operation to either execute s_t or s_f, depending on the value of the expression.

If Instruction

$$\frac{a \ is \ fresh}{\begin{array}{l} \Gamma \vdash \langle p :: \textbf{if } e \textbf{ then } s_t \textbf{ else } s_f \textbf{ end};s_p,\sigma\rangle \rightarrow \\ \quad \langle p :: \texttt{eval}(a,e); \\ \qquad \texttt{wait}(a); \\ \qquad \texttt{provided } a.data \texttt{ then} \\ \qquad\quad s_t \\ \qquad \texttt{else} \\ \qquad\quad s_f \\ \qquad \texttt{end}; \\ \qquad s_p,\sigma\rangle \end{array}}$$

The **until** e **loop** s_l **end** instruction executes a sequence of s_l instructions until the expression e evaluates to true. If e is true initially, then s_l never gets executed. There is one inference rule for this instruction. First, the instruction evaluates e using a fresh channel a. Then it waits for a notification on a. Next, it uses the provided operation to check whether e evaluates to true or false. If e is true, then it is done. Otherwise, it executes s_l followed by another **until** e **loop** s_l **end** operation.

Loop Instruction

$$\frac{a \; is \; fresh}{\begin{aligned} &\Gamma \vdash \langle p :: \textbf{until } e \textbf{ loop } s_l \textbf{ end}; s_p, \sigma \rangle \rightarrow \\ &\quad \langle p :: \texttt{eval}(a,e); \\ &\quad\quad \texttt{wait}(a); \\ &\quad\quad \texttt{provided } a.\textit{data} \texttt{ then} \\ &\quad\quad\quad \texttt{nop} \\ &\quad\quad \texttt{else} \\ &\quad\quad\quad s_l; \textbf{until } e \textbf{ loop } s_l \textbf{ end} \\ &\quad\quad \texttt{end}; \\ &\quad\quad s_p, \sigma \rangle \end{aligned}}$$

Assignment instructions. An assignment instruction $b := e$ assigns the value of the expression e to the entity b. The instruction first evaluates the expression e and then waits for a notification on a fresh channel a. Once it gets this notification, it uses the write operation to set the value to the entity b.

Assignment

$$\frac{a \; is \; fresh}{\Gamma \vdash \langle p :: b := e; s_p, \sigma \rangle \rightarrow \langle p :: \texttt{eval}(a,e); \texttt{wait}(a); \texttt{write}(b.name, a.data); s_p, \sigma \rangle}$$

5.5 Termination

The system terminates when it reaches a configuration where all action queues are empty, i.e., when there is no more work to do.

6 Conclusion

In this paper we have presented a formal specification of the SCOOP model, based on operational semantics. We have demonstrated that this level of rigor is necessary if the specification is to be used as a guideline for an implementation. In particular, we were able to clarify a number of omissions and ambiguities in the available informal specification, which had gone undetected in other formalizations:

- Are processor locks fine-grained enough? We require request queue locks and call stack locks.
- Which locks must be passed? Which locks can be passed? We pass all the locks we actually have. We pass these locks both for normal lock passing and for separate callbacks.
- How do we move object structures from one processor to another processor without violating the invariant? The deep import operation must be used.
- When do we set the status of a fresh once routine to non-fresh? The status of the once routine must be set to non-fresh before deep importing.
- When can a postcondition be evaluated asynchronously? The postcondition can be evaluated asynchronously if every feature call in the postcondition only requires a lock that was obtained in the synchronization step and if the postcondition does not involve lock passing.

Because of the complexity of the SCOOP model, our resulting specification is large, the management of which is a challenge for a fully formal development. To address this problem, we used abstract data types and a notation with an object-oriented flavor, which made the specification more readable and more easily extendable, without sacrificing any of the rigors of operational semantics. Furthermore, we introduced a distinction between two kinds of statements, namely instructions (user syntax) and operations (run-time syntax). This made it possible to treat within one inference system both the actual language elements and the implementation details of the runtime system, and to distinguish clearly between them.

The main application of this work is to guide the implementation of the SCOOP model. This has led to a successful implementation of SCOOP on top of the Eiffel language, which supersedes the previous prototype implementation and is publicly available [31]. The SCOOP model can however be implemented on top of any object-oriented language (support for contracts, as offered by Java or Spec#, is beneficial), and our work also facilitates such future implementation efforts. In the case of Java, first steps towards such an implementation have been taken [33], which could certainly be supported by our work.

A number of other applications of our semantics can be envisioned. First, the semantics can be used to prove correct various properties of the model which have so far only been postulated, such as absence of object-level data races and type safety (absence of traitors). In light of the complexity of the full model, these properties are no longer obvious. For example, as processor locks serve as an abstraction only, it must be shown that locks are not misused in situations such as separate callbacks, which involve call stack locks. Second, our operational semantics can also be used to prove correct an axiomatic semantics for the SCOOP model, which is planned for future work. In the case of sequential Eiffel, a similar development is documented in [26]. Third, we feel our semantics is detailed enough that its rules can directly be implemented as an interpreter for SCOOP programs. Such an interpreter could serve as a true reference implementation, which could in turn be used for conformance checking of real implementations.

Acknowledgments. We thank Stephan van Staden for interesting discussions on the lock model. This work is part of the SCOOP project at ETH Zurich, which has benefited from grants from the Hasler Foundation, the Swiss National Foundation, Microsoft (Multicore award) and ETH (ETHIIRA).

References

1. Ábrahám, E., de Boer, F.S., de Roever, W.-P., Steffen, M.: A compositional operational semantics for JavaMT. In: Dershowitz, N. (ed.) Verification: Theory and Practice. LNCS, vol. 2772, pp. 290–303. Springer, Heidelberg (2004)
2. Allen, E., Chase, D., Luchangco, V., Maessen, J.W., Steele Jr., G.L.: Object-oriented units of measurement. In: Conference on Object Oriented Programming Systems Languages and Applications, pp. 384–403 (2004)
3. Benton, N., Cardelli, L., Fournet, C.: Modern concurrency abstractions for C#. ACM Transactions on Programming Languages and Systems 26(5), 269–804 (2004)
4. Blumofe, R.D., Joerg, C.F., Kuszmaul, B.C., Leiserson, C.E., Randall, K.H., Zhou, Y.: Cilk: An efficient multithreaded runtime system. ACM SIGPLAN Notices 30(8), 207–216 (1995)

5. Brooke, P.J., Paige, R.F., Jacob, J.L.: A CSP model of Eiffel's SCOOP. Formal Aspects of Computing 19(4), 487–512 (2007)
6. Cenciarelli, P., Knapp, A., Reus, B., Wirsing, M.: An Event-Based Structural Operational Semantics of Multi-threaded Java. In: Alves-Foss, J. (ed.) Formal Syntax and Semantics of Java. LNCS, vol. 1523, pp. 157–200. Springer, Heidelberg (1999)
7. Charles, P., Grothoff, C., Saraswat, V., Donawa, C., Kielstra, A., Ebcioglu, K., von Praun, C., Sarkar, V.: X10: An object-oriented approach to non-uniform cluster computing. In: Conference on Object Oriented Programming Systems Languages and Applications, pp. 519–538 (2005)
8. Coffman, E.G., Elphick, M.J., Shoshani, A.: System deadlocks. ACM Computing Surveys 3(2), 67–78 (1971)
9. ECMA: ECMA-367 Eiffel: Analysis, design and programming language 2nd edn. Tech. rep., ECMA International (2006)
10. Ericsson Erlang website (2011), http://www.erlang.org/
11. Fournet, C., Gonthier, G.: The reflexive CHAM and the join-calculus. In: ACM SIGPLAN-SIGACT Symposium on Principles of Programming Languages, pp. 372–385 (1996)
12. Gelernter, D., Carriero, N., Chandran, S., Chang, S.: Parallel programming in Linda. In: International Conference on Parallel Processing, pp. 255–263 (1985)
13. Hoare, C.A.R.: Communicating Sequential Processes. Prentice Hall (1985)
14. International Organization for Standardization: ISO/IEC 8652:1995 Ada. Tech. rep., International Organization for Standardization (1995)
15. Joyner, M., Chamberlain, B.L., Deitz, S.J.: Iterators in Chapel. In: International Parallel and Distributed Processing Symposium/International Parallel Processing Symposium (2006)
16. Khoshafian, S., Copeland, G.P.: Object identity. In: Conference on Object Oriented Programming Systems Languages and Applications. pp. 406–416 (1986)
17. Klein, G., Nipkow, T.: A machine-checked model for a Java-like language, virtual machine and compiler. ACM Transactions on Programming Languages and Systems 28(4), 619–695 (2006)
18. Liskov, B., Zilles, S.: Programming with abstract data types. ACM SIGPLAN Notices 9(4), 50–59 (1974)
19. Lochbihler, A.: Type safe nondeterminism – A formal semantics of Java threads. In: International Workshop on Foundations of Object-Oriented Languages (2008)
20. Meyer, B.: A three-level approach to data structure description, and notational framework. In: ACM-NBS Workshop on Data Abstraction, Databases and Conceptual Modelling, pp. 164–166 (1981)
21. Meyer, B.: Object-Oriented Software Construction, 2nd edn. Prentice-Hall (1997)
22. Microsoft Axum website (2011), http://msdn.microsoft.com/en-us/devlabs/dd795202.aspx/
23. Milner, R.: Communicating and mobile systems: the π-calculus. Cambridge University Press (1999)
24. Morandi, B., Nanz, S., Meyer, B.: A comprehensive operational semantics of the SCOOP programming model (2011), http://arxiv.org/abs/1101.1038v1
25. Nienaltowski, P.: Practical framework for contract-based concurrent object-oriented programming. Ph.D. thesis, ETH Zurich (2007)
26. Nordio, M., Calcagno, C., Müller, P., Meyer, B.: A Sound and Complete Program Logic for Eiffel. In: Oriol, M., Meyer, B. (eds.) TOOLS EUROPE 2009. LNBIP, vol. 33, pp. 195–214. Springer, Heidelberg (2009)
27. Odersky, M.: The Scala language specification version 2.8. Tech. rep., Swiss Federal Institute of Technology Lausanne (2010)
28. Ostroff, J.S., Torshizi, F.A., Huang, H.F., Schoeller, B.: Beyond contracts for concurrency. Formal Aspects of Computing 21(4), 319–346 (2008)

29. Plotkin, G.D.: A structural approach to operational semantics. The Journal of Logic and Algebraic Programming 60–61, 17–139 (2004)
30. Schmidt, H.W., Chen, J.: Reasoning about concurrent objects. In: Asia-Pacific Software Engineering Conference, p. 86 (1995)
31. SCOOP website (2011), `http://scoop.origo.ethz.ch/`
32. SGS-THOMSON Microelectronics Limited: occam 2.1 reference manual. Tech. rep., SGS-THOMSON Microelectronics Limited (1995)
33. Torshizi, F., Ostroff, J.S., Paige, R.F., Chechik, M.: The SCOOP concurrency model in Java-like languages. In: Communicating Process Architectures, pp. 155–178. IOS (2009)

On the Integration of Software Testing and Formal Analysis

Pietro Braione, Giovanni Denaro, and Mauro Pezzè

Dipartimento di Informatica, Sistemistica e Comunicazione
Università di Milano-Bicocca
P.zza dell'Ateneo Nuovo, 1
I-20126 Milano, Italy
{braione,denaro,pezze}@disco.unimib.it

Abstract. The software industry favors dynamic testing over static analysis of software, because traditional static software analysis techniques do not adequately balance automation, precision and scalability. Recently several researchers have combined static and dynamic techniques to overcome these problems. Undergoing efforts include concolic execution, testing-based correctness prove, execution driven abstract interpretation and dynamic invariant generation.

This paper summarizes the state of the art about combining dynamic testing and static analysis, and designs a roadmap towards a modern approach to software V&V that enhances dynamic testing with static analysis techniques. In particular, this paper surveys the most promising approaches to combine dynamic testing and static program analysis. It classifies the techniques against a framework of combination patterns, to facilitate the identification of commonalities and complementarities between the techniques. It quantifies analytically the gain that stems from the most important combination patterns. It provides a roadmap for future research.

1 Introduction

The complexity and ubiquity of current software systems increases the already high costs of deployed software bugs. This happens in many application domains that span from mass-diffused software, like operating and embedded systems, to software systems that manage huge investments and human lives, like e-commerce systems and flight controllers. Current design and development techniques do not adequately match the strict integrity requirements of these systems, regardless of the effort allocated to detect and remove faults from software before deployment.

The leading software industry privileges dynamic *testing* over *program analysis* techniques for locating failures and removing faults, because testing scales better, is effective in exposing many failures with a limited initial effort, and samples only actual executions, thus avoiding false positives. On the downside, the efficacy of testing is limited by the fact that testing is based on the observation of a finite, *underapproximating* sample of the possible program behaviours,

B. Meyer and M. Nordio (Eds.): LASER Summer School 2008-2010, LNCS 7007, pp. 158–193, 2012.

and thus cannot reason on the whole execution space. A relevant consequence is the weak relationship between testing effort and software quality, which implies that planning what to test, how to test it and when to stop testing is still mostly a matter of human judgement and simple heuristics. In practice, as testing effort grows, eliciting erroneous behaviours by means of new test cases becomes increasingy harder. Finally, testing steers software behaviour by acting on inputs. This implies that errors that are not triggered by some input, like synchronization errors in concurrent software, do not typically surface during testing.

On the other side, static *analysis* techniques rely on mathematical models of program behaviour and infer properties from them, thus complementing testing. While testing cannot reason on the whole execution space, static analysis is potentially able to detect the absence of specific categories of errors from software systems. This is because the models used in software analysis *overapproximate* the possible behaviours of a program, and can deduce invariant software properties holding on all the executions. This also means that the faults detected with a static analysis may be *spurious*, and must be confirmed on the actual program. Also, current static analysis techniques do not adequately meet automation, precision and scalability requirements. This derives from the fact that no single abstraction suits all the combinations of verification problems and target systems. Current analysis techniques suffer from one or more of the following problems: do not scale well to industry-size software systems, miss relevant bugs, flood the user by spurious error warnings, require on-line manual assistance. Consequently, static analysis techniques find scarce industrial applications mostly limited to special-purpose applications.

Recent research focused on combining static and dynamic analysis techniques to benefit from the advantages and reduce the problems. Combined approaches test and analyze the same program, and share the information produced by one technique to improve the results of the other. Testing provides exact information about feasible behaviours, thus it can be used as a cost-effective way to build precise models. Analysis provides hints about the regions of the program state space that may contain faults, thus it can be used to steer testing towards faulty regions for distinguishing actual from spurious faults. Together, testing and analysis may yield fully automated, sound verification procedures more precise, scalable and automatic than either testing or analysis alone.

Triggered by encouraging preliminary results, research on combining static and dynamic techniques has proliferated in the literature of the last ten years. Most of the literature presents specific combinations of static and dynamic techniques without providing a general framework. The absence of a deep understanding of the general advantages of combining different kinds of techniques hinders the ability of exploiting new interaction patterns within the context of combination of different techniques. Many questions remain unanswered: What are the structural features of the basic analysis and testing techniques available in literature? How do these features impact on the precision, convergence and performance of the techniques? When two techniques may interplay? Which information should they share to interplay? How does this interplay improve precision, convergence or performance? How can we *design* a combination between techniques in a way that yields a predictable advantage? How can we discover new combination patterns? Giving an answer to some of these questions can highlight the commonalities among different combined techniques and can provide the foundations for new tools for designing better testing, analysis and verification techniques.

This paper moves a first step in the direction of answering some of the above questions. We propose a vocabulary of concepts which, in our vision, allow to motivate, understand and evaluate the interactions between static and dynamic techniques. These concepts are grounded on a definition of *technique* as a way to explore the reachable state space of a program, and will characterize different techniques in terms of how they restrict the ideal but infeasible exhaustive exploration to make exploration feasible. The framework allows us to motivate and explain a number of combination patterns between techniques emerging from current literature. We assess the advantage of these combination patterns informally, and we propose some preliminary ideas about a more quantitative assessment. All these concepts are grounded on current research by considering some state-of-the-research static/dynamic tools as case studies and guides for identifying the combination patterns.

The paper is organized as follows. Section 2 defines the category of programs, analysis problems and techniques that are considered in the rest of the paper. Section 3 introduces and classifies basic state space exploration techniques, on which combined approaches are based, with a special attention to testing, symbolic execution and predicate abstraction. Section 4 introduces the concept of synergies between techniques, as the way techniques exchange information about the program state space, identifies a set of synergies that recur across three representative combined techniques from literature, and discusses their aims in terms of improved performance or completeness. Section 5 considers the problem of assessing in a more quantitative way how combined techniques improve over purely static or dynamic ones, and calculates the performance gain that derives form a specific synergy pattern, by isolating its effect in two combined techniques among those surveyed in Section 4. Finally, Section 6 draws some conclusions and outlines an agenda for future research.

2   Preliminaries: Programs, Properties and Analysis

This section sets the scope of the paper and introduces some preliminary definitions that will be used in the next sections: What do we consider as software programs, which category of correctness problems are we dealing with, what is a technique for analyzing the program correctness.

2.1   Programs

We consider software systems written in an *imperative* programming language. An imperative program transforms an initial *program state* into a final one.

A program state is a mapping from a finite set of *program variables* $\mathbf{X} \stackrel{\text{def}}{=} \{x_0, \ldots, x_n\}$ to a set of *values* $\mathbf{V}$. We write $\mathbf{S} \stackrel{\text{def}}{=} \mathbf{X} \to \mathbf{V}$ for the set of program states over $\mathbf{X}$, v for a generic value in $\mathbf{V}$, and s for a generic program state in $\mathbf{S}$. Our only assumption on $\mathbf{V}$ is that it contains the boolean values *true* and *false* (in the examples $\mathbf{V}$ contains also the set of the natural numbers).

The programming language we consider is a simplified variant of Dijkstra's language of the guarded commands [10] in the style of Chandy and Misra's UNITY [6]. Henceforth, $\mathbf{P}$ indicates the set of the possible programs, and p a generic program in $\mathbf{P}$. A program is a set of guarded assignments $g(x_0, \ldots, x_n) \mapsto x_0, \ldots, x_n := f(x_0, \ldots, x_n)$, where f and g (the *guard*) are *expressions* over program variables. We write $\mathbf{E}$ for the set of the possible expressions. If we abstract from the notation, a guarded assignment can be considered as the pair of the expressions (f, g). Therefore, p is a subset of $\mathbf{E}^2$ ($p \subseteq \mathbf{E}^2$) and $\mathbf{P}$ is the powerset of $(\mathbf{E}^2)$ ($\mathbf{P} \stackrel{\text{def}}{=} \mathcal{P}(\mathbf{E}^2)$). We make no assumptions on $\mathbf{E}$.

A program executes by selecting a statement among all the statements whose guards evaluates to *true* in the current state, and executing its assignment. This process is repeated until all the guards evaluate to *false* (possibly diverging). We formally define this by assuming the existence of suitable evaluation functions $[\![f]\!]$ and $[\![g]\!]$, yielding the values assumed by f and g in a state. We abstract from the concrete evaluation procedures. We only assume that the evaluation of f in a state yields another state, and the evaluation of g in a state yields either *true* or *false*—formally, $[\![f]\!] : \mathbf{S} \to \mathbf{S}$ and $[\![g]\!] : \mathbf{S} \to \{true, false\}$. When $[\![g]\!]s = true$ we say that (f, g) is *enabled* by s. We now define the *single-step operational semantics* of a program p, $[\![p]\!] \subseteq \mathbf{S} \times p \times \mathbf{S}$, as follows:

$$(s, (f, g), s') \in [\![p]\!] \text{ iff } [\![g]\!]s = true \text{ and } s' = [\![f]\!]s.$$

We write $s \xrightarrow{(f,g)} s'$ instead of $(s, (f, g), s') \in [\![p]\!]$, and $s \xrightarrow{p} s'$ to mean that $s \xrightarrow{(f,g)} s'$ for some $(f, g) \in p$ (we also drop the p subscript when the program that we are considering is evident from the context). The one-step operational semantics of a program defines a labelled transition system whose states are program states, whose labels are statements, and whose labelled transitions connect states with the effects of the guarded commands on them. The reflective and transitive closure of the semantic function, $\left(\xrightarrow{p} \right)^*$, associates each state s with all its successors in an arbitrary number of states. These states are said to be the *reachable* state space of p starting from s.

The programming language we are considering differs from most mainstream imperative programming languages in that it does not have control flow statements such as conditionals, loops and sequencing. This is not a limit because control flow can be encoded explicitly by introducing a program variable l which stores the current location in the program. Figure 1 exemplifies how a C program is translated to an equivalent one in the guarded command language.

```
while (x != 0) {
    if (x % 2 == 0) {
        x = x - 2;
    } else {
        x = 3 * x + 1;
    }
}
```

$$l = 1 \wedge x \neq 0 \mapsto l := 2$$
$$[\,]\quad l = 1 \wedge x = 0 \mapsto l := 8$$
$$[\,]\quad l = 2 \wedge x \bmod 2 = 0 \mapsto l := 3$$
$$[\,]\quad l = 2 \wedge x \bmod 2 \neq 0 \mapsto l := 5$$
$$[\,]\quad l = 3 \mapsto x := x - 2, l := 7$$
$$[\,]\quad l = 5 \mapsto x := 3x + 1, l := 7$$
$$[\,]\quad l = 7 \mapsto l := 1$$

Fig. 1. A C program (left) and the equivalent program in the guarded command language (right)

2.2 Detecting Errors in Programs

Automatic program verification aims to determine properties valid for all or some of the possible executions of a program. In this paper we consider a specific instance of the automatic verification problem, which aims to determine the specific class of *reachability* properties. A reachability problem can be stated as follows: Given a program p, a set $I \subseteq S$ of *initial states* and a set $O \subseteq S$ of *correct states*, determine whether or not the reachable state space of p is entirely contained in the set of correct states. In formal terms, we want to determine whether there exist $s \in I$ and $s' \notin O$ such that $s \left(\xrightarrow{p} \right)^{*} s'$. The complement of O is the set of the *failure states*.

(Un)reachability properties are a kind of *safety* properties. Safety properties state that during any possible program computation "something bad" never happens. More formally, a computation violates a safety property if there is a finite prefix ("something bad") which is not shared with at least one other computation that does not violate it. In the case of reachability this happens whenever a computation hits a failure state. In this case we say that the program under analysis is *incorrect* w.r.t. the property, and *correct* otherwise.

A *(verification) technique* is a procedure that takes as input a program p and two specifications of the sets I and O, and tries to decide whether an error state is reachable from a state in I. Being reachability undecidable in the general case, a verification technique does not produce a conclusive answer on all combinations of its inputs. To account for this we consider as possible answers one of CORRECT, INCORRECT, INCONCLUSIVE, meaning that p is correct, incorrect w.r.t. the reachability problem, and that the technique has failed in deciding about correctness, respectively. Some techniques are *partial*, i.e., they diverge on some possible inputs. Additionally, we assume that a technique is always *sound* with respect to both CORRECT and INCORRECT—i.e., whenever a technique returns CORRECT (respectively, INCORRECT), the program is indeed correct (respectively, incorrect). This is equivalent to assuming that there is no discrepancy between the true program semantics and the semantics assumed by the technique when it reasons about the program—an assumption that often does not hold in practice, but that allows us to abstract away from issues that are not relevant to our tractation.

We now introduce some terminology about the relevant properties of verification techniques. We say that a technique is *complete w.r.t. correct (incorrect) programs* if, whenever a program is correct (incorrect) w.r.t. an arbitrary reachability problem, the technique answers CORRECT (INCORRECT). From the undecidability of the reachability problem follows that every verification technique has some degree of incompleteness either w.r.t. correctness or incorrectness. In the worst case a technique may be *void w.r.t. correct (incorrect) programs* i.e., fails in producing any CORRECT (INCORRECT) answer. We will say that a technique is *more complete* than another one whenever the former converges to a conclusive answer on more inputs than the latter (we may refine the statement by saying that the technique is more complete w.r.t. correctness, incorrectness or both).

When a technique does not produce a conclusive answer, i.e. either CORRECT or INCORRECT, it may either converge to INCONCLUSIVE or fail to converge. The two situations are not, of course, equivalent in practice since a diverging computation cannot be in general distinguished by a human from a very long converging computation. We say that a technique *converges more* than another one whenever the former converges (albeit not necessarily to a conclusive answer) on more inputs than the latter. Finally, we say that a technique is *more precise* than another one whenever the former is more complete and converges more than the latter.

3 Exploring the Space of Program Executions

This section introduces and classifies the basic analysis and testing techniques that are used and combined to prove software properties. Here we propose a taxonomy that helps us comparing the various approaches with respect to completeness and convergence. This, in turns, motivates the combination patterns arising between basic techniques, which is investigated in the next section. We propose the taxonomy focusing on three categories of basic explorative techniques that are commonly exploited in combinations of static and dynamic approaches: testing, symbolic execution, and predicate abstraction.

3.1 Full Exhaustive State Space Exploration

A state s_e is reachable from some initial state s_0 if there exists at least one *finite* sequence of computation steps $s_0 \xrightarrow{p} s_1 \xrightarrow{p} \ldots \xrightarrow{p} s_e$. Thus, an intuitively simple way to investigate a set of reachable states is to look for such finite computations. On the above rationale, techniques based on state space exploration *unroll* the reachable program state space at increasing (but finite) depth, through real or simulated program execution. The process is iterated until either an error state is found, in which case the program is rejected, or all the reachable program states have been explored, in which case the program is accepted. Testing, explicit-state or symbolic model checking, and symbolic execution are different declinations of this paradigms.

```
Explore(p,I,O):
-- p is a program, a set of statements (f,g)
-- I is the set of initial states
-- O is the set of safe states
  S := I
  loop:
    if S ⊄ O return INCORRECT
    S' := Post(p,S)
    if S' ⊆ S return CORRECT
    S := S' ∪ S
```

Fig. 2. Full exhaustive state space exploration

Figure 2 drafts the skeleton of the approach to full exhaustive state space exploration, which can be considered either the ideal exhaustive testing (if the program is deterministic) or explicit-state model checking (if the program is non-deterministic)[1]. The procedure relies on the definition of the *post-states transformer* $\text{Post} : \mathbf{P} \times \mathcal{P}(\mathbf{S}) \to \mathcal{P}(\mathbf{S})$ that is defined as:

$$\text{Post}(p, S) \stackrel{\text{def}}{=} \bigcup_{s \in S} \{s' \in \mathbf{S} \mid s \stackrel{p}{\to} s'\} \quad \text{for } S \subseteq \mathbf{S}.$$

Intuitively, $\text{Post}(p, S)$ contains all and only the successors of some state in S, according to $\stackrel{p}{\to}$. The reachable state space of p starting fron I is $\bigcup_{k \geq 0} \text{Post}^k(p, I)$, where $\text{Post}^0(p, I) \stackrel{\text{def}}{=} I$ and $\text{Post}^{k+1}(p, I) \stackrel{\text{def}}{=} \text{Post}(p, \text{Post}^k(p, I))$. This can be seen as the least fixpoint of the function[2] $f(S) \stackrel{\text{def}}{=} \text{Post}(p, S) \cup I : \mathcal{P}(\mathbf{S}) \to \mathcal{P}(\mathbf{S})$. The procedure calculates this fixpoint by iterating through a loop which, at the n-th iteration, calculates into the variable S the underapproximation of the reachable state space $\bigcup_{0 \leq k < n} \text{Post}^k(p, I)$ and performs two termination checks. The loop is structured as follows:

Check for failure: if S contains a failure state, the procedure stops and returns INCORRECT;

Compute successors: the successors of S are calculated and stored in S';

Check for success: if all the successors are already in S, then the whole state space has been explored without finding a failure state: The procedure stops and returns CORRECT;

Update the computation state: The successors are added to S, yielding

$$\bigcup_{0 \leq k < n+1} \text{Post}^k(p, I).$$

---

[1] A program is *deterministic* whenever $|\text{Post}(p, \{s\})| \leq 1$.

[2] The fact is easily proved by taking into account that Post preserves union, i.e., $\text{Post}(p, S \cup S') = \text{Post}(p, S) \cup \text{Post}(p, S')$.

The procedure converges on all the incorrect programs, and on the correct programs with finite-depth reachable state space[3]. This asymmetry is a bit annoying, since most interesting programs have not a finite-depth reachable state space, and is a hallmark of dynamic techniques such as testing.

3.2   Reducing the Exploration Scope

Even if we assume convergence (when the state space is finite), the fully exhaustive state space exploration is impractical, as the typical size of a program state space quickly explodes also for relatively simple programs. Many techniques work around the state-explosion problem by discarding some of the information discovered during the exploration according to one of the following three strategies:

depth-bounded exploration, which consists in observing only finite computations and prefixes of computations, up to some predefined length.

width-bounded exploration, which consists in analyzing a subset of the states discovered at a given exploration step.

non-monotonic exploration, which consists in forgetting the states discovered at previous iterations, and retaining only the states at the current exploration depth.

Figure 3 presents the pseudocode for reduced state space exploration techniques. In the figure, we write $(-)_\subseteq : \mathcal{P}(\mathbf{S}) \to \mathcal{P}(\mathbf{S})$ to indicate a nontrivial reductive function, i.e., having the properties:

$$S_\subseteq \subseteq S, \quad S \neq \emptyset \text{ implies } S_\subseteq \neq \emptyset.$$

Informally, $S_\subseteq$ returns a nonempty subset of S (unless S is empty).

Depth-bounded exploration always converges, which can be considered a practical advantage by itself. On the other hand, whenever an error state does not exist within the depth bound, an INCONCLUSIVE answer is mandatory to preserve soundness. In other words, depth-bounded exploration is void w.r.t. correct programs with a reachable state space deeper than the bound. As an example, all the programs with a finite reachable state space (for instance, finite state automata) fall in this class whenever the state space has size greater than the depth bound.

Width-bounded exploration is hardly comparable with full exhaustive one. Under some assumptions, it may even be more precise than the latter w.r.t. some classes of programs. This happens when we assume that an optimal oracle performs sampling by discarding as many correct diverging computations as possible, and by retaining (when it exists) at least one incorrect computation. In this case, width-bounded exploration converges better than full exhaustive exploration w.r.t. some classes of correct programs with finite computations, and produces a conclusive answer on all the inputs where it converges. At the opposite

---

[3] A program's reachable state space has finite depth n (from I) when it is $\bigcup_{0 \leq k < n} \text{Post}^k(p, I)$.

```
ExploreDepthBounded(p,I,O,maxDepth):
-- maxDepth >0 is an integer, the maximum depth of the exploration
  S := I
  depth := 0
  loop:
    if S ⊄ O return INCORRECT
    if depth ≥ maxDepth return INCONCLUSIVE else depth := depth + 1
    S' := Post(p,S)
    if S' ⊆ S return CORRECT
    S := S' ∪ S

ExploreWidthBounded(p,I,O,maxWidth):
-- maxWidth >0 is an integer, the maximum width of the exploration
  (−)⊆ := some reductive function s.t. |S⊆| = min(maxWidth,S)
  S := I⊆
  exact := (S = I)
  loop:
    if S ⊄ O return INCORRECT
    S' := Post(p,S)⊆
    exact := exact ∧ (S' = Post(p,S))
    if S' ⊆ S:
      if exact return CORRECT else return INCONCLUSIVE
    S := S' ∪ S

ExploreNonmonotone(p,I,O):
  S := I
  loop:
    if S ⊄ O return INCORRECT
    S' := Post(p,S)
    if S' ⊆ S return CORRECT
    S := S' − S
```

Fig. 3. Reduced state space exploration

end of the spectrum, an adverse oracle may discard computations leading to error states and retain diverging correct computations. In this case, width-bounded exploration converges less well and is less precise than full exhaustive exploration. We choose not to make any assumption on how sampling selects states, which reflects practical situations where no a priori knowledge exists about either the program's reachable state space, or sampling. Consistently, the procedure in Figure 3 produces an INCONCLUSIVE answer whenever the sampling misses some states. This yields a procedure which is always less precise (but may converge better) than full exhaustive exploration. Width bounds allow to limit the size of S' but not the size of S, for which either depth bounds or nonmonotony are necessary.

Non-monotonic exploration focuses on minimizing the memory occupation of a possibly exhaustive search, rather than limiting the scope of the exploration. The rationale is that if the the reachability space of a program is large, a same state will unlikely be visited twice. On this rationale, non-monotonic exploration trades the cost in time of exploring some states more than once, against memory occupation. This is done by storing only the states at depth n which are not also at depth $n-1$. The space saving is paid in terms of precision, since missing the memory of visited states reduces convergence. Indeed, a non-monotonic exploration diverges on correct programs (even finite-state ones) with at least an infinite computation with cycle length greater than 1. As an example, the C program `while (1) { x := x + 1; }` diverges this way.

```
ExploreTesting (p,I,O):
  S := choose S s.t. S ⊆ I and S is finite
  exact := (S = I)
  loop:
    if S ⊄ O return INCORRECT
    S' := ∪ₛ∈ₛ choose s' s.t. s' ∈ Post(p, {s})
    exact := exact ∧ (S' = Post(p, S))
    if S' ⊆ S:
      if exact return CORRECT else return INCONCLUSIVE
    S := S' - S
```

Fig. 4. State space exploration by means of testing

Figure 4 summarizes how testing explores the state space. Testing starts from a finite set of initial states (test cases), and for each of them at each step chooses exactly one successor to explore. These can be seen as a both non-monotonic and width-bounded exploration (bound = 1). Testing does not bound the depth of execution, and thus may diverge. An interesting observation is that, differently from purely non-monotonic and purely width-bounded explorations, testing may converge with inconclusive answers. This can happen because, when sampling discards a state, this is lost because of non-monotony.

3.3 Exploring via Auxiliary Spaces

The approaches summarized in the former section deal with the state explosion problem by limiting the set of examined states, thus producing partial results. Another class of approaches handles infinity directly either in width by intensionality or in depth by abstraction. These approaches exploit the idea of recasting the exploration in an auxiliary space, with better properties than the original program state space.

Intensionality. Full exhaustive search strategies assume an *extensional* (*explicit-state*) representation of sets of program states. Representing a set as the enumeration of its members requires the same storage size of the set that must be represented. Consequently, the implementations of explicit-state approaches do not scale with the size of the analyzed program, and cannot analyze exhaustively programs with infinitely many reachable states. *Intensional* (*symbolic-state*) approaches deal with the state explosion problem by describing sets of states that share common features with sentences in a formal language, or equivalent formalisms like ordered binary decision diagrams [4]. As an example, the formula $x > 0$ describes intensionally the infinite set of all and only the states which assign a positive value to the variable x. Intensional representations have complementary properties with respect to extensional ones, stemming from the fact that the size of a symbolic formula is loosely correlated with the size of the set it represents. Symbolic-state techniques can represent very large, and even infinite, sets of states with a short formula, but sometimes may use large formulas to represent small, or even empty, sets of states. Moreover, the same set of states may have many, even infinite, different symbolic representations that may be hard to compare. Indeed, the most relevant decision problems (equivalence and inclusion) become computationally hard, or even undecidable, for most symbolic languages.

Abstraction. Abstraction limits the fully exhaustive exploration of the state space of a program by partitioning the space of the possibly infinite program states into a (possibly finite) number of subsets, and by analyzing only a finite number of representative behaviours for each set. As an example, let us consider the program from Figure 1, which for the reader's comfort has been reported on the left side of Figure 5. If we relax all the statements' guards by dropping all the clauses on x, and at the same time we remove all the assignments to x, we obtain the finite-state program reported on the right side of Figure 5. There is a precise relationship between the possible behaviours of the two programs, which allows e.g. to conclude that the program on the left side of Figure 5 will never set l to 9 because the program on the right, its *control abstraction*, does not. In a sense which will be made explicit later in this section, each behaviour of the abstract program provides information on an infinite subset of the possible behaviours of the original program (the abstract program *overapproximates* the concrete one).

Abstraction techniques trade convergence against completeness, and this trade-off typically is on the incorrect side. This reflects the original aim of abstraction-based exploration techniques, i.e., proving programs correct. Classic abstract exploration always converges, and is void w.r.t. incorrect programs, while testing may not converge and is void w.r.t. correct programs. The degree of completeness of abstract exploration w.r.t. correct programs strongly depends on how the

$$
\begin{array}{ll}
l = 1 \wedge x \neq 0 \mapsto l := 2 & l = 1 \mapsto l := 2 \\
[]\ \ l = 1 \wedge x = 0 \mapsto l := 8 & []\ \ l = 1 \mapsto l := 8 \\
[]\ \ l = 2 \wedge x \mod 2 = 0 \mapsto l := 3 & []\ \ l = 2 \mapsto l := 3 \\
[]\ \ l = 2 \wedge x \mod 2 \neq 0 \mapsto l := 5 & []\ \ l = 2 \mapsto l := 5 \\
[]\ \ l = 3 \mapsto x := x - 2, l := 7 & []\ \ l = 3 \mapsto l := 7 \\
[]\ \ l = 5 \mapsto x := 3x + 1, l := 7 & []\ \ l = 5 \mapsto l := 7 \\
[]\ \ l = 7 \mapsto l := 1 & []\ \ l = 7 \mapsto l := 1
\end{array}
$$

Fig. 5. The guarded command program from Figure 1 (left) and its control abstraction (right)

program is abstracted. In the previous example, the control abstraction does not allow to decide whether the program may reach a state with $x < 0$.

Unifying the concepts. Intensionality and abstraction are different and independent concepts that can be unified by means of abstract interpretation [9]. Abstract interpretation is a general theory that defines how a correct fixpoint calculation on a lattice approximates a fixpoint calculation on a different lattice.

To unify intensionality and abstraction, we start by considering, for a program p and a set of initial states I, the function $f(S) \stackrel{\text{def}}{=} \text{Post}(p, S) \cup I$, which is a continuous function over the complete powerset lattice of program states. The least fixpoint of $f(S)$ represents the set of the reachable state space of the program. It exists and is equal to $\bigcup_{k \geq 0} \text{Post}^k(p, I)$. The fully exhaustive reachability procedure is therefore sound, in that it calculates this fixpoint whenever the iterative procedure converges.

We now consider a structure A composed by a different complete lattice $\mathcal{T}_A$, whose elements are interpreted as sets of states, together with a "translation" of Post into $\mathcal{T}_A$. More precisely,

$$A = (\mathcal{T}, [\![-]\!], \text{Post}_A),$$

where

- $\mathcal{T} = (\mathbf{T}, \top, \bot, \sqcup, \sqsubseteq)$ is a complete join-semilattice,
- $[\![-]\!] : \mathbf{T} \to \mathcal{P}(\mathbf{S})$ is monotone and preserves bottom and top ($[\![\top]\!] = \mathbf{S}$, $[\![\bot]\!] = \emptyset$),
- $\text{Post}_A : \mathbf{P} \times \mathbf{T} \to \mathbf{T}$ is monotone and has the property:

$$\text{Post}(p, [\![I_A]\!]) \subseteq [\![\text{Post}_A(p, I_A)]\!].$$

Intuitively, $[\![-]\!]$ assigns a meaning (a set of program states) to every element of $\mathbf{T}$, and Post_A overapproximates Post over $\mathbf{T}$.

The algorithm described in Figure 6 implements the algorithm for full exhaustive exploration from Figure 2 on $\mathcal{T}$, and calculates a safe overapproximation of S into S_A that upon convergence is a safe overapproximation of the reachable state space. Indeed, it can be easily proved that[4], whenever I_A overapproximates I (i.e., $I \subseteq [\![I_A]\!]$), it is:

$$\bigcup_{0 \leq k < n} \text{Post}^k(p, I) \subseteq [\![\bigsqcup_{0 \leq k < n} \text{Post}_A^k(p, I_A)]\!]$$

and:

$$\bigcup_{k \geq 0} \text{Post}^k(p, I) \subseteq [\![\bigsqcup_{k \geq 0} \text{Post}_A^k(p, I_A)]\!].$$

---

[4] We must take into account that monotony of $[\![-]\!]$ implies that $\bigcup_{S_A \in T} [\![S_A]\!] \subseteq [\![\bigsqcup_{S_A \in T} S_A]\!]$, for all $T \subseteq \mathbf{T}$.

Note that the abstract state space exploration procedure requires to initialize S_A by an arbitrary over-approximation I. In some cases, a monotonic map exists $[\![-]\!]^- : \mathcal{P}(\mathbf{S}) \to \mathbf{T}$ that, applied to a set of concrete states, produce an abstract over-approximation of it:

$$S \subseteq [\![[\![S]\!]^-]\!].$$

One would also expect that $[\![-]\!]^-$, when applied to a set of concrete states which is perfectly described by an abstract value S_A, returns such value. We will be less demanding, and be content when $[\![-]\!]^-$ returns an underapproximation of S_A:

$$[\![[\![S_A]\!]]\!]^- \sqsubseteq S_A.$$

Any pair of monotonic maps enjoying the above properties forms what is commonly known as a *Galois connection*, of which $[\![-]\!]^-$ is said to be the *abstraction* and $[\![-]\!]$ the *concretization* maps respectively. A Galois connection satisfies many properties, among which:

- $[\![-]\!]^-$ completely preserves joins, i.e., $\bigsqcup_{S \in T} [\![S]\!]^- = [\![\bigcup_{S \in T} S]\!]^-$, for all $T \subseteq \mathcal{P}(\mathbf{S})$,
- $[\![S]\!]^-$ is the *smallest* abstract value which covers S,
- $[\![S_A]\!]$ is the *greatest* set of states which can be soundly approximated by S_A.

The last property is simply a restatement of the fact that $[\![S_A]\!]$ is the meaning, or extension, of S_A.

Recasting the fixpoint computation into a simpler lattice $\mathcal{T}$ can solve the infinity issues. The reachable state space is, in the general case, uncomputable, but when $\mathcal{T}$ has finite height, the procedure always converges. When this happens because the abstract invariance termination check succeeds, the procedure finds a safe program invariant in $\mathcal{T}$ that contains the reachable state space, and answers CORRECT. When the abstract reachability termination check succeeds, nothing can be said about program correctness, unless A is *exact* (i.e., all of $[\![\text{Post}_A]\!]$, $[\![I_A]\!]$, and $[\![O_A]\!]$ are equal to their concrete counterparts). Correspondingly, the procedure returns either INCONCLUSIVE or INCORRECT.

Example: Symbolic execution. All the symbolic analyses can be formalized by means of abstract interpretation as illustrated above. As an example, we discuss *symbolic execution*, a well known technique introduced in the seventies [15].

While an ordinary program execution computes program states over concrete initial values (integers in our example language), symbolic execution summarizes infinite sets of such computations by computing program states over symbolic initial values. Symbolic execution produces *symbolic states*. A symbolic state maps the program variables to symbolic expressions that describe the current values of the variables as functions of their initial values. In our example guarded command language, a symbolic computation step fires simultaneously all the guarded assignments over an initial symbolic state and cumulates the resulting symbolic states. Firing a guarded assignment over a symbolic state updates the mapping of program variables to symbolic expressions to reflect the effect of the

```
ExploreAbstract (p,I,O,A):
```
-- $A \stackrel{\text{def}}{=} (\mathcal{T}, [\![-]\!], \text{Post}_A)$
```
  S_A  := some  I_A from  T s.t.  I ⊆ [[I_A]]
  O_A  := some  O_A from  T s.t.  [[O_A]] ⊆ O
  exact := ([[S_A]] = I)  ∧  ([[O_A]] = O)
  loop:
    if  S_A ⋢ O_A:
       if exact return  INCORRECT else  return  INCONCLUSIVE
    S'_A := Post_A(p, S_A)
    exact := exact ∧  ([[S'_A]] = Post(p, [[S_A]]))
    if  S'_A ⊑ S_A return  CORRECT
    S_A  := S'_A ⊔ S_A
```

Fig. 6. Abstract state space exploration

assignment. It also computes a *path condition* associated to each symbolic state. The path condition is a predicate that is computed as the logical "and" of all the guards in the sequence of assignments used to produce the state, and represents the assumption on the initial values of the variable for the state to exist. When a symbolic state has a contradictory path condition, it is discarded.

We can formalize symbolic execution by defining symbolic states as members of the set $\mathbf{S}_{sy} \stackrel{\text{def}}{=} (\mathbf{X} \to \mathbf{E}) \times \mathbf{E}$, whose elements are mappings of variables X to expressions E joint with a path condition E. For example, the symbolic state $(\{x \mapsto 2\,x+4\}, x > 0)$ represents a set of concrete states where the value of x is twice plus four its initial value, which in turn was an arbitrary positive integer. The initial symbolic state is a pair (id, *init*), where id is the identity map on variables (i.e., maps each variable to itself) and *init* is an expression having I as *extension*, where the extension of an expression $e \in \mathbf{E}$ is the set $\langle e \rangle$ of all and only the states where the expression evaluates to true:

$$\langle e \rangle \stackrel{\text{def}}{=} \{s \in \mathbf{S} \mid [\![e]\!]\, s = true\}\,,$$

and $\langle init \rangle = I$.

To define the meaning of sets of symbolic states, we first introduce an auxiliary translation function:

$$\ulcorner (\sigma, \gamma) \urcorner \stackrel{\text{def}}{=} \exists \mathbf{X}_0 . \gamma[\mathbf{X}_0/\mathbf{X}] \;\wedge\; \mathbf{X} = \sigma[\mathbf{X}_0/\mathbf{X}]\,.$$

The translation essentially states the existence of an initial (program) state that satisfies the guard of a symbolic state, and is transformed by the associated symbolic map into the final (program) state. As an example,

$$\ulcorner (\{x \mapsto 2\,x+4\}, x > 0) \urcorner = \exists x_0 . x_0 > 0 \wedge x = 2\,x_0 + 4\,.$$

We can now define the meaning of a set of symbolic states as the function $[\![-]\!] : \mathcal{P}(\mathbf{S}_{sy}) \to \mathcal{P}(\mathbf{S})$ defined as follows:

$$[\![S_{sy}]\!] \stackrel{\text{def}}{=} \bigcup_{s_{sy} \in S_{sy}} \langle \ulcorner s_{sy} \urcorner \rangle\,,$$

where the extension of a formula ϕ is, again, the set $\langle\phi\rangle$ of all and only the states which satisfy it:

$$\langle\phi\rangle \stackrel{\text{def}}{=} \{s \in \mathbf{S} \mid s \models \phi\}\,.$$

Finally, we define the symbolic post-state transformer by first introducing, for all $(\sigma, \gamma), (\sigma', \gamma') \in \mathbf{S}_{sy}$, a symbolic state transition relation:

$$(\sigma, \gamma) \xrightarrow{(f,g)} (\sigma', \gamma') \text{ iff } \sigma' = \llbracket f \rrbracket\,\sigma,\ \gamma' = \gamma \wedge \llbracket g \rrbracket\,\sigma \text{ and } \gamma' \text{ is satisfiable.}$$

As usual we write $(\sigma, \gamma) \xrightarrow{p} (\sigma', \gamma')$ to signify that $(\sigma, \gamma) \xrightarrow{(f,g)} (\sigma', \gamma')$ for some $(f, g) \in p$. The semantic functions $\llbracket f \rrbracket : (\mathbf{X} \to \mathbf{E}) \to (\mathbf{X} \to \mathbf{E})$ and $\llbracket g \rrbracket : (\mathbf{X} \to \mathbf{E}) \to \mathbf{E}$ are defined as plain syntactic substitutions of all the program variables x with the corresponding expressions $\sigma(x)$ into f and g:

$$\llbracket f \rrbracket\,\sigma \stackrel{\text{def}}{=} f[\sigma(\mathbf{X})/\mathbf{X}]\,, \qquad \llbracket g \rrbracket\,\sigma \stackrel{\text{def}}{=} g[\sigma(\mathbf{X})/\mathbf{X}]\,.$$

Now we can define the symbolic post-state transformer $\text{Post}_{sy} : \mathbf{P} \times \mathcal{P}(\mathbf{S}_{sy}) \to \mathcal{P}(\mathbf{S}_{sy})$ as:

$$\text{Post}_{sy}(p, T) \stackrel{\text{def}}{=} \bigcup_{(\sigma,\gamma)\in T} \{(\sigma', \gamma') \in \mathbf{S}_{sy} \mid (\sigma, \gamma) \xrightarrow{p} (\sigma', \gamma')\}\,.$$

Figure 7 shows an algorithm that explores the state space via symbolic execution. We define $\ulcorner S_{sy} \urcorner \stackrel{\text{def}}{=} \bigvee_{s_{sy}\in S_{sy}} \ulcorner s_{sy} \urcorner$ for finite sets S_{sy}. Both S_{sy} and S'_{sy} are always finite because S_{sy} is initially finite, and Post_{sy} creates at most one symbolic state per program statement. The algorithm translates sets of symbolic states to first-order sentences (although more convenient translations may be exploited in practice), and assumes the availability of an oracle that can decide over the validity of the first-order sentences. With these assumptions the encoding is exact, symbolic reachability is as precise as a fully exhaustive exploration, and thus diverges on the same class of programs.

```
ExploreSymbolicExecution(p,I,O):
   S_sy := {(id, init)} for some init ∈ E s.t. ⟨init⟩ = I
   ok  := some ok ∈ E s.t. ⟨ok⟩ = O
   loop:
      if ⌜S_sy⌝ ⟹ ok is not valid:
         return INCORRECT
      S'_sy := Post_sy(p, S_sy)
      if ⌜S'_sy⌝ ⟹ ⌜S_sy⌝ is valid:
         return CORRECT
      S_sy := S'_sy ∪ S_sy
```

Fig. 7. State space exploration by means of symbolic execution

In general, the symbolic exploration of a program may diverge differently from a fully exhaustive exploration, since a symbolic computation aggregates a possibly infinite set of concrete states that may behave differently with respect to divergence. As an example, the C program `while (x > 0) { x = x − 1; }` produces the infinite symbolic computation $(\{x \mapsto x\}, true) \xrightarrow{p} (\{x \mapsto x − 1\}, x > 0) \xrightarrow{p} (\{x \mapsto x − 2\}, x > 1) \xrightarrow{p} \ldots$ that represents the set of all the computations from states with $x > 0$, none of which is infinite[5].

In practice, symbolic execution must rely on incomplete theorem provers for deciding over logical statements. The actual precision of symbolic execution is strongly affected by these "hard points":

Check for failure: decide whether a symbolic state contains an error state;
Compute the successors: decide whether a path condition is satisfiable;
Check for success: decide whether a set of symbolic states is subsumed by another set of symbolic states.

The problem of checking reachability is sometimes tackled by encoding error states within the control flow (error states are all and only the states at a given location). In these cases, error states are identified by simply observing the current locations of the symbolic states, and the problem is therefore collapsed with that of computing the symbolic successors. The problem of computing the symbolic successors requires a decision procedure for checking the satisfiability of the path conditions. Path conditions are typically existential quantifications of conjunctions of atomic clauses, and thus the problem is less hard than full first-order logic satisfiability checking. The problem of efficiently detecting symbolic invariance (i.e., checking symbolic equivalence of states) is hard and has not been solved satisfactorily yet. Most approaches do not detect invariance at all.

Example: Predicate abstractions. Predicate abstractions exploit finite sets of predicates to interpret the state space of a program abstractly. The abstract lattice is the boolean lattice built over the set of predicates, which has finite height.

Let $H \stackrel{\text{def}}{=} \{h_0, \ldots h_{m-1}\} \subseteq \mathbf{E}$ a set of predicates with finite size m. We define the lattice of predicate abstraction over H as the powerset lattice over the powerset of the possible predicates, $\mathcal{P}(\mathcal{P}(H))$. The abstract lattice elements are usually interpreted as sets of *abstract states*, in analogy with the concrete powerset lattice of (concrete) program states. The meaning of an abstract state $\sigma \in \mathcal{P}(H)$ is the set of all and only the concrete states which verify the predicates in σ, and falsify all the other predicates. We formalize this interpretation by a translation function $\ulcorner - \urcorner$ defined as follows:

$$\ulcorner \sigma \urcorner \stackrel{\text{def}}{=} (\bigwedge_{h \in \sigma} h) \wedge (\bigwedge_{h \notin \sigma} \neg h), \quad \ulcorner \Sigma \urcorner \stackrel{\text{def}}{=} \bigvee_{\sigma \in \Sigma} \ulcorner \sigma \urcorner.$$

---

[5] While this shows that symbolic execution loses information about program termination, such imprecision is irrelevant in the context of this paper, where we consider only reachability properties.

The meaning of a lattice element $\Sigma \in \mathcal{P}(\mathcal{P}(H))$ is, quite simply, the extension of its translation, $[\![\Sigma]\!] \stackrel{\text{def}}{=} \langle \ulcorner \Sigma \urcorner \rangle$, where we define the extension of a formula ϕ analogously to our previous definition of extension of an expression:

$$\langle \phi \rangle \stackrel{\text{def}}{=} \{s \in \mathbf{S} \mid s \models \phi\}.$$

As an example, let us consider $H \stackrel{\text{def}}{=} \{h_0, h_1, h_2\}$ and $\Sigma \stackrel{\text{def}}{=} \{\{h_0, h_1\}, \{h_0, h_2\}\}$. Then, the meaning of Σ is the extension of $\ulcorner \Sigma \urcorner = (h_0 \wedge h_1 \wedge \neg h_2) \vee (h_0 \wedge \neg h_1 \wedge h_2)$. A lattice elements can alternatively be seen as a set of bitvectors, where each position corresponds to a predicate in H, and the corresponding bit indicates the predicate truth value. As an example, the above defined Σ can be considered as the bitvector set $\{110, 101\}$.

```
ExplorePredicateAbstraction(p,I,O,H):
    S_H := some Σ ∈ P(P(H)) s.t. I ⊆ {s ∈ S | s ⊨ ⌜Σ⌝}
    O_H := some Σ ∈ P(P(H)) s.t. {s ∈ S | s ⊨ ⌜Σ⌝} ⊆ O
    loop:
        if S_H ⊄ O_H return INCONCLUSIVE
        S'_H := Post_H(p, S_H)
        if S'_H ⊆ S_H return CORRECT
        S_H := S'_H ∪ S_H
```

Fig. 8. State space exploration by means of predicate abstraction

Figure 8 shows the state space exploration via predicate abstraction. The lattice of predicate abstraction being finite, the procedure always converges. Lattice operations are very simple to implement, for instance by means of ordered binary decision diagrams. The critical part of the procedure is the construction of Post_H. Indeed, an optimal Post_H exists, namely, the *existential* abstraction $\text{Post}_H^{\exists}$:

$$\text{Post}_H^{\exists}(p, \Sigma) \stackrel{\text{def}}{=} \bigcup_{\sigma \in \Sigma} \{\sigma' \in \mathcal{P}(H) \mid \sigma \xrightarrow{p} \sigma'\},$$

where

$$\sigma \xrightarrow{p} \sigma' \text{ iff } \text{Post}(p, [\![\sigma]\!]) \cap [\![\sigma']\!] \neq \emptyset.$$

In other words, $\sigma \xrightarrow{p} \sigma'$ iff exist $s \in [\![\sigma]\!], s' \in [\![\sigma']\!]$ such that $s \xrightarrow{p} s'$. The existential abstraction is not computable in the general case, but any sound Post_H must contain it (i.e., $\text{Post}_H^{\exists}(p, \Sigma) \subseteq \text{Post}_H(p, \Sigma)$) yielding a sound, albeit less precise, analysis. If we assume the availability of an oracle that can decide the underlying predicate logic, we can build the existential abstraction, for instance through symbolic execution:

$$\sigma \xrightarrow{p} \sigma' \text{ iff } \ulcorner \text{Post}_{sy}(p, \{(\text{id}, \ulcorner \sigma \urcorner)\}) \urcorner \wedge \ulcorner \sigma' \urcorner \not\equiv \text{false}.$$

For the sake of simplicity we define the *strongest postcondition predicate transformer* $\text{sp}(p, \phi)$ as:

$$\mathrm{sp}(p, \phi) \stackrel{\mathrm{def}}{=} \ulcorner \mathrm{Post}_{sy}(p, \{(\mathrm{id}, \phi)\}) \urcorner .$$

Intuitively, $\mathrm{sp}(p, \phi)$ is the strongest predicate satisfied by the post-states of the extension of ϕ—i.e., the predicate whose extension is precisely the set of such post-states. Its dual is the *weakest liberal precondition predicate transformer* $\mathrm{wlp}(p, \phi)$ that yields the weakest predicate satisfied by the states whose post-states satisfy ϕ.

```
PostPredicateAbstraction(p, H, Σ):
  result := ∅
  for all σ ∈ Σ:
    for all σ' ∈ P(H):
      if a theorem prover is able to prove that
      sp(p,⌜σ⌝) ⟹ ¬⌜σ'⌝ is valid (or, equivalently,
      that ⌜σ⌝ ⟹ wlp(p,¬⌜σ'⌝) is valid):
        skip
      else:
        result := result ∪ {σ'}
  return result
```

Fig. 9. Computing the abstract post-state transformer for predicate abstraction

The properties summarized above allow us to devise an algorithm to compute the abstract post-state transformer (see a draft in Figure 9). Soundness is ensured by considering all abstract states feasible unless the theorem prover proves the contrary. The precision of the resulting abstract post-state transformer depends on the precision of the theorem prover. The hard step of the procedure is deciding the validity of a formula with shape $\mathrm{sp}(p, \phi_0) \implies \phi_1$, a problem that can be proved equivalent to the (typically easier) problem of deciding the validity of the formula $\phi_0 \implies \mathrm{wlp}(p, \phi_1)$.

3.4 Classification of Basic Techniques

The categories introduced in this section allow us to classify practical state space exploration techniques usually indicated by terms like "model checking", "testing", etc. Table 1 summarizes the taxonomy that we briefly comment below.

Testing. As discussed above, testing is a non-monotonic and width-bounded state space exploration, but there exist variants where the exploration is also depth-bounded. The ideal "exhaustive testing" that consists of executing the program for all the possible inputs is still a non-monotonic and width-bounded state space exploration, with no width bound on S at iteration 0 (i.e., initially $S:=I$). A fully exhaustive exploration is still more precise than exhaustive testing, coinciding with the latter when the program is deterministic and I is finite (when I is not finite, exhaustive testing is infeasible).

Table 1. Features of the basic techniques

Technique	Symbolic	Abstract	Depth bounded	Width bounded	non Monotonic
Testing	No	No	No$^-$	Yes	Yes
Exhaustive testing	No	No	No$^-$	No	Yes
Symbolic execution	Yes	No	Yes$^-$	Yes$^-$	Yes$^-$
Abstract reachability	Yes	Yes	No	No	No
Model checking	Both	No	No	No	No$^-$
Bounded model checking	Yes	No	Yes	No	No

Legend:
Yes/No: Yes/No by definition, Yes$^-$/No$^-$: Yes/No in most cases, Both: Either ways

Symbolic execution. State space exploration via practical symbolic execution approaches is typically non-monotonic (conveniently since detection of symbolic loops is hard, and sets of symbolic states are usually represented in an extensional fashion), depth-bounded (to avoid divergence) and in some cases width-bounded (to reduce the exploration scope).

Abstract reachability. State space exploration via predicate abstraction is both symbolic and abstract. The techniques take advantage of the finite size of the abstract state space and the loss in precision by abstraction to explore the abstract state space in full and monotonically.

Model checking. Model checking is a family of techniques that validate a system against a specification of some program property, typically expressed in temporal logic, and produce a counterexample computation if the system violates the property. From the reachability viewpoint, a model checking procedure explores the program state space fully and exhaustively, either symbolically or explicitly, and is typically width-unbounded, depth-unbounded and monotonic. Bounded model checking is a form of depth-bounded symbolic exploration for finite-state systems. It starts from a specification of the system Post in propositional logic, "unrolls" it up to some finite depth, joins it with clauses establishing that the first state is initial and the last state is an error state, and uses a SAT solver to decide the satisfiability of the resulting formula. In the positive case, a SAT solver may produce a satisfying assignment, which can be interpreted as a finite computation leading to an error state.

4   Combining Techniques by Synergies

Testing and formal analysis techniques trade the precision of state space exploration against tractability and speed by means of different approximation strategies that we discussed in the previous section. Approximation criteria typically yield poor results except for very narrow classes of inputs. For this reason, best practice suggests to uses various techniques based on different approximation criteria, to compensate the respective deficiencies. Some recent research work shows that combining different techniques by sharing information about the state space can increase the benefits of heterogeneity. This section reviews some of the most popular approaches that combine techniques by sharing information about the state space, highlights the patterns that characterize the information sharing, and pinpoints the relative advantages. In this way, we draft a framework of the *synergies* between state exploration techniques as they are enacted by modern combined approaches.

4.1 A Note on "Static" and "Dynamic" Techniques

While this paper focuses mostly on the interplay between static and dynamic techniques, we do not explicitly characterized what makes a technique "static" or "dynamic", but we rely on the intuition that dynamic techniques refer to direct program execution, while static techniques refer to reasoning over models of program behaviour. We will assume that dynamic techniques are extensional, concrete, nonmonotonic, width-bounded, and possibly depth-bounded. Testing, the paradigmatic dynamic technique, has all these features, while the presence of width bound rules out techniques as the explicit-state exploration performed by the VeriSoft software model checker [11]. We assume that static techniques are either symbolic or abstract, but we will not assume them to be monotonic, width- or depth-unbounded.

4.2 Synergies between Techniques

Throughout this paper we consider synergies between state space exploration techniques. Synergies arise when different state space exploration techniques share or exchange information about the program state space. Sharing information is necessary, but not sufficient for igniting mutual synergies. For example, we do not consider synergetic two techniques A and B, if B simply uses information about the program state space produced by A. A synergy must also explain how such knowledge is integrated into the state space exploration performed by B, and how such integration contributes to improve the exploration chore of either A, or B, or both.

Synergies between techniques can improve the trade-off between precision, tractability and speed on the target of the analysis, often yielding combined techniques with better convergence and efficiency than their single components. This happens because synergies may:

- Improve the knowledge of the program state space by fusing the knowledge coming from different techniques.
- Accelerate the exploration of the program state space by delegating different regions of the state space to the technique which may explore it more efficiently;

Now we discuss more in detail how synergies may cope with the main sources of inefficiency and incompleteness for static and dynamic techniques. The discussion is informal, and is better substantiated later in this section through the analysis of a number of examples from recent literature.

Trading off over- and under-approximation. As highlighted in Section 3, practical techniques reason on the program state space by approximation, in the forms of either over-approximation, which is void w.r.t. incorrect programs, or under-approximation, which is void w.r.t. correct programs. Modern techniques rely at the same time on both over- and under-approximating exploration of the state space. The combination of the two forms of approximation can improve the exploration of the state space when each one *guides* the other. Under-approximating techniques can benefit from techniques that reason on the state space at a coarser grain, since they provide hints for accelerating the finer exploration towards regions of the state space more likely to contain an error state. Dually, when a concrete analysis proves that a region is free from erroneous behaviours, the over-approximated exploration can progress beyond this infeasible region, thus improving completeness.

Improving performance of symbolic reasoning. Static techniques are based on symbolic reasoning that underlies their expressiveness, but reduces performance and completeness. For example, symbolic execution requires deciding whether a symbolic post-state has an empty extension, in which case the symbolic state is pruned. Failing in pruning infeasible symbolic states may lead to unnecessary exploration and false alarms. Exploration based on predicate abstraction requires deciding whether an abstract states is unreachable from any of the abstract states that we could not prove unreachable. The cost of not proving that an abstract state is unreachable is a degradation of the precision of the model, which may at worst become unusable. Both procedures require to decide whether some symbolic formulas are satisfiable, a problem undecidable for most logical languages, and computationally hard for all the others. The consequence is that symbolic reasoning is a source of either incompleteness, or performance loss, or both.

A simple way of reducing the amount of invocations of a decision procedure is by exploiting concrete states. A concrete state implicitly proves satisfiable all the formulas that evaluate *true* in it (together with the negation of all the formulas that evaluate to *false*). Therefore the concrete states generated by a dynamic technique can be used to prove satisfiable the formulas arising from a static one. This approach is potentially useful since dynamic techniques are very efficient generators of concrete states, albeit with bias towards depth rather than width of exploration. Even when a state does not satisfy a formula of interest, it may satisfy some of its subformulas. Some techniques exploit this fact either to reduce the complexity of a formula by weakening/strengthening it (whenever a weaker or stronger formula than the original one is acceptable), or to build a candidate solution of a complex formula from the solution of one of its subformulas.

A small catalog of synergies. Here we introduce a simple catalog of the synergies we detected by surveying the recent literature. We will use the taxonomy in the next section to characterize the different examples.

- *Feeding of reachable states (FRS)*: A technique soundly feeds a translation of some of its reachable states into a coarser one. This is usually done to reduce the exploration chore of the coarser technique by providing it with information about the program state space that has already been computed, albeit at a different granularity (in which case the latter can delegate search on the uncovered abstract states to a finer technique by frontier abduction, FA);
- *Frontier abduction (FA)*: A technique feeds part of its frontier[6] into a finer technique, to delegate to the latter technique the exploration of the abduced frontier slice. The advantage may stem either because the finer technique is more efficient than the coarser one in exploring the frontier (in which case the results are afterwards ported to the coarser technique by FRS), or because the coarser technique may continue the analysis when the finer technique is stuck by invariance in an inconclusive way;
- *Refinement by unreachable region (RUR)*: Whenever an abstract region R is proved unreachable from a region Q by a more precise technique, the abstraction of the coarser technique can be refined by superimposing to it any set of predicates sufficient for showing the region unreachable (for instance, a predicate whose extension is precisely Q).
- *Constraining by region (CR)*: A technique constrains a finer one to analyze an abstract region it has detected. This is usually done when an abstract technique is stuck by reachability in an inconclusive way, and allows to determine feasible behaviours within the abstract region. It is typically followed by either FA (for efficiently searching within the region when some feasible behaviour exists) or RUR (when the region is unfeasible);
- *Formula construction by satisfiability (FCS)*: Whenever a symbolic technique must build a satisfiable formula from a set of clauses, it can exploit the existence of a concrete state which satisfies some of them to build it, or some relaxation of it. This has at least two applications: building a short formula from a long one (useful while performing refinement), and building a formula that can be solved automatically from a formula that cannot (useful while performing frontier abduction).

4.3   Detecting Synergies in Combined Techniques: A Brief Survey

Here we survey popular approaches that combine different testing, static analysis and formal verification techniques, with the goal of exemplifying the different possible synergies.

---

[6] With the word *frontier* we indicate a region of the state space which a technique has discovered, but of which has not yet calculated the successors. This loose definition is consistent with the many uses of the word in the related literature.

Directed testing. Directed testing aims to exercise all executable control-flow paths of a program under test systematically and automatically [12,16,17].[7] In directed testing, a controller supervises the generation of test cases to ensure that new test cases exercise control-flow paths not-yet-executed.

Directed testing uses a technique called *dynamic symbolic execution*, or *concolic execution*[8] that combines concrete execution of test cases with symbolic execution along the same execution paths. It starts with a set of randomly generated test inputs, and iterates through concolic execution and test input generation. While executing test cases, concolic execution produces the path conditions that represent the executed paths. The controller exploits these path conditions to generate new test cases that execute unexplored paths. It first identifies a branching point that contains a not-yet-executed branch in the executed paths (if none, the analysis terminates since all executable paths have been explored). Then, it considers all the clauses in a path condition up to that branching point, and negates the last clause to obtain a path condition that correspond to a not-yet-executed branch. Finally, it solves the identified path condition to generate a new test input (if none, the branch is infeasible, and the controller tries to identify another candidate not-yet-executed branch).

```
1  ExploreConcolic (p,I,O):
2     S := I_⊆ ; S_sy := {(id, init)} for some init ∈ E s.t. ⟨init⟩ = I
3     loop:
4        if S ⊄ O return INCORRECT
5        S' := Post(p,S)_⊆
6        if S' ⊆ S:
7           φ := ⌜S_sy⌝ ; φ' := sp(p,φ)
8           if φ' ⟹ φ return CORRECT
9           S' := ⟨φ' ∧ ¬φ⟩_⊆
10       S'_sy := Post_co(p, S_sy, S')
11       S := S' − S ; S_sy := S'_sy ∪ S_sy
```

Fig. 10. Concolic execution

Figure 10 illustrates the concolic execution approach underlying directed testing approaches, recast on the reachability problem. The presentation abstracts from details like the order of the visit of the concrete state space, to focus on the main characteristics of the approach, thus accounting for all the features invariant across the different implementations available in literature.

The approach in Figure 10 maintains a set of reachable concrete states, S, and a set of reachable symbolic states, S_{sy}. The set of concrete states is updated by either concrete execution or test input generation, the set of symbolic states

---

[7] In practice, this goal often implies exercising as many paths as possible up to some predefined testing budget, since the number of control-flow paths is infinite for most programs.

[8] Concolic = *concrete* + symb*olic*.

is always updated by feeding reachable states from S. The set S is initialized with a set of initial states that represent random test input (line 2), and S' is a selection of a nontrivial subset of $\text{Post}(p, S)$ (line 5). If such a subset does not exist ($S' \subseteq S$), the approach generates new test inputs from S_{sy} by frontier abduction (lines 7–9).

The approach adds new reachable symbolic states with a Post_{co} operator that is defined by means of a new symbolic state transition relation that requires successors to be *supported* by some set of concrete states S':

$$(\sigma, \gamma) \xrightarrow[S']{(f,g)} (\sigma', \gamma') \ \text{iff} \ \sigma' = [\![f]\!]\sigma, \ \gamma' = \gamma \wedge [\![g]\!]\sigma \ \text{and}$$

$$[\![\gamma']\!]s' = true \ \text{for some} \ s' \in S'.$$

As we can see, the new symbolic state transition relation requires the target path condition be satisfied by a concrete state in S' (thus simplifying the computation). The corresponding Post_{co} operator can be easily defined as follows:

$$\text{Post}_{co}(p, T, S') \overset{\text{def}}{=} \bigcup_{(\sigma, \gamma) \in T} \{(\sigma', \gamma') \in \mathbf{S}_{sy} \mid (\sigma, \gamma) \xrightarrow[S']{p} (\sigma', \gamma')\},$$

and can be interpreted as an abstraction operator $[\![-]\!]^{-}_{S_{sy}}$ from the concrete to the symbolic state space that selects the smallest set of symbolic states that are supported by a corresponding concrete one. By defining $[\![S']\!]^{-}_{S_{sy}} \overset{\text{def}}{=} \text{Post}_{co}(p, S_{sy}, S')$, the FRS (feeding of reachable states) nature of concolic execution is captured by the sequence of operations:

$$S'_{sy} := [\![S']\!]^{-}_{S_{sy}} \ ; \ S_{sy} := S'_{sy} \cup S_{sy}.$$

The loop in Figure 10 (lines 3–11) first computes the successors of the reachable symbolic states S_{sy} by exploiting the symbolic post-state transformer (line 7). This is the computationally most expensive step of the whole procedure, but it is inevitable to overcome the fact that testing is width-bounded. Then, it builds the frontier as a predicate satisfied by all the concrete post-states of $[\![S_{sy}]\!]$ that are not in $[\![S_{sy}]\!]$, selects some concrete frontier states, and abduces them to form the set of concrete post-states S' (line 9). This last step ensures progress, since it forces the execution of a sequence of statements different from the sequences executed until then. The procedure is based on the assumption that a firing sequence that produces an error state, produce *only* error states. Under this assumption, we can stop exploring symbolic states as soon as we find a non-erroneous concrete state in their extensions. The FA (frontier abduction) nature of concolic execution is captured by the sequence of statements:

$$S' := \langle \phi' \wedge \neg \phi \rangle_{\subseteq} \ ; \ S := S' - S.$$

Directed testing and classic symbolic execution share the goal of increasing code coverage, but direct testing is more effective, because while classic symbolic execution needs to prove the feasibility of each branch along the explored paths, directed testing discovers most branches by testing, and thus can safely assume feasibility. As discussed in Section 5, directed testing can improve the efficiency up to 50% over classic symbolic execution, needing up to 50% less calls to an external solver than classic symbolic execution.

Dynamic abstract interpretation. The dynamic abstract interpretation approach proposed by Yorsh, Ball and Sagiv in 2006 and that we will refer to as the YORSH-BALL-SAGIV procedure is based on a combination of dynamic and static analysis claimed to be more efficient than the traditional approach of statically calculating the abstract transformer [18]. In a nutshell, the YORSH-BALL-SAGIV procedure aims to compute the most-precise abstract property with respect to an abstraction, without explicitly computing the corresponding most-precise abstract transformer. The YORSH-BALL-SAGIV procedure is parametric with respect to the categories of abstractions. Here we describe the YORSH-BALL-SAGIV procedure by assuming a predicate abstraction with predicates in H.

The YORSH-BALL-SAGIV procedure alternates program execution and theorem proving. Whenever the program is executed for some (possibly random) input, all traversed concrete states s are abstracted to the corresponding abstract ones via a suitable abstraction map $[\![-]\!]_H^-$:

$$\beta_H(s) \overset{\text{def}}{=} \{\{h \in H \mid s \models h\}\}, \quad [\![S]\!]_H \overset{\text{def}}{=} \bigcup_{s \in S} \beta_H(s).$$

$[\![-]\!]_H^-$ can be easily computed when S is finite (which is always the case with testing) by evaluating all the predicates in H against all the concrete states in S. The YORSH-BALL-SAGIV procedure cumulates the abstract states incrementally cumulated throughout concrete execution, to build the currently reached abstract region. At any point of the analysis, for example when the execution terminates or does not produce new abstract states, the current set of abstract states can be checked for invariance, to understand whether it covers the reachable state space of the program under analysis. This check is done by querying a theorem prover on whether any post-state of any concrete state in the computed abstract region is still in the same region. If this is the case, the procedure can terminate since it has computed an invariant for the program that covers its reachable state space. Otherwise, there is at least one concrete state that can be found by a suitable solver such that (1) it is not in the computed the abstract region, and (2) it is a successor of some state in the computed abstract region. Concrete execution of the program starting from such state feeds back a new iteration of the analysis, possibly discovering new reachable abstract states.

Figure 11 illustrates the YORSH-BALL-SAGIV procedure for an arbitrary abstraction A by referring to the reachability problem. The structure of the procedure shares the structure of concolic execution (Figure 10), reflecting the fact that the two procedures work similarly. They compute a set of reachable states with concrete execution, use the concrete states to build a set of abstract states, and when the concrete execution is stuck because of inconclusive invariance, they exploit frontier abduction to feed concrete execution of fresh states. Like concolic execution, the YORSH-BALL-SAGIV procedure has the nature of both

```
ExploreBallYorshSagiv (p,I,O,A):
  S  := I⊆ ; S_A := ⟦S⟧⁻_A
  loop:
    if  S ⊄ O return INCONCLUSIVE
    S' := Post(p,S)⊆
    if  S' ⊆ S:
      φ  := ⌈S_A⌉ ; φ' := sp(p,φ)
      if φ' ⟹ φ return CORRECT
      S' := ⟨φ' ∧ ¬φ⟩⊆
    S'_A := ⟦S'⟧⁻_A
    S  := S' − S ;  S_A  := S'_A ⊔ S_A
```

Fig. 11. YORSH-BALL-SAGIV procedure

a feeding of reachable states (FRS) and a frontier abduction (FA) approach, as illustrated by the formulas:

$$S'_A := \llbracket S' \rrbracket^-_A \; ; \; S_A := S'_A \sqcup S_A \,,$$

and:

$$S' := \langle \phi' \wedge \neg\phi \rangle_{\subseteq} \; ; \; S := S' - S \,.$$

The frontier is built by symbolically analyzing the abstract region S_A, which (trivially) constrains symbolic execution by the statement:

$$\phi := \ulcorner S_A \urcorner \; ; \; \phi' := \mathrm{sp}(p,\phi) \,.$$

In general, the YORSH-BALL-SAGIV procedure converges when the height of the lattice of abstract program properties is finite, as in the case of predicate abstraction. When the height of the lattice is finite and the procedure is adequately supported by a theorem prover and a solver, the YORSH-BALL-SAGIV procedure computes an abstract property that covers as many states as the most-precise (i.e., existential) abstract interpreter.

The readers should notice that the concrete states computed by checking invariance are not necessarily reachable program states, and this is in line with the over-approximation of the most-precise abstract interpreter. The more the abstract states discovered by concrete execution, the more the YORSH-BALL-SAGIV procedure is efficient with respect to a completely static approach like the predicate abstraction approach illustrated in Figures 8 and 9. The YORSH-BALL-SAGIV procedure improves on speed, while maintaining the same precision. We discuss this point in detail in Section 5.

We conclude with a final remark that apply to both the YORSH-BALL-SAGIV procedure and concolic execution: The invariance check and frontier abduction consider, essentially, the same predicates. Both problems are tantamount to deciding whether the predicate $\phi' \wedge \neg\phi$ has at least a solution. When we can find a solution, it is an abduced frontier, since it ensures progress towards a yet uncovered abstract state, that can be added to S_A.

Static/dynamic verification. The static/dynamic verification approach DASH recently introduced by Beckman et al. computes the reachability of (faulty) statements of programs [3]. Given a program p and a target statement in p, DASH searches for either a test case that executes the target statement, or a proof that such statement is unreachable in p. DASH searches for a test case that executes the target statement by exploring program paths increasingly closer to it, by means of directed testing. It tries to prove that the target statement is unreachable by progressively refining a finite abstract model that conservatively overapproximates all transitions between the program statements, until the model eventually contains no abstract trace that includes the target statement. The two searches interplay as DASH stores the abstract states supported by the concrete states generated by testing, and uses such information to direct and coordinate test case generation and model refinement.

DASH initially assumes an abstract model equivalent to the static control flow graph of the program, and generates a random test case. Then DASH iterates through the following steps until either the target statement becomes unreachable in the current abstract model, or it is executed by a test case. DASH identifies a frontier transition within the abstract model, i.e. a transition that belongs to some abstract trace that goes from the program entry to the target statement[9], and connects the last abstract state σ_1 covered by at least a test case t, to the first abstract state σ_2 not covered by any test case. Next, it executes t concolically up to state σ_1, augments the obtained path condition with the clause to cross the frontier to σ_2, and checks for its satisfiability with an automatic solver. A solution, when found by the solver, is a new test case that covers σ_2, thus progressing in the search for a feasible path towards the target statement. If the solver does not find a solution, DASH eliminates the infeasible abstract trace from the model by conservatively refining σ_1 along the frontier transition.

Figure 12 illustrates how DASH refines the model (Figure 12 (b)), given a frontier transition from an abstract state σ_1 covered by a concrete state s to a state σ_2 (Figure 12 (a)). From the definition of frontier it follows that σ_1 is supported by a concrete state s generated by a test t, σ_2 is not supported by any concrete state, and no state reaching σ_1 along t can reach σ_2. DASH splits σ_1 into two new states annotated with refinement predicates r and its negation respectively[10]. The predicate r is satisfied by all the concrete states that may have a post-state in σ_2, thus $\neg r$ is satisfied by all the concrete states that have *no* post-states in σ_2 (including s)[11]. Consequently, σ_2 may be reachable from the region with extension $r \wedge \ulcorner \sigma_1 \urcorner$, but not from the region with extension $\neg r \wedge \ulcorner \sigma_1 \urcorner$. This sets the frontier one step backwards, and the problem of proving

---

[9] Such a transition is guaranteed to exist, until the termination conditions are not met.

[10] Note that, if a frontier state σ_2 includes a refinement predicate, DASH can generate a test case that satisfy it. For this reason, concolic execution adds the refinement predicate of σ_2 to the current path condition.

[11] When the program is deterministic, *every* concrete state that supports σ_1 must satisfy $\neg r$: otherwise, its only possible successor would support σ_2 thatis not supported by the definition of frontier.

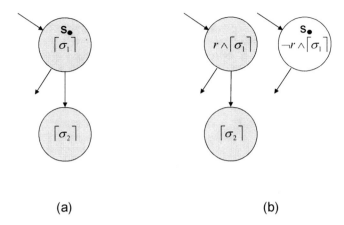

Fig. 12. Refining an infeasible transition (Abstract states are annotated with the predicates signifying their extensions)

the reachability of σ_2 is reduced to the problem of proving the reachability of $r \wedge \ulcorner \sigma_1 \urcorner$. When σ_2 is unreachable, subsequent iterations of DASH may propagate the frontier back beyond the entry state of the model. In such case, DASH safely concludes that such a frontier is infeasible and safely removes the frontier edge from the model without splitting the source node.

Figure 13 illustrates the DASH approach by considering predicate abstraction as the framework for abstraction refinement. The abstraction captures the sets of initial and error states, by including two predicates $init$ and ok with extension I and O respectively. Similarly to concolic execution and to the YORSH-BALL-SAGIV procedure, DASH starts from a set of random test cases, executes them, and collects the corresponding reachable symbolic and abstract states exploiting the feeding of reachable states (FRS) synergy (lines 7 and 20 in Figure 21). If testing reveals an error state, DASH terminates signaling `INCORRECT` (line 6). Otherwise, DASH explores exhaustively the abstract space (lines 9–11) starting from the region discovered through the FRS synergy. This exploration builds either a safe invariant in S_H or an abstract region that contains an error state. In the first case DASH concludes with `CORRECT` (line 11), in the latter case, DASH progresses (lines 12–19), since neither testing nor abstract verification have produced a conclusive answer yet.

In DASH, test case generation and refinement exploit S_H to guarantee that the analysis progresses towards the final goal. Test case generation progresses the search towards a reachable error state by generating a test case that traverses at least an abstract state in S_H (not necessarily the abstract error state) that has not been already traversed by some state in S. Such constraint is expressed by a predicate ϕ_{new} that is conjoined to the symbolic post-states to be explored (line 15, left part). ϕ_{new} is defined in line 14 as any predicate which is nontrivial (whenever possible) and stronger than the whole uncovered abstract region. We introduce at the purpose a strengthening function $(-)_\Rightarrow$, enjoying the same properties as sampling:

```
1   ExploreDASH(p,I,O):
2     H  := {init,ok}  ;  O_H  :=  {{init,ok},{ok}}
3     S  := I_⊆  ;  S_sy  :=  {(id,init)}  ;  S_H := [[S]]_H^-
4       where init,ok ∈ E s.t. ⟨init⟩ = I, ⟨ok⟩ = O
5     loop:
6       if S ⊄ O return INCORRECT
7       S'  := Post(p,S)_⊆  ;  S'_H  :=  [[S']]_H^-
8       if S' ⊆ S:
9         if S_H ⊑ O_H:
10          S'_H  :=  Post_H(p,S_H)
11          if S'_H ⊑ S_H return CORRECT
12        else:
13          φ  := ⌜S_sy⌝  ;  φ'  :=  sp(p,φ)
14          φ_new  :=  (⌜S_H⌝ ∧ ¬ ⌜[[S]]_H^-⌝)_⇒
15          S'  := ⟨φ' ∧ φ_new⟩_⊆  ;  S'_H  :=  [[S']]_H^-
16          if S' = ∅:
17            r  :=¬ wlp(p,¬φ_new)  ;  H  :=  H ∪ {r}
18            O_H  :=  {σ ∈ P(H) | ok ∈ σ}
19            S_H  :=  [[S]]_H^-
20      S'_sy  := Post_co(p,S_sy,S')
21      S  := S' ∪ S  ;  S_sy  :=  S'_sy ⊔ S_sy  ;  S_H  :=  S'_H ⊔ S_H
```

Fig. 13. DASH

$$\phi_\Rightarrow \implies \phi, \quad \phi \not\equiv false \text{ implies } \phi_\Rightarrow \not\equiv false.$$

Strengthening reflects the previous informal description of DASH, where only a single abstract error trace, rather than the whole frontier, is considered for test case generation. The region $\phi' \wedge \phi_{new}$ is abduced to concrete execution (line 15). If abduction does not progress the analysis, then no successor of a state in S_{sy} can support the abstract states in ϕ_{new}. DASH exploits this information to refine the model by adding a refinement predicate, i.e., the weakest precondition of $\neg\phi_{new}$, to H (line 17). The refinement predicate is satisfied by all (and only) the states with no successors in ϕ_{new}. Figure 13 does not highlight the fact that DASH calculates $\text{Post}_{H \cup \{r\}}$ syntactically, i.e., without invoking a theorem prover. More precisely, it splits the abstract states along r, it replicates $\text{Post}_{H \cup \{r\}}$ on all the split states, and then it cancels all the transitions from the abstract states where r is false, to abstract states where ϕ_{new} is true. While this is an especially limited form of refinement, it has the advantage of being computationally inexpensive, and is sufficient to ensure that test case generation will not retry to support these abstract states along the same frontier.

In DASH any discovered symbolic state is always supported by at least one concrete state (as in concolic execution), and any discovered abstract states may be supported or not (but during testing surely is) by a concrete state. In formulas:

$$[[S]]_{S_{sy}}^- = S_{sy}, \quad [[S]]_H^- \sqsubseteq S_H,$$

and $[\![S]\!]_H^- = S_H$ at all iterations which execute line 7. When DASH cannot generate a test case that supports a non yet supported abstract state, the model is refined by removing the unfeasible abstract transitions, thus ensuring progress of either abstract state space exploration or test case generation in the following steps.

DASH is based on several synergies: FRS (feeding of reachable states) from testing to symbolic exploration:

$$S'_{sy} := [\![S']\!]_{S_{sy}}^- \; ; \; S_{sy} := S'_{sy} \cup S_{sy} \, ,$$

and from testing to abstract exploration:

$$S'_H := [\![S']\!]_H^- \; ; \; S_H := S'_H \sqcup S_H \, ,$$

CR (constraining by region) from abstract exploration and testing to symbolic exploration:

$$\phi_{new} := (\ulcorner S_H \urcorner \wedge \neg \ulcorner [\![S]\!]_H^- \urcorner)_{\Rightarrow} \, ,$$

FA (frontier abduction) to testing:

$$S' := \langle \phi' \wedge \phi_{new} \rangle_{\subseteq} \; ; \; S := S' \cup S \, ,$$

and RUR (refinement by unreachable region) from symbolic exploration to abstract exploration:

$$r := \neg \, \mathrm{wlp}(p, \neg \phi_{new}) \; ; \; H := H \cup \{r\} \; ; \; O_H := [\![O]\!]^{op,-} \; ; \; S_H := [\![S]\!]_H^- \, .$$

5   Quantifying the Advantage of Synergies

Section 4 defined synergies between techniques, proposed a simple taxonomy of synergies, and discussed the different synergies by means fo three state-of-art approaches. A taxonomy is a key step towards comparing different approaches both qualitatively and quantitatively. To quantifying the advantage of combined techniques, we must put special care in isolating the effects of a specific component among the others, in identifying techniques that do not leverage the synergy to compare against, and in choosing appropriate metrics.

This section reports our preliminary insight about quantifying the performance gain that the joint use of frontier abdution and feeding of reachable states (FA+FRS) may introduce into an abstract exploration, with respect to techniques that perform the abstract exploration statically. The value of FA+FRS can be paramount because the satisfiability checks (required by abstract static analyses to guarantee soundness and avoid false-positive results) is the most expensive step, since the SAT problem is NP complete in the general case [8]. Many papers that discuss and experiment with static analyses, report that the time complexity of the algorithms is dominated by the calls to the automatic solver [14]. Combined techniques guarantee the satisfiability of the abstract traces by construction, and thus eliminate such performance costs.

This section shows that, thanks to FA+FRS, combined exploration techniques require less calls to constrain solvers than equivalent static techniques, and tries to analytically quantify the difference. Similar quantifications can be provided for the other synergies indicated in Section 4, thus leading to a complete comparison of different approaches.

5.1   Directed Testing

Here we try to analytically quantify the benefit of FA+FRS when exploited for directed testing, as in DART and CUTE [12,16], and we compare the results with purely static global symbolic execution, as in JAVA PATHFINDER and SAVE [1,7].

To isolate the effects of FA+FRS and avoid the influences of the mutual effects of different optimizations we draw (with no loss of generality) on the following assumptions:

- We assume an ideal sound and complete prover and a fully deterministic program;
- We assume that any other optimization that may derive from synergies other than FA and FRS is switched off[12];
- We assume that the considered pure-static and static-dynamic analysis procedures explore the program paths in exactly the same order.

To be more precise, we refer to the following versions of the concolic and symbolic exploration procedures presented in the previous sections:

Concolic exploration

1. Let M be an initially empty symbolic execution model of the program state space, (the tree of all the static program paths with all branches along them tagged as potentially feasible);
2. Concretely execute the program on an input and update M by tagging all the branches on the path as feasible;
3. Identify a path to a potentially feasible and not-yet executed branch b, with all predecessors tagged as feasible; stop if no such branch exists;
4. Symbolically execute the program along the path to the branch b identified at step 3, and solve the path condition to a satisfying assignment; If the solver fails (returns *unsatisfiable*), annotate b as infeasible along the path, and iterate from step 3; Otherwise, iterate from step 2 by considering the returned satisfying assignment as a new input.

Static symbolic exploration

1. Let M be a, initially empty, symbolic execution model of the program state space, as for concolic exploration step 1;

---

[12] For example, common concolic analyses use the values from concrete states to simplify (approximate) the symbolic formulas of the corresponding symbolic states [12,16]. We deliberately ignore this and other similar optimizations.

2. Symbolically execute in-depth the program along a path in M, by checking for each branching point the satisfiability of a branch (say b_1) out of the two possible branches b_1 and b_2; If b_1 is satisfiable, proceed the execution through b_1, else proceed through b_2; Update M by tagging all the feasible and unfeasible branches on the path;

3. Identify a path to a never executed, potentially feasible branch b, with all predecessors tagged as feasible, in the same order as for concolic exploration; stop if no such branch exists;

4. Decide whether the path condition along the path to b identified at step 3 is satisfiable; If it is not, annotate b as infeasible along the path, otherwise, annotate b as feasible along the path. Iterate from step 3.

To compare the two classes of approaches, we assume that both symbolic and concolic explorations select program paths and branches in the same order (steps 2–3 in both cases referring to the descriptions above). The path exploration order of concolic execution depends on the test cases generated by a solver as solutions of a satisfiability problem. Since the solver may pick different solutions, the exploration order may vary if we repeat multiple times the analysis of the same program. The exploration order of static symbolic exploration depends on the analyzer that may freely decide which branch to explore first. However, for all directed testing explorations of a program, there exists a global symbolic execution that explores the program paths in the same order. By assuming the same exploration order for the two approaches, we aim to eliminate the effect of the exploration order on performance.

We quantify the performance of the different approaches as the number of calls to the theorem prover. Since all branching points of the class of deterministic programs that we consider lead to either one or two feasible paths, a pure symbolic execution calls the prover as most twice for each branching point. When both branches are feasible (two-way branching point), two calls are necessary—one call to confirm the feasibility of each branch. When one of the branches is infeasible (one-way branching point), pure symbolic execution calls the solver either once or twice, depending on whether or not the infeasible branch is discovered first, and thus the feasibility of the other path can be directly inferred without the need of the second theorem prover call. We conservatively assume that both cases can happen with 50% probability, independently on the evaluation order of branches. The concolic approach, on the other hand, calls the prover only once for each branching point, since the feasibility of one of the branches derives from the fact that has been covered by the concrete execution, and is thus a benefit of the FRS synergy.

Under the above assumptions, we can compute both the average number of calls to the solver during static symbolic execution ($SolverCalls_{Static}$) and during concolic execution ($SolverCalls_{Concolic}$), and the relative gain G that derives from FA+FRS. Let B_{1way} and B_{2way} be the number of one- and two-way branching points analyzed so far, respectively, we have:

$$SolverCalls_{Static} = \frac{B_{1way}}{2} + 2\,\frac{B_{1way}}{2} + 2B_{2way}\,,$$
$$SolverCalls_{Concolic} = B_{1way} + B_{2way}\,,$$

and consequently:

$$G = SolverCalls_{Static} - SolverCalls_{Concolic} = \frac{B_{1way}}{2} + B_{2way}\,.$$

We can then conclude that the gain is always positive, and depends on the number of one- and two-way branching points of the program. The structure of the program state space strongly affects the yield of FA+FRS—the "narrower" the program state space is, the more symbolic states a test case is able to discover on average, and thus the less must be discovered by invoking the solver.

5.2   Dynamic Abstract Interpretation

Here we try to quantify the benefit of FA+FRS as exploited in YORSH-BALL-SAGIV [18], and compare it with purely static abstract interpretation used to build a (possibly optimal) abstract trasformer, as done for example by SLAM [2]. As in the former case, we assume an ideal sound and complete prover, a fully deterministic program, the presence of no synergies other than FA+FRS, and the same order of exploration of the abstract program states.

To be more precise, we refer to the following versions of the static/dynamic and static procedures presented in the previous sections:

Static/dynamic abstract exploration

1. Let S_A be a set of abstract states initialized to a possibly empty set of the initial abstract states;
2. Concretely execute the program with an input, and extend S_A with the abstract states supported by the concrete states reached during the concrete execution;
3. Solve the constraints associated to the abstract states up to a satisfying assignment $sp(p, \ulcorner S_A \urcorner) \wedge \neg \ulcorner S_A \urcorner$; If the solver fails (returns *unsatisfiable*), stop; Otherwise, iterate from step 2 by considering the returned satisfying assignment as a new input.

Static abstract exploration

1. Let S_A be a set of abstract states initialized to a possibly empty set of the initial abstract states;
2. Solve the constraints associated to the abstract states up to a satisfying assignment $sp(p, \ulcorner S_A \urcorner) \wedge \neg \ulcorner S_A \urcorner$; If solver fails (returns *unsatisfiable*), stop; Otherwise add the abstract state supported by the returned satisfying assignment to S_A, and iterate this step.

As above, we assume that the static/dynamic and the static abstract approaches explore abstract state in the same order. Under these assumptions, the static approach calls the solver once at each step to compute each abstract state except for the initial ones, and once at the end to verify the transitive closure. Thus, if the final abstraction contains N abstract states out of which I are initial states that do not result in a call to the solver, the static approach calls the solver $N - I + 1$ times. The static/dynamic approach calls the solver once for each new state, and once at the end to discover abstract invariance. It does not call the solver for the $0 \leq C < N - I$ reachable abstract states discovered by concrete execution, thus resulting in a total of $N - I - C + 1$ calls. In summary:

$$SolverCalls_{Static} = N - I + 1 \,,$$
$$SolverCalls_{S/D} = N - I - C + 1 \,,$$

and consequently:

$$G = SolverCalls_{Static} - SolverCalls_{S/D} = C \,.$$

The gain of the static/dynamic procedure over the purely static one is the number of abstract states discovered by concrete execution. This again depends on the shape of the abstract state space: Narrow structures enable discovering more abstract states with a single test case, thus yielding higher gains.

6   Conclusions and Future Work

This paper discusses the synergies between static and dynamic approaches and proposes a way of quantifying the gain that derives from the synergy of the different approaches, exemplifying it on some popular proposals. The paper makes some simplifying assumptions that have a limited impact on the generality of the results presented in this paper. In this concluding section, we discuss the main assumptions to indicate possible directions for future work.

Different kinds of safety properties. This paper focuses on reachability properties of programs. Reachability has the desirable feature of being both simple conceptually and relevant in practice, and is an important kind of *safety* property. Safety properties express the fact that "something bad will not happen", and their violation can be detected by observing a finite prefix of infinite violating computations. A wide range of safety properties are customarily considered in software engineering, for instance assertions and code contracts (preconditions, postconditions, invariants). Focusing on reachability alone may appear somehow reductive. From a purely theoretical viewpoint, every safety property can be expressed as an equivalent reachability one over an instrumented version of the program under analysis. As an example, assertions can be encoded as guarded assignments that set a flag when the assertion is violated. In practice, there exists specialized approaches that detect violations of a safety specification expressed in a specification language, like JML [5]. These methods can be studied orthogonally to the state space exploration techniques which are the main topic of this paper.

Liveness properties. We do not consider *liveness* properties either. Liveness properties state that every program computation eventually does "something useful".

Termination is the prototypical liveness property. Differently from safety properties, observing a finite prefix of a program computation does not give any information about whether the computation violates or not a liveness property—the computation must be considered as a whole. For this reason, the techniques for verifying liveness properties differ from the ones for safety properties. Another consequence of this fact is that liveness analysis does not substantially benefit from testing, which is bound to inspecting finite prefixes of program executions. To the best of our knowledge, all the techniques in literature for deciding liveness properties of software are purely static.

Concurrency. From the viewpoint of safety properties, concurrent systems are essentially equivalent to nondeterministic ones. The guarded command language admits bounded nondeterminism, the kind of nondeterminism of concurrent systems that have a finite number of threads. In this paper we do not assume determinism, unless in few parts where the assumption is explicitly stated. In practice, concurrency and nondeterminism usually means that the runtime support of the language (the scheduler) can choose the next state among a set of possible successors. This hinders the effectiveness of testing, which acts only through program inputs, in steering the behaviour of programs towards errors. This issues is tackled by combined approaches either by controlling the scheduling or by backtracking. In the first case, the analysis uses some additional inputs to control the scheduler, in the second case, the analysis stores unvisited states to analyze them later. Both approaches can be seen as implementations of the combination techniques discussed in this paper.

Procedures, encapsulation, polymorphism, dynamic dispatch. The simple programming language that we consider does not offer any constructs for structuring large-scale programs, such as procedural abstraction, information hiding, type inheritance, dynamic dispatching, etc. While these constructs are always present in real software, most of the combined approaches available in literature are essentially interprocedural. The main reason is that interprocedural static analysis is a notoriously hard problem (testing, on the other hand, is easily performed both in an intraprocedural and interprocedural fashion). Some recent efforts are available in literature, which exploit the static/dynamic combination to improve interprocedural static analysis, and may deserve future attention [13].

Acknowledgements. This work is partially supported by the European Community under the call FP7-ICT-2009-5 – project acronym PINCETTE, project number 257647. The authors are solely responsible for the content of this paper. It does not represent the opinion of the European Community, and the European Community is not responsible for any use that might be made of data appearing therein.

References

1. Anand, S., Păsăreanu, C.S., Visser, W.: JPF–SE: A Symbolic Execution Extension to Java pathFinder. In: Grumberg, O., Huth, M. (eds.) TACAS 2007. LNCS, vol. 4424, pp. 134–138. Springer, Heidelberg (2007)

2. Ball, T., Rajamani, S.K.: Automatically Validating Temporal Safety Properties of Interfaces. In: Dwyer, M.B. (ed.) SPIN 2001. LNCS, vol. 2057, pp. 103–122. Springer, Heidelberg (2001)
3. Beckman, N.E., Nori, A.V., Rajamani, S.K., Simmons, R.J.: Proofs from tests. In: 2008 International Symposium on Software Testing and Analysis, pp. 3–14. ACM (2008)
4. Bryant, R.E.: Graph-based algorithms for boolean function manipulation. IEEE Transactions on Computers C-35(8), 677–691 (1986)
5. Chalin, P., Kiniry, J.R., Leavens, G.T., Poll, E.: Beyond Assertions: Advanced Specification and Verification with JML and eSC/Java2. In: de Boer, F.S., Bonsangue, M.M., Graf, S., de Roever, W.-P. (eds.) FMCO 2005. LNCS, vol. 4111, pp. 342–363. Springer, Heidelberg (2006)
6. Chandy, K.M., Misra, J.: Parallel Program Design: A Foundation. Addison-Wesley (1988)
7. Coen-Porisini, A., Denaro, G., Ghezzi, C., Pezzè, M.: Using symbolic execution for verifying safety-critical systems. In: Joint 8th European Software Engineering Conference and 9th ACM SIGSOFT Symposium on the Foundations of Software Engineering, pp. 142–151. ACM (2001)
8. Cook, S.A.: The complexity of theorem-proving procedures. In: Proceedings of the 3rd Annual ACM Symposium on Theory of Computing, pp. 151–158 (1971)
9. Cousot, P., Cousot, R.: Abstract interpretation: a unified lattice model for static analysis of programs by construction or approximation of fixpoints. In: Proceedings of the 4th ACM SIGACT-SIGPLAN Symposium on Principles of Programming Languages (POPL 1977), pp. 238–252. ACM, New York (1977)
10. Dijkstra, E.W.: A Discipline of Programming. Prentice-Hall (1976)
11. Godefroid, P.: Model checking for programming languages using VeriSoft. In: Proceeding of the 24th ACM SIGACT-SIGPLAN Symposium on Principles of Programming Languages (POPL 1997), pp. 174–186 (1997)
12. Godefroid, P., Klarlund, N., Sen, K.: DART: directed automated random testing. In: 2005 ACM SIGPLAN Conference on Programming Language Design and Implementation, pp. 213–223. ACM (2005)
13. Godefroid, P., Nori, A.V., Rajamani, S.K., Tetali, S.D.: Compositional may-must program analysis: Unleashing the power of alternation. In: 37th ACM SIGACT-SIGPLAN Symposium on Principles of Programming Languages, pp. 43–55. ACM (2010)
14. Henzinger, T.A., Jhala, R., Majumdar, R., Sutre, G.: Lazy abstraction. In: Proceeding of the 29th ACM SIGACT-SIGPLAN Symposium on Principles of Programming Languages (POPL 2002), pp. 58–70 (2002)
15. King, J.C.: Symbolic execution and program testing. Communications of the ACM 19(7), 385–394 (1976)
16. Sen, K., Marinov, D., Agha, G.: CUTE: a concolic unit testing engine for C. In: 10th European Software Engineering Conference Held Jointly with 13th ACM SIGSOFT International Symposium on Foundations of Software Engineering, pp. 263–272. ACM (2005)
17. Tillmann, N., de Halleux, J.: Pex–White Box Test Generation for.NET. In: Beckert, B., Hähnle, R. (eds.) TAP 2008. LNCS, vol. 4966, pp. 134–153. Springer, Heidelberg (2008)
18. Yorsh, G., Ball, T., Sagiv, M.: Testing, abstraction, theorem proving: Better together! In: 2006 International Symposium on Software Testing and Analysis, pp. 145–156 (2006)

Is Branch Coverage a Good Measure of Testing Effectiveness?

Yi Wei[1], Bertrand Meyer[1], and Manuel Oriol[2]

[1] Chair of Software Engineering, ETH Zurich, Switzerland
{yi.wei,bertrand.meyer}@inf.ethz.ch
[2] Department of Computer Science, University of York, United Kindom
manuel@cs.york.ac.uk

Abstract. Most approaches to testing use branch coverage to decide on the quality of a given test suite. The intuition is that covering branches relates directly to uncovering faults. The empirical study reported here applied random testing to 14 Eiffel classes for a total of 2520 hours and recorded the number of uncovered faults and the branch coverage over time. For the tested classes, (1) random testing reaches 93% branch coverage (2) it exercises almost the same set of branches every time, (3) it detects different faults from execution to execution, (4) during the first 10 minutes of testing, while branch coverage increases rapidly, there is a strong correlation between branch coverage and the number of uncovered faults, (5) over 50% of the faults are detected at a time where branch coverage hardly changes, and the correlation between branch coverage and the number of uncovered faults is weak.

These results provide evidence that branch coverage is not a good stopping criterion for random testing. They also show that branch coverage is not a good indicator for the effectiveness of a test suite.

Keywords: random testing, branch coverage, experimental evaluation.

1 Introduction

Various studies[11,4] show that random testing is an effective way of detecting faults. Random testing is also attractive because it is easy to implement and widely applicable. For example, when insufficient information is available to perform systematic testing, random testing is more practical than any alternative [10]. Many practitioners think that, to evaluate the effectiveness of a strategy, branch coverage –the percentage of branches of the program that the test suite exercises – is the criterion of choice. It is a weaker indicator of test suite quality than other coverage criteria such as predicate coverage or path coverage [15]. Branch coverage is widely used because of its ease of implementation and its low overhead on the execution of the program [18] under test. As an example the European Cooperation for Space Standardization (ECSS) gives 100% branch coverage as one of the measures to assure the quality of a critical software [6].[1]

Many practitioners and researchers dismiss random testing because it only achieves low branch coverage. We used AutoTest [4], an automatic, random-based testing tool

---

[1] Section 6.2.3.2.

B. Meyer and M. Nordio (Eds.): LASER Summer School 2008-2010, LNCS 7007, pp. 194–212, 2012.
© Springer-Verlag Berlin Heidelberg 2012

for Eiffel, to gain insights on three questions: (1) the actual branch coverage achieved by testing Eiffel classes with AutoTest, (2) whether the achieved branch coverage correlates with the number of bugs found in the code, (3) whether branch coverage is a good stopping criterion for random testing. Despite the popularity of both random testing and branch coverage, there is little data available on the topic.

We tested 14 Eiffel classes using our fully automated random testing tool AutoTest for 2520 hours. AutoTest tested each class in 30 runs with each run 6 hour long. For each run, we recorded the exercised branches and faults detected over time. The main results are:

- Random testing reaches 93% branch coverage on average.
- Different test runs with different seeds for the pseudo-random number generator of the same class exercise almost the same branches, but detect different faults.
- At the beginning of the testing session, branch coverage and faults both increase dramatically and are strongly correlated.
- 90% of all the exercised branches are exercised in the first 10 minutes. After 10 minutes, the branch coverage level increases slowly. After 30 minutes, branch coverage further increases by only 4%.
- Over 50% of faults are detected after 30 minutes.
- There is a weak correlation between number of faults found and coverage over the 2520 hours of testing.

The main implication of these results is that branch coverage is an inadequate stopping criterion for random testing. As AutoTest conveniently builds test suites randomly as it tests the code, the branch coverage achieved at any point in time corresponds to the branch coverage of the test suite built since the beginning of the testing session. Because there is a strong correlation between faults uncovered and branch coverage when coverage increases, higher branch coverage implies uncovering more faults. However, half of the faults can be further discovered with hardly any increase in coverage. This confirms that branch coverage by itself is not in general a good indicator of the quality of a test suite.

A package is available online[2] containing the source code of the AutoTest tool and instructions to reproduce the experiment.

Section 2 describes the design of our experiment. Section 3 presents our results. We discuss the results in Section 4 and the threats to validity in Section 5. We present related work in Section 6 and conclude in Section 7.

2   Experiment Design

The experiment on which we base our results consists in running automated random testing sessions of Eiffel classes. We first describe contract-based unit testing for object-oriented (O–O) programs, then introduce AutoTest, and present the classes under test, the testing time and the computing infrastructure.

---

[2] http://se.inf.ethz.ch/people/wei/download/branch_coverage.zip

2.1   Contract-Based Unit Testing for O–O Programs

In O–O programs, a unit test can be assimilated to a routine (method) call on an instance using previously created instances as arguments. Test engineers write unit tests and check that the result of calls are equal to pre-calculated values. In a Hoare-triple style this means that a unit test can be modelled as (v, o, o_1,... are variables, $init_o$,$init_{o_1}$... expressions that return instances, m the routine called, and v_0 a value):

$$\{\}o := init_o; o_1 := init_{o_1}; ...; v := o.m(o_1, ..., o_n)\{v = v_0\}$$

In a contract-enabled environment, routines are equipped with contracts from the start:

$$\{Pre\}o.m(o_1, ..., o_n)\{Post\}$$

Unit tests can rely on contracts to check the validity of the call. It then consists only of writing the code to initialize instances that would satisfy the precondition of the routine:

$$\{\}o := init_o; o_1 := init_{o_1}; ...\{Pre\}$$

In this article we use contract-based automated random testing. In such an approach the testing infrastructure automatically takes care of this last part. In practice, it generates the sequence of instructions at random and proceeds with the call.

When making a call, if the generated instances do not satisfy the precondition of the routine, the result of the call is ignored and not counted as a test. After the precondition is checked, any contract violation or any exception triggered in the actual call then corresponds to a failure in the program.

As the random testing tool is not able to avoid executing similar test cases, it might uncover the same failure multiple times. Thus, it maps failures to faults by defining a fault as a unique triple:

$$< m, line\ number\ of\ the\ failure, type\ of\ exception >$$

When tests are executed, branch coverage is calculated in a straightforward manner as:

$$Branch\ Coverage = \frac{Number\ of\ exercised\ branches}{Number\ of\ branches}$$

2.2   The AutoTest Tool

This section presents a general view of how AutoTest works. More detailed explanations on AutoTest are available in previous publications [4].

AutoTest is a tool implementing a random testing strategy for Eiffel and is integrated to EiffelStudio 6.3 [2]. Given a set of classes and a time frame, AutoTest tries to test all their public routines in the time frame.

To generate test cases for routines in specified classes, AutoTest repeatedly performs the following three steps:

Select routine. AutoTest maintains the number of times that each routine has been tested, then it randomly selects one of the least tested routines as the next routine under test, thus trying to test routines in a fair way.

Prepare objects. To prepare objects needed for calling the selected routine, AutoTest distinguishes two cases: basic types and reference types.

For each basic type such as INTEGER, DOUBLE and BOOLEAN, AutoTest maintains a predefined value set. For example, for INTEGER, the predefined value set is $0, +/-1, +/-2, +/-10, +/-100, maximum$ and $minimum$ $integers$. It then chooses at random either to pick a predefined value or to generate it at random.

AutoTest also maintains an object pool with instances created for all types. When selecting a value of a reference type, it either tries to create a new instance of a conforming type by calling a constructor at random or it retrieves a conforming value from the object pool. This allows AutoTest to use old objects that may have had many routines called on them, resulting in states that would otherwise be unreachable.

Invoke routine under test. Eventually, the routine under test is called with the selected target object and arguments. The result of the execution, possible exceptions and its branch coverage information is recorded for later use.

2.3   Experiment Setup

Class selection. We chose the classes under test from the library EiffelBase [1] version 5.6. EiffelBase is production code that provides basic data structures and IO functionalities. It is used in almost every Eiffel program. The quality of its contracts should therefore be better than average Eiffel libraries. This is an important point because we assume the contracts to be correct. In order to increase the representativeness of the test subjects, we tried to pick classes with various code structure and intended semantics. Table 1 shows the main metrics for the chosen classes. Note that the branches shown in

Table 1. Metrics for tested classes

Class	LOC	Routines	Contract assertions	Faults	Branches	Branch Coverage
ACTIVE_LIST	2433	157	261	16	222	92%
ARRAY	1263	92	131	23	118	98%
ARRAYED_LIST	2251	148	255	22	219	94%
ARRAYED_SET	2603	161	297	20	189	96%
ARRAYED_STACK	2362	152	264	10	113	96%
BINARY_SEARCH_TREE	2019	137	143	42	296	83%
BINARY_SEARCH_TREE_SET	1367	89	119	10	123	92%
BINARY_TREE	1546	114	127	47	240	85%
FIXED_LIST	1924	133	204	23	146	90%
HASH_TABLE	1824	137	177	22	177	95%
HEAP_PRIORITY_QUEUE	1536	103	146	10	133	96%
LINKED_CIRCULAR	1928	136	184	37	190	92%
LINKED_LIST	1953	115	180	12	238	92%
PART_SORTED_TWO_WAY_LIST	2293	129	205	34	248	94%
Average	**1950**	**129**	**192**	**23**	**189**	**93%**
Total	**27302**	**1803**	**2693**	**328**	**2652**	**93%**

Table 1 is the number of testable branches, obtained by subtracting dead branches from the total number of branches in the corresponding class.

Test runs. We tested each class in 30 runs with different seeds with each run 6 hour long. This supposedly made the test runs long enough so that branch coverage level reaches a plateau. But we found out that even after 16 hours, random testing is still capable of exercising some new branches with a very low probability. We chose 6 hour runs because the branch coverage level already increases very slowly after that, and because 6 hours corresponds to an overnight testing session.

Computing infrastructure. We conducted the experiment on 9 PCs with Pentium 4 at 3.2GHz, 1GB of RAM, running Linux Red Hat Enterprise 4. The version of AutoTest used in the experiment is modified to include instrumentation for monitoring the branch coverage. AutoTest was the only CPU intensive program running during testing.

3   Results

This section presents results that answer five main questions:

1. Is the level of the branch coverage achieved by random testing predictable?
2. Is the branch coverage exercised by random testing similar from one test run to another?
3. Is the number of faults discovered by random testing predictable?
4. Are the faults uncovered by different test runs similar?
5. Is there a correlation between the level of coverage and the number of faults uncovered?

3.1   Predictability of Coverage Level

Because AutoTest might not be able to test all branches of a class due to its random nature, it is unlikely that testing sessions achieve total coverage, or even just constant results over all tested classes. As an example, it might be extremely difficult to satisfy a complex precondition guarding a routine with such a random approach. Another example is that the visibility of a routine might not let AutoTest test it freely.

This intuition is confirmed by the results presented in Figure 1 which shows the median of the branch coverage level for each class over time. The branch coverage level ranges from 0 to 1. As a first result, we can see that the branch coverage of some classes reaches a plateau at less than 0.85 while most of them have a plateau at or above 0.9. The thick curve in Figure 1 is the median of medians of the branch coverage level of all the classes. Over all 14 classes, the branch coverage level achieved after 6 hours of testing ranges from 0.82 to 0.98. On average, the branch coverage level is 0.93, with a standard deviation of 0.04, corresponding to 4.67% of the median.

While the maximum coverage is variable from one class to another, the actual evolution of branch coverage compared to the maximum coverage achieved through random testing is similar: 93% of all exercised branches are exercised in the first 10 minutes, 96% in 30 minutes, and 97% in the first hour. Section 4 contains an analysis of branches not exercised.

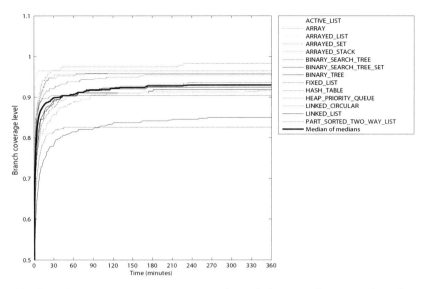

Fig. 1. Medians of the branch coverage level for each class over time and their median

In short, the branch coverage level achieved by random testing depends on the structure of the class under test and increases very fast in the first 10 minutes of testing and then very slowly afterwards.

3.2 Similarity of Coverage

Another important question is whether different test runs for the same class exercise different branches. Since we are more interested in branches difficult to exercise, the more specific question is: Do different test runs for the same class leave the same set of branches not visited? To answer this question, we need to measure the difference between the sets of branches not visited in two test runs for the same class. We use an array per testing run, containing a flag for each branch indicating whether it was visited.

To measure the difference between two sets of non-visited branches, it is appropriate to use the Hamming distance [12]: the number of positions, in two strings of equal lengths, where symbols differ. For example, the Hamming distance between 1011101 and 1001001 is 2 since the values differ at two positions, 3 and 5.

For the purposes of this study, a branch is said to be "difficult to exercise" if and only if it has not been exercised at least once through the 30 runs for that class.

The *difficult branch coverage vector* of a test run for a class with n difficult branches is a vector of n elements, where the i-th element is a flag for the i-th difficult branch in that class, with one of the following value: 0, indicating that the corresponding branch has not been exercised in that test run, or 1, indicating that the corresponding branch has been exercised in that test run.

The *difficult branch coverage distance* D_{BC} between two vectors u and v of the a class with N_b difficult branches is the Hamming distance between them:

$$D_{BC} = \sum_{i=1}^{N_b} u_i \oplus v_i$$

where u_i and v_i are the values at the i-th position of u and v respectively, and $\oplus$ is exclusive or. D_{BC} is in the range between 0 and N_b. The larger the distance, the more different branches are covered by these two runs.

The *difficult branch coverage similarity* is defined as:

$$\frac{N_b - D_{BC}}{N_b}$$

The intention of the similarity is that the smaller the branch coverage distance, the higher the similarity and the similarity should range between 0 and 1. The similarity among $k > 2$ vectors is calculated as the median of the similarity values between each two vectors: there are $\frac{k(k-1)}{2}$ pairs of k vectors, for each pair, a similarity value is calculated, and the overall similarity is the median of those $\frac{k(k-1)}{2}$ values.

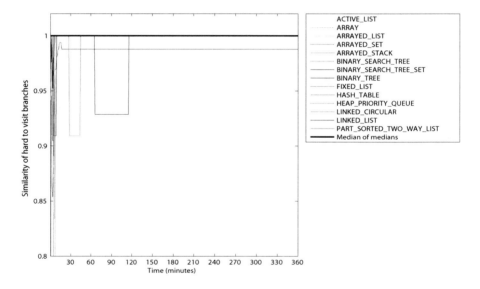

Fig. 2. The branch coverage similarity for each class over time; their median

Figure 2 shows the difficult branch coverage similarity for each class over time. The thick curve is the median of the difficult branch coverage similarity over all classes. Figure 2 reveals that the similarity of difficult branch coverage is already 1 only after a few minutes of testing, Figure 3 shows the standard deviation of the branch coverage similarity for each class. It reveals that the standard deviation of difficult branch coverage similarity is almost 0.

The high median of similarity means that in general, the set of branches from a class that are difficult to exercise are very similar from test run to test run (for the

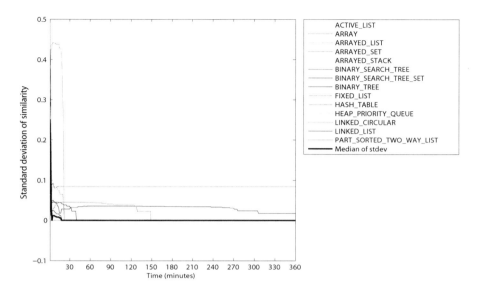

Fig. 3. Standard deviation of the branch coverage similarity for each class over time; their median

same class), the small standard deviation means that this phenomenon was constantly observed through all the runs.

The consequence drawn from Figure 2 and Figure 3 is that if a branch is not exercised by a test run, it is unlikely that it will be exercised by other runs for the same class. In other words, applying random testing with different seeds to the same class does not improve branch coverage for that class. Branches not exercised in one run are not visited in subsequent runs.

3.3   Predictability of Number of Faults

The question of predictability of the number of faults found by random testing was already addressed in a previous study [5]. The new results confirm that study and extend it to longer testing sessions (6-hour sessions rather than 90-minute ones), they are also using the most recent version of AutoTest which benefits from significant performance improvements. The median of the number of faults detected for each class over time is plotted in Figure 4. Note that all the faults found are real faults in a widely used Eiffel library. This also shows that our testing tool is effective at finding faults. Figure 4 shows that 54% of the faults are detected in the first 10 minutes, 70% in 30 minutes, and 78% in 1 hour. About 22% of the faults are detected after 1 hour. This means that after 30 minutes of testing, 70% of the faults have been detected even though only 4% additional branches have been exercised.

Different classes contain different numbers of faults. To compare fault detection across different classes, we use the normalized number of faults, obtained by dividing the number of faults detected by each test run by the total number of faults found in all test runs for that particular class. The number of normalized faults for a particular

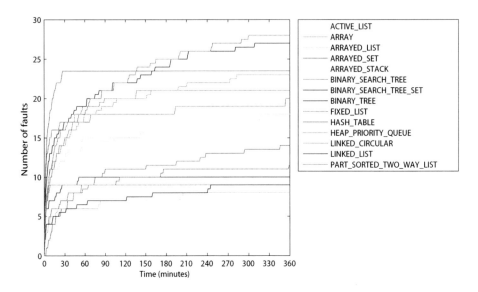

Fig. 4. Medians of the number of faults detected in each class over time

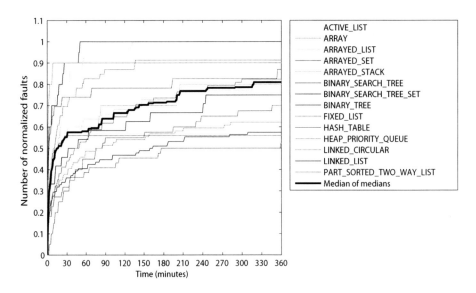

Fig. 5. Medians of the normalized number of faults detected for each class over time; their median

test run represents the percentage of faults found in that test run against all faults that we know in the class. The medians of the number of the normalized faults detected over time for each class are shown in Figure 5. The thick curve is the median of the medians of the number of normalized faults detected over time for all classes.

For most of the classes, the median does not reach 1. This indicates different runs detect different faults (since median 1 would mean that every run finds the same faults).

3.4   Similarity of Faults

As in the case of the branch coverage level, we are interested in the similarity of detected faults for the same class among test runs. The detected faults are similar when different test runs find the same faults. Definitions of distances, similarity and fault detection vector, similar to those of section 3.2, are appropriate.

The *fault detection vector* of a class in a particular test run is a vector of n elements, with n being the total number of faults detected for that class over all runs. Because we do not know the actual number of faults in a class, we can only use the total number of faults found by AutoTest. Each vector element is 1 if the corresponding fault has been detected and 0 otherwise.

Given two fault detection vectors r and s for the same class, in which the total number of found faults is N_f, the *fault detection distance* D_f between r and s is defined as

$$D_f = \sum_{i=1}^{N_f} r_i \oplus s_i$$

where r_i and s_i is the value at the i-th position of r and s respectively. D_f is in the range between $0..N_f$.

The *fault detection similarity* between them is then defined as:

$$\frac{N_f - D_f}{N_f}$$

The fault detection similarity ranges from 0 to 1. The larger the similarity, the more faults are detected in both test runs or in neither. Fault detection similarity among more than two vectors is calculated similarly to branch coverage similarity.

Figure 6 shows the similarity of detected faults in different test runs for each class. The median of the fault detection similarity for all classes (the thick curve) ranges from 0.84 to 0.90. The figure indicates that most of the faults can be detected in every test run, but (because the median does not reach 1.0) in order to get as many faults as possible, multiple test runs for that class are necessary. Figure 7 shows the standard deviation of the fault detection similarity for each class. The median (the thick curve) ranges from 0.07 to 0.05, corresponding to 8% to 5% of the median for all classes.

This implies that most faults are discovered by most testing runs, but several runs produce better results. The choice of seed has a stronger impact on fault detection than on branch coverage.

3.5   Correlation between Branch Coverage and Number of Faults

Here we take a closer look at the correlation between branch coverage and the number of detected faults. Although higher coverage does uncover more faults overall, it is clearly not sufficient an indicator.

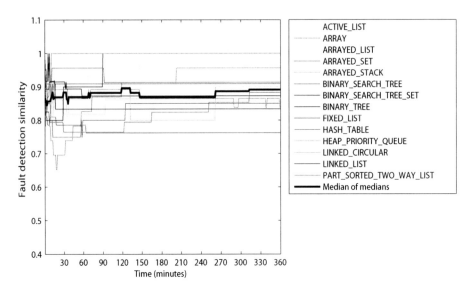

Fig. 6. Fault detection similarity for each class over time; their median

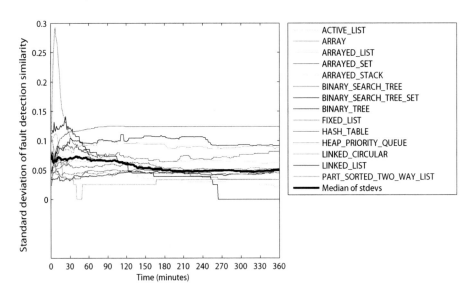

Fig. 7. Standard deviation of the fault detection similarity for each class over time; their median

To study the correlation between branch coverage level and fault detection ability, Figure 8 superimposes the median of the branch coverage level and the median of the normalized number of faults for the tested classes. In the first few minutes of testing, when the branch coverage level increases quickly, faults are also found quickly. After a while, the increase of branch coverage slows down. The speed of fault detection also

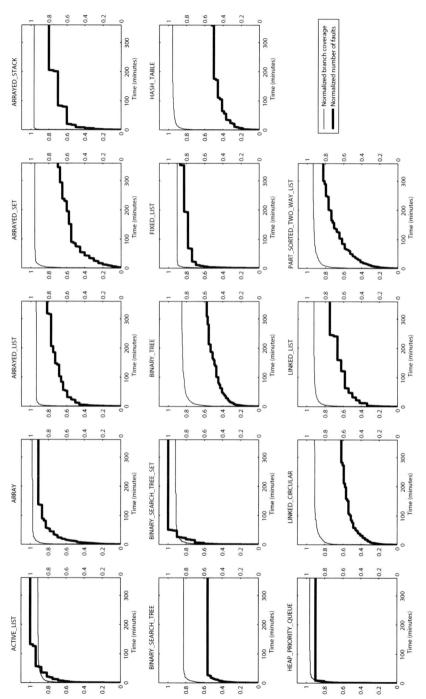

Fig. 8. Median of the branch coverage level and median of the normalized number of faults for each class over time

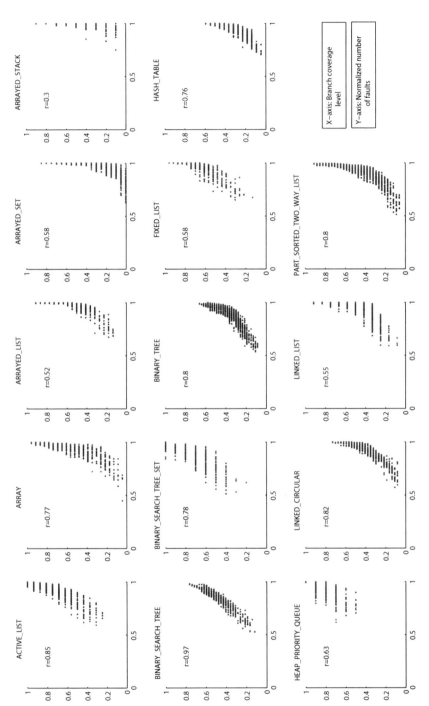

Fig. 9. Correlation between the branch coverage level and the normalized number of faults for each class over 360 minutes

decreases, although less dramatically. After 30 minutes, the branch coverage level only increases slightly, but many faults are detected in that period.

We also calculated the correlation between branch coverage and normalized number of faults. It varies much from class to class, 0.3 to 0.97 and there seems to be no common pattern among the tested classes as shown in Figure 9.

The implications of these results are twofold: (1) when coverage increases, faults discovered increase as well, (2) when coverage stagnates, faults are still found. Thus increasing the branch coverage clearly increases the number of faults found. It is however clearly not sufficient to have a high value of the branch coverage to assess the quality of a testing session.

The next section further elaborates on these findings as well as their limitations.

4 Discussion

The results of the previous section provide material for answering three questions:

- Is branch coverage a good stopping criterion for random testing?
- Is it a good measure of testing effectiveness?
- What are the unexercised branches?

4.1 Branch Coverage as Stopping Criterion for Random Testing

Since in general, random testing cannot achieve 100% branch coverage in finite time, total branch coverage is not a feasible stopping criterion. In practice, the percentage of code coverage is often used as an adequacy criterion: the higher the percentage, the more adequate the testing [19]; and testing can be stopped if the generated test suite reached a certain level of adequacy. In our experiments, after 1 hour, the branch coverage level hardly increases, so it will be unpractical to extend the testing time until reaching full coverage. Instead, the only reasonable way to use branch coverage would be to evaluate the expectation of finding new faults. As shown in the previous section, the number of faults evolves closely with the coverage only in the first few minutes of testing. On testing sessions longer than 10 minutes, the correlation degrades. In fact, about 50% of the faults are found in a period where the branch coverage level hardly increases any more. This means that branch coverage is not a good predictor for the number of faults remaining to be found.

The correlation greatly varies from class to class. For some classes such as BINARY_SEARCH_TREE, the correlation coefficient is 0.98 and the correlation is almost linear, but for others such as ARRAYED_STACK the correlation is weak (0.3), especially with longer testing sessions. This variation on the class under test reduces the precision if branch coverage is used as a stopping criterion.

Random testing also detects different faults in different test runs while it exercises almost the same branches. This confirms that multiple restarts drastically improves the number of faults found [5]: to find as many faults as possible, a class should be random-tested multiple times with different seeds, even if the same branches are exercised every time.

Our conclusion is that branch coverage alone cannot be used as a stopping criterion for random testing.

4.2 Branch Coverage as Measure of Testing Effectiveness

To assess branch coverage as a measure of testing effectiveness, one must understand that running random testing longer is the same as adding new test cases into a test suite. The reason is that testing for a longer time means that more routine calls are executed on the class under test. Each routine call is actually the last line of a test case that contains all previous calls participating to the state of data used in the call (see [14] for a detailed explanation of test case construction and simplification). To push the analogy further, testing a class in different runs is the same as providing different test suites for that class.

Our experiments test production code in which the existing number of faults is unknown. They do not seed faults in the code but merely tested the discrepancy between the contracts and the code. As a result, it is not possible to use the ratio of detected faults against the total number of faults to measure the effectiveness of testing. Instead, we assess testing effectiveness through two parameters: the number of faults detected and the speed at which those faults are detected.

Two results show that different faults can be detected at the same level of branch coverage: (1) in a test run, new faults were detected in a period where branch coverage hardly changes; (2) in different test runs for the same class, different faults were detected while almost the same branches were exercised. In other words, different test suites satisfying the same branch coverage criterion may detect different faults.

These two observations indicate that test adequacy in terms of branch coverage level is highly predictable, not only in how many branches are covered, but also in what the covered branches are. Applying random testing to a class always yields the same level of branch coverage adequacy. Also, for all the tested classes, the branch coverage adequacy level stabilizes after some time (1 hour in our case).

Although we do not know how many faults remain in tested classes, it was astonishing to discover that over 50% of found faults only appear in the period when branch coverage stagnates.

These results provide evidence of the lack of reliability [8] of branch coverage criterion achieved by random testing. Reliability requires that a test criterion always produce consistent results. In the experiments reported here, this goal requires that two test runs achieving the same branch coverage of a class should deliver similar numbers of faults. But the results show that the number of faults found in different test runs will differ from each other by at least 50%.

What about the speed of fault detection? In the first few minutes of random testing, branch coverage increases quickly, and the number of faults increases accordingly, with a strong correlation. This means that branch coverage is good in measuring testing effectiveness in the first few minutes. But after a while, the branch coverage level hardly increases, the fault detection speed also slows down but less dramatically than the branch coverage level. In fact, many faults are detected in the period where the branch coverage hardly changes. This means in the later period, branch coverage is not a good measure for testing effectiveness.

In general, to detect as many faults as possible, branch coverage is necessary but not sufficient.

4.3   Branches Not Exercised

We analyzed the 179 branches in all 14 classes that were not exercised in our experiments. Among these branches, there are 116 distinct branches, and 63 duplicated branches because they appear in inherited routines. Table 2 shows the reasons why certain branches were not exercised and the percentage of branches not exercised that fall into that each reason. In Table 2 the categories are as follows:

Table 2. Branches not exercised

Reason	% of branches
Branch condition not satisfied	45.6%
Linear constraint not satisfied	12.9%
Call site not exercised	13.7%
Unsatisfiable branches	13.7%
Crash before branch	8.6%
Implementation limitation	2.5%
Concurrent context needed	1.7%

Branch condition not satisfied: branch not exercised because its branch condition is not met. This is the most common case.

Linear constraint not satisfied: in the branch condition there is a linear constraint, and they were not satisfied by the random strategy. This is actually a special case of branch condition, but important on its own because a random strategy usually has great difficulty satisfying these constraints.

Call site not exercised: no calls of a routine containing the branch were executed.

Unsatisfiable branch: the branch depends on conditions that can never be satisfied.

Fault before branch: there was always a fault found before exercised.

Implementation limitation: branch not exercised because of a limitation of AutoTest.

Concurrent context needed: the branch is only exercisable when tested in a concurrent context. But our experiments were conducted in a sequential setting.

Table 2 shows that 58.5% of the branches not exercised fall into the first two reasons (*Branch condition not satisfied, linear constraint not satisfied*).

A follow-up question would be how to satisfy these branch conditions. A common solution to satisfy branch conditions is to use symbolic execution to collect path conditions and propagate them up to the routine entry. Symbolic executors however induce a large overhead in the general case.

We analyzed branches falling into the first two categories to see how often a symbolic executor would help: in 32.3% of cases, we need a symbolic executor to propagate path conditions, for the remaining 67.7%, it is only needed to concatenate all dominating path conditions and select inputs at the routine entry – a linear constraint solver is needed when there is linear constraint in the concatenated path condition. Even if in some cases it is not possible to solve the constraints, it seems useful to investigate further this lead.

For *Faults before branch*, the faults should either be fixed first or avoided while testing. For the *Implementation limitation* and *Concurrent context needed* categories, we need to further improve AutoTest.

5   Threats to Validity

Four observations may raise questions about the result.

Representativeness of chosen classes. Despite being chosen from the widely used Eiffel library EiffelBase and varying in terms of various code metrics and intended semantics, the chosen classes may not be fully representative of general O–O programs.

3 **Representativeness of AutoTest's variant of random testing.** We tried to keep the algorithm of AutoTest as general as possible, but other implementations of random testing may produce different results.

Branch coverage below 100%. We do not know whether the correlation between branch coverage and number of faults still holds when all branches are exercised. We consider this very likely, since if we considered the application trimmed of all the branches that were not visited, we would then achieve 100% branch coverage in most cases.

Size of test suite. A recent formal analysis [3] of random testing showed that the number of tests made has a great influence on the results found with random testing. It might be possible that while our study relies on many more tests than previous ones, we did not execute enough tests. We consider this unlikely because of the high similarity of the faults found in the present experiments.

6   Related Work

Intuitively, random testing cannot compete in terms of effectiveness with systematic testing because it is less likely that randomly selected inputs will be interesting enough to reveal faults in the program under test. Some studies [17,16] have shown that random testing is as effective as some systematic methods such as partition testing. Our results also showed that random testing is effective: in the experiment, random testing detected 328 faults in 14 classes in EiffelBase library while in the past 3 years, only 28 faults were reported by users.

Ciupa et al. [5] investigated the predictability of random testing and showed that in terms of the number of faults detected over time, random testing is predictable. Figure 5 and Figure 6 confirm those results.

Many studies compare branch coverage for assessing the effectiveness of test strategies. With other criteria in. Frankl et al. [7] compared the branch coverage criterion with the all-uses criterion and concluded that for their programs, all-uses adequate test sets performs better than branch adequate test sets, and branch adequate test sets do not perform significantly better than null-adequate test sets, which are test sets containing randomly selected test cases without any adequacy requirement. The present study focuses more on the branch coverage level achieved by random testing in a certain amount of time and the number of faults found in that period.

Hutchins et al. [13] also compared the effectiveness of the branch coverage criterion and the all-uses criterion. They found that for both criteria, test sets achieving coverage levels over 90% showed significantly better fault detection than randomly selected test sets of the same size. This means that a lot of faults could be detected when the coverage level approaches 100%. They also concluded that in terms of effectiveness, there is no winner between branch coverage and all-uses criterion. Our results on the correlation between the branch coverage level and the number of detected faults also shows a similar pattern: many faults are detected at higher coverage levels, in our experiment, however, the branch coverage level did not reach 100%, while in their study, manually written test sets guaranteed total branch coverage. Also, in their study, programs under test were seeded with faults, while in our experiment, programs were tested as they are.

Gupta et al. [9] compared the effectiveness (the ability to detect faults) and efficiency (the average cost for detecting a fault) of three code coverage criteria: predicate coverage, branch coverage and block coverage. They found that predicate coverage is the most effective but the least efficient, block coverage is the least effective but most efficient, while branch coverage is between predicate coverage and block coverage in terms of both effectiveness and efficiency. Their results suggest that branch coverage is the best among those three criteria for getting better results with moderate testing efforts.

7   Conclusions and Future Work

This article has shown that the branch coverage level achieved by random testing varies depending on the structure of the program under test but was very high on the classes we tested (93% on average). Most of the branches exercised by random testing are exercised very quickly (in the first 10 minutes of testing) regardless of the class under test. For the same class, branches exercised in different test runs are almost the same. Different test runs on the same class detect roughly 10% different faults.

Our results also confirm that branch coverage in general is not a good indicator of the quality of a test suite. In the experiments, more than 50% of the faults are uncovered while coverage is at a plateau. Although many studies showed the weakness of branch coverage, there is little evidence showing that random testing finds new faults while the branch coverage stagnates.

Our results indicate that branch coverage is not a good stopping criterion for random testing. One should test a program in multiple test runs to find as many faults as possible even though by doing so the branch coverage level will not be increased in general. Also, one should not stop random testing, even if the branch coverage level stops increasing or only increases very slowly.

For the continuation of this work, we are investigating how to reach even higher branch coverage (100% or very close), and how to devise a good stopping criterion for random testing.

Acknowledgement. We thank Ilinca Ciupa, Andreas Leitner, Simon Poulding, and Stephan van Staden for their insightful comments.

References

1. EiffelBase. Eiffel Software, http://www.eiffel.com/libraries/base.html
2. EiffelStudio. Eiffel Software, http://www.eiffel.com/
3. Arcuri, A., Iqbal, M., Briand, L.: Formal analysis of the effectiveness and predictability of random testing. In: Proceedings of the 19th International Symposium on Software Testing and Analysis, pp. 219–230. ACM (2010)
4. Ciupa, I., Leitner, A., Oriol, M., Meyer, B.: Experimental assessment of random testing for object-oriented software. In: Proceedings of the International Symposium on Software Testing and Analysis 2007 (ISSTA 2007), pp. 84–94 (2007)
5. Ciupa, I., Pretschner, A., Leitner, A., Oriol, M., Meyer, B.: On the predictability of random tests for object-oriented software. In: First International Conference on Software Testing, Verification, and Validation 2008 (ICST 2008), pp. 72–81 (2008)
6. European Cooperation for Space Coordination. Space product assurance - Software product assurance, ECSS-Q-ST-80C. ESA Requirements and Standards Division (2009)
7. Frankl, P., Weiss, S.: An experimental comparison of the effectiveness of branch testing and data flow testing. IEEE Transactions on Software Engineering 19(8), 774–787 (1993)
8. Goodenough, J.B., Gerhart, S.L.: Toward a theory of test data selection. IEEE Trans. Software Eng. 1(2), 156–173 (1975)
9. Gupta, A., Jalote, P.: An approach for experimentally evaluating effectiveness and efficiency of coverage criteria for software testing. Int. J. Softw. Tools Technol. Transf. 10(2), 145–160 (2008)
10. Hamlet, D.: When only random testing will do. In: RT 2006: Proceedings of the 1st international workshop on Random testing, pp. 1–9. ACM, New York (2006)
11. Hamlet, R.: Random testing. In: Encyclopedia of Software Engineering, pp. 970–978. Wiley (1994)
12. Hamming, R.W.: Error detecting and error correcting codes. The Bell System Technical Journal 26(2), 147–160 (1950)
13. Hutchins, M., Foster, H., Goradia, T., Ostrand, T.: Experiments of the effectiveness of dataflow- and controlflow-based test adequacy criteria. In: ICSE 1994: Proceedings of the 16th International Conference on Software Engineering, pp. 191–200. IEEE Computer Society Press, Los Alamitos (1994)
14. Leitner, A., Oriol, M., Zeller, A., Ciupa, I., Meyer, B.: Efficient unit test case minimization. In: Proceedings of the 22nd IEEE/ACM International Conference on Automated Software Engineering (ASE 2007), pp. 417–420 (2007)
15. Myers, G.J.: The Art of Software Testing, 2nd edn. John Wiley and Sons (2004)
16. Ntafos, S.: On random and partition testing. In: ISSTA 1998: Proceedings of the 1998 ACM SIGSOFT International Symposium on Software Testing and Analysis, pp. 42–48. ACM, New York (1998)
17. Weyuker, E., Jeng, B.: Analyzing partition testing strategies. IEEE Transactions on Software Engineering 17(7), 703–711 (1991)
18. Yang, Q., Li, J.J., Weiss, D.: A survey of coverage based testing tools. In: AST 2006: Proceedings of the 2006 International Workshop on Automation of Software Test, pp. 99–103. ACM, New York (2006)
19. Zhu, H., Hall, P.A.V., May, J.H.R.: Software unit test coverage and adequacy. ACM Comput. Surv. 29(4), 366–427 (1997)

Author Index